The Back to Basics Cookbook

The
Back to Basics
Cookbook

Maureen Tatlow

Illustrations by Eva Byrne

Gill & Macmillan

Gill & Macmillan Ltd
12 Hume Avenue, Park West
Dublin 12
with associated companies throughout the world
www.gillmacmillan.ie
© Maureen Tatlow 2000
0 7171 2933 0

Illustrations by Eva Byrne

Design by Slick Fish
Print origination by Design Image
Printed by ColourBooks Ltd, Dublin

This book is typeset in Frutiger and Garamond.

A CIP catalogue record for this book is available from the British Library.

1 3 5 4 2

For Anne Willett, in whose
kitchens at Volta House and
Le Thil this all began, with love
and thanks

contents

Conversion Tables   viii
Acknowledgments   ix
Back to Basics   1
Follow Your Nose   2

EGGS   4
Boil an Egg (or Why Not To)   4
Omelettes   6
Poach, Scramble, Fry   8

PASTA   10

POTATOES   16
Boiled Potatoes   17
Fried Potatoes   20
Roast Potatoes   22
Potato Gratins   24

RICE AND OTHER GRAINS   26
Rice   26
Quick Grains   29

FISH AND SHELLFISH
Fried Fish   31
Steamed Fish   34
Mussels   36
Squid   38

MEAT AND POULTRY   40
Steaks and Chops   40
Roast Chicken   44
Roasting Meat   48
Gravy   52
Poached Chicken and Lamb   54
Stew   58
Stir-fry   62
Char-grill   65

SALADS   68

VEGETABLES   74
Roasting Vegetables   74
Steaming Vegetables   76
Stir-frying Vegetables   78
Brassicas   80
Roots   82

SOUP AND STOCK   84
Soup   84
Stock   88

SOME SAUCES   92
Salsas and Relishes   92
White Sauce   95
Mayonnaise   98

DOING THINGS WITH EGGS   102
Pancakes   102
Egg Whites and Meringues   106
Soufflés   108

A LITTLE BAKING   110
Quick Breads   110
Yeast Bread, Focaccia, Pizza   113
Shortcrust Pastry and a few Tarts   118

FOR AFTERS   122
Fruit Salad   122
Chocolate   125
Steamed Pudding   128
Cakes   129

Select Bibliography   132
Index   134

conversion tables

For simplicity, clarity and accuracy, my recipes are all in metric, so for the die-hard pounds-and-ouncers amongst you, I've devised these conversions. The more usual rounded-off conversions can be very misleading; I've seen 8 oz translated into everything from 200 g to 250 g, so do be wary if you use other conversion charts.

If the numbers in these charts look a little arbitrary, that's because I've given the conversions necessary for the recipes in this book. In general, I've stuck as close to the accurate conversion as possible without getting into silly territory like 4/5 oz. Use your own common sense about how accurate you need to be. As a rule of thumb, go for stringent accuracy with small quantities, and when baking.

Weights

metric	imperial
20 g	$\frac{3}{4}$ oz
25	1
30	1
40	1½
50	2
60	2
65	2
75	2½
80	3
85	3
90	3
100	3½
110	4
115	4
120	4
125	4½
130	4½
140	5
150	5
170	6
175	6
200	7
220	7½
225	8
230	8
240	8½
250	9
275	10
285	10
300	10½
325	11½
350	12½
375	13
400	14
425	15
450	16 oz (1 lb)
475	1 lb 1 oz
500	1 lb 1½ oz
550	1 lb 3½ oz
600	1 lb 5 oz
700	1 lb 9 oz
750	1 lb 10½ oz
800	1 lb 12 oz
900	2 lb
1 kg	2 lb 3 oz
1.1 kg	2 lb 7 oz
1.2 kg	2 lb 10½ oz
1.3 kg	2 lb 14 oz
1.4 kg	3 lb 1½ oz
1.5 kg	3 lb 5 oz
1.8 kg	4 lb
2 kg	4 lb 6½ oz
3 kg	6 lb 10 oz

Volumes

Remember that a pint has 20 fl oz. If you use cup measures from other recipes, 1 cup = 8 fl oz, 225 ml.

50 ml	2 fl oz
60 ml	2
75	2½
80	3
100	3½
115	4
125	4½
140	5 fl oz (¼ pint)
150	5½
175	6
200	7
225	8
250	9
275	9½
300	10 fl oz (½ pint)
310	11
330	11½
350	12
375	13
400	14
425	15 fl oz (¾ pint)
450	16
475	17
500	17½
510	18
540	19
570	20 fl oz (1 pint)
600	1 pint 1 fl oz
625	1 pint 2 fl oz
660	1 pint 3 fl oz
1 litre	1¾ pints
1.1 litres	1 pint 19 fl oz
1.2 litres	2 pints 2 fl oz
1.3 litres	2 pints 6 fl oz
1.4 litres	2 pints 9 fl oz
1.5 litres	2 pints 13 fl oz
2 litres	3½ pints

Measures

cm	inches
½	⅕
1	⅖
2	⅘
2½	1
3	1
5	2
6	2⅓
11	4⅓
15	6
18	7
20	8
21	8
22	8⅔
23	9
24	9⅓
26	10
28	11
30	11⅔
32	12½
33	13

acknowledgments

Thanks to
All my readers who wrote and asked for this book; I hope you enjoy it!

And also to . . .
Didi Tatlow, Orla Broderick, Peggy O'Brien and Evelyn Bracken, who gave so much time to reading the manuscript and making such a difference

Ros Dee for going with the idea of the series in the *Sunday Tribune* in the first place, as well as all your support, and time off to finish writing

Myrtle Allen and Darina Allen for the basics from Ballymaloe

Mum for starting us on the right track all those years ago with the cooking of the Sunday lunches, Dad for giving us all the questioning and writing bug, and Mum and Dad for space to write, once again

And above all, to Conor. It simply couldn't have happened without you there to encourage, help, eat and enjoy

back to basics

This book is about little things which make a big difference.

It started back in 1997, in my column on food and cooking in the *Sunday Tribune*. I had decided to take an occasional look at the simplest of kitchen jobs, the ordinary ones which everyone takes for granted but which can — and do — go wrong for every cook. I wanted to explain the basic things which many of you asked me about, like how exactly to cook rice, or roast potatoes, and get them right.

They were the very things which had caused me grief in my early cooking years, the days when it was just me and a recipe in the kitchen, and there was no one to lean over my shoulder and show me how. I was supposed to be completing a Masters thesis on Reformation and Enlightenment studies, but instead I was spending my time seeking elucidation about far more pressing matters. Why was it that my steaks or chops or fried eggs stuck to the pan? How did a bread dough simply fail to rise; why did a cake sink? My pastry was tough, or soggy, or sometimes even both (improbable, but true). I remember standing helplessly with a bowl of egg whites tucked under my arm and whisking and whisking, and they frothed a little but they never fluffed up, and I just didn't know what I was doing wrong.

So several years later, when I had abandoned the thesis and become a food writer instead, I thought it was about time to explore those niggly details, the ones which are so obvious that they hardly merit a mention in recipes. They are the basics which I had discovered over years of cooking in my own kitchen, working on my own recipes, and of watching and working with many other inspiring cooks. They are the basics which can make all the difference between a bit of a disaster and a truly yummy dinner.

I had no idea when it started that 'Back to Basics' would eventually run for three years, but requests from readers to cover topics kept coming, so the series kept going. I've added some more topics to the book, and I have added many recipes too, recipes for everyone from complete beginners to those who are already pretty confident in the kitchen.

The extra recipes are also there because, ultimately, this book is not about techniques, even though it does explain plenty of them along the way. This book is about that delicious dinner, whether it's just for you, for your family or for a big crowd of friends. It's about the pleasures of cooking; because once you get the basics right, you can stop feeling anxious and start to have some fun. It is all about that exciting moment in the kitchen when words on a page combine with ingredients, and they metamorphose into a succession of tastes and flavours. It is all about the conviviality, the comfort, the pleasures which good food brings.

Trust your tastebuds, smell the smells, use your fingers, and enjoy.

follow your nose

The recipe is a peculiar thing. We take it quite for granted, assuming it is a set of simple, mechanical instructions, and we expect it to be infallible.

Of course this is nonsense. The recipe, as any other prose form, is bound by its conventions; it is constrained by requirements for brevity, and often characterised by its very own language — a world where things tend to 'pop' into ovens, and the onions always fry until 'golden brown'.

As for the infallibility: I hate to say it, but there's no such thing. Every pan, every hob, every oven and every cook is different, and fresh ingredients vary from day to day as well, but if recipes were to point to every possible pitfall and variation, they would be interminable. All a recipe can ever do is point the way. After that, it's over to you.

Don't let this worry you; it's where the fun of cooking begins. In this book, I've tried to fill in many of the gaps that recipe shorthand leaves out, but there's one important, often unspoken, factor which is worth bearing in mind:

When you cook, you need to use your ears, your tongue and your nose.

At a time when more and more people are learning to cook from the telly and from books, rather than in their mothers' kitchens, so much of the sensory experience of cooking is being forgotten. Consider those 'golden brown' onions. How many umpteen times have we all followed that instruction for frying onions to make them tasty? Yet this standard recipe shorthand is most inexpressive. It acknowledges that you use your sight at the stove, but it leaves out the rest.

First, let's listen. Recipes do occasionally mention sound. You might have tapped the base of a cooked loaf of bread and listened for the hollow knock, as opposed to the dead thud that you'd hear if it contained still-uncooked wet dough. You might have been told, after a yeast dough had risen, to knead until the squeaking stopped, and then you would know that you had forced out the excess air bubbles. If you've cooked Indian food, you may have heated spices until they popped.

But it needn't end there, with obvious sounds like those. The good cook uses her ears in the kitchen all the time. Sound is one of the first warnings you will get; listening in the kitchen helps you to avert disaster.

Take this example: when you're frying meat, you must hear a violently sparky sizzle when it hits a hot pan. If you don't hear this, your dinner is in trouble. If your ears pick up a dispiriting wet sigh, as cold meat encounters a lukewarm pan, the meat will ooze its juices, it'll stew rather than fry, and the food will never acquire those tasty, yummy caramelised flavours which are created when the pan and oil are hot enough. (What to do? Tip the meat out, heat the pan till it's hotter, and start over again.)

Frying onions? You need to listen too. This time, you're in trouble if you hear vehemently noisy crackles when the onions land in the oil. You'll have to do something fast, or they'll burn to bitterness before they have deepened to sweet, dark gold. (Whip the pan off the heat instantly, to allow it to cool off.)

Making a sauce? Keep your ears open too. If you don't, you'll miss the tell-tale evidence: that indignant spluttering of a sauce drying just before it burns, or the prickly crackle you hear when you stir a sauce which is sticking to the base of a pot.

Sounds are useful, but smell and taste are even better.

Taste may seem obvious, but it does surprise me how often I see people following a recipe and then serving up a dish — without having tasted it first. Always taste to check! It may need more salt, or a dash of pepper. Perhaps a squirt of lemon juice will lift the flavour of a sauce. No recipe can finish a dish for you. That's up to your judgment and discernment.

And as for smell: we use it all the time when cooking, if only we knew it, for smell is an indispensable partner of taste. Indeed much of what we think of as taste is actually a message coming to us from our noses: while the tongue can pick out a few chemical substances, the nose is far more sensitive. It is alive to hundreds.

Smell will tell you when those onions are right; as they fry, they become gradually more bitter. Do you need them sweet, or tinged with pungency? Your nose knows the golden moment better than your eyes ever will. Let the smell of a dish in progress guide you, not recipe timings. As each stage of cooking is reached, your nose will let you know.

This is the biggest problem with the microwave, and the reason I don't much care for cooking with one. Encased in that coffin, all the fun, the stimulation, the nuances of cooking are removed; making food is reduced to keying in numbers. For the same reason, cooking (and indeed eating) when you have a cold, removes most of the pleasure of the experience.

Why is the experience of smell so powerful, so persuasive and evocative? It may have something to do with the fact that smell was where our first thoughts began; the frontal lobes of our brain, the areas in which association and higher mental processes take place, actually evolved from the original junction between the brain and the olfactory nerve. As science writer Lyall Watson put it: 'We think because we *smelled*.' This may be why smelling when you cook can be more helpful than reading.

Next time you cook, be sceptical of that recipe. Use your head; watch and listen; taste all the time; and don't be afraid to follow your nose.

eggs

BOIL AN EGG

Perhaps you're looking forward to a sunny summer lunch. Tucked in with those green beans, the bright tomatoes and the wrinkled, inky black olives of a big Niçoise Salad you'd like the eggs to glow, saffron-yolked and slightly sticky. Or perhaps it's breakfast time, and you want to dig through shell and tender white, for the core of liquid gold, and dip in some sticks of buttered toast.

If so, you need to know how to boil your egg.

Or rather, you need to know how not to.

NOT BOILING THE EGG

Not boiling an egg was news to me too, but boiling is too hot; it makes the white rubbery. If you cook the egg gently, the white will stay tender as the yolk cooks to your liking.

Put eggs straight from the fridge in a small heavy pan and cover them completely with cold water. On the hob, bring the water up quickly to a rapid, fat-bubbled, rumbling boil. Put on a tight-fitting lid and take the pan off the heat.

Timings for large eggs:

- For **really soft eggs**, wait **3½ minutes**. You'll have a partially cooked white and a runny yolk. Wait **4–4½ minutes** for a nearly firm white and runny yolk.

- For beautiful, **sticky-yolked hard-cooked eggs for eating cold,** wait **6 minutes**. Immediately cool them in several changes of cold water, until quite cold. Peel right away (but don't cut them until you're just about to eat). The result? Tender whites and firm but sticky, dark yellow yolks. Delicious.

- **If you want to eat the hard-cooked sticky-yolked egg hot,** you must leave it in the water for **6½–7 minutes**. (The egg for eating cold needs less time in hot water because it will go on cooking as it cools.)

- For **harder-cooked eggs** (light yellow at the edge of the yolks), leave the eggs in the water for **9–10 minutes**. Cool and peel as above.

- If your eggs are smaller or larger, adjust timings accordingly.

The yucky green ring

In his wondrous book of food, chemistry and good sense, *On Food and Cooking*, Harold McGee explains the chemistry of this horrid thing, the bane of childhood picnics (he also explains why boiling makes eggs go rubbery). The Yucky Green Ring is a harmless formation of ferrous sulphide which afflicts overboiled, not-so-fresh eggs. To prevent it, when hard-cooking eggs:

- Use reasonably fresh eggs.
- Don't cook them for any longer than necessary.
- Plunge into cold water immediately (this also, happily, makes them easier to peel).
- Peel immediately they are cold.

SALADE not-quite-NIÇOISE

Bright green beans, salty wrinkled black olives, sticky-yolked hard-boiled eggs, waxy little potatoes, ripe red tomatoes, and some best tuna. That's Niçoise Salad, right? Wrong. Those in the know are anguished at the travesty, insisting there are no cooked vegetables whatsoever in a true Niçoise. Does it matter? Not at all; it's still delicious . . .

Quantities may be varied according to availability and the cook's mood.

SERVES ABOUT 4

4 large or 8 small waxy potatoes
4 large fresh free-range eggs
250 g French beans
1 fennel bulb (optional)
250 g cherry tomatoes
1 small lettuce
a few handfuls of black olives
a tin of best tuna

Vinaigrette

100 ml extra-virgin olive oil
2 tbsp wine vinegar
1 clove crushed garlic
a few fresh basil leaves
salt and pepper

Steam the potatoes. Cook 6-minute eggs as described above; cool and peel. Quarter them lengthways.

Top and tail the French beans. Steam them for a minute (just long enough to take off the raw edge), then lay them out in a single layer to stop them cooking. Cut the base and tough stalks off the fennel and slice very finely. Halve the cherry tomatoes. Slice the cooled steamed potatoes.

Arrange all the ingredients attractively on a platter, starting with the lettuce leaves. Shake up the vinaigrette ingredients in a jam jar; pour it over the vegetables. (You may not need all of it.) Eat soon after dressing the salad.

Tip: Best tuna: The best tuna is often a French or Spanish brand, packed in olive oil — though even that is no guarantee of quality; some olive-oil-packed ones taste coarse and smell distressingly reminiscent of cat-food. My favourites? **Ortiz** for a real treat, or the widely available **John West Light Tuna Slices** (in sunflower oil).

Other things to do with sticky-yolked eggs:

Make a **Peanut Sambal**, for a platter of mixed steamed vegetables and hard-cooked sticky-yolked eggs, p. 77; or a **Salsa Verde**, p. 94, to serve with them as a simple starter.

A GOOD EGG

Free-range
Use a free-range egg. Their shells are stronger, and they often taste better — if they come from a well-cared-for flock, the lucky hens will have a varied diet and the result will show in the egg. At the very least, you will be spared that aftertaste of unease, at the thought of caged hens suffering pain so that we can have the dubious benefit of paying a few pence less for their eggs.

Fresh?
If you want a soft-boiled yolk to dip your spoon into, then be sure you have a very fresh egg. Egg boxes — irritatingly — give only 'best before' dates, but don't say when the egg was laid. Subtract 28 days from the 'best before' date to discover this.

However, you don't want the very freshest eggs if you're going to peel them: the white will stick to the shell and leave you with a scabby mess. For hard-boiling and peeling, an egg should be at least three days old. (But it shouldn't be ancient either: see 'The yucky green ring' above!)

Healthy
If you want to soft-boil an egg, or leave it sticky-yolked, it's best to use eggs from salmonella-tested flocks (eggs which have the Quality Assured label are from tested flocks) or from a farmer whom you know and whom you can trust (who uses safe feed and buys salmonella-tested chicks only). Young children, pregnant women, the ill and the elderly should avoid soft eggs and all egg dishes which haven't been well cooked.

Storage
Keep your eggs in the fridge. This keeps them freshest, slowing down their deterioration. It would also inhibit the growth of salmonella, should there unfortunately be any in the egg.

omelettes

Let's take the eggy cooking a step further this time. A boiled egg for supper spells survival, but if you can turn eggs into an omelette, you can go beyond bare sustenance. You can treat yourself, and you can treat others. And really that's what cooking is all about.

The omelette has a bit of a fearsome reputation, but don't let that put you off trying it. It is the ultimate quick supper: it takes 10 seconds. A full half-minute if you're a slowcoach. Add a minute or two to make the salad, or some toast; a moment to pour the wine; and you're done.

The eggs
The omelette is a showcase for eggs: just-set, golden and buttery on the outside; lusciously, oozingly soft within. So go for good, fresh free-range eggs.

The pan
Omelettes have the reputation of needing a never-washed, perfectly seasoned cast-iron pan handed down through generations. Piffle. A non-stick frying pan will do just as well; just be sure to use a heavyish one, which will cook more reliably.

What does matter a great deal, however, is the size of the pan. (Confusion reigns here. Most cookbooks, when telling you about omelette-making, give a pan size which measures the base. Most pan manufacturers like to give the larger top measurement.)

For a 2–3 egg omelette, use a pan which measures about 23–6 cm across the top, 15–18 cm across the base. Any larger, and you'll

have a thin and leathery pancake. Any smaller, and you'll have a thick eggy wedge.

The butter
Purists require unsalted, clarified butter. I much prefer salty butter, straight from the pack. I like its flavour and I like the way it darkens to a nutty brown, speckling and flavouring the outside of the omelette. However, it does mean you have to watch the temperature of the pan with care.

(If you want to live less dangerously, clarify some butter. Melt it in a pan, then pour into a small bowl. It will settle into 3 layers. The top is the hardened froth of salt. Scoop it off and discard it. The middle is the butter, which you will use. Underneath are the milk solids, the bits which burn so easily; discard these too.)

The filling
The best eggs and butter on their own taste so good, so don't crowd them out with more than 1 or 2 tbsp of filling:
— **grated cheese** (such as Gruyère, Manchego, Gabriel, Desmond or Parmesan — freshly grated only, please)
— **chopped ham, smoked salmon**, or perhaps a little bit of cooked **flaked fish**
— **chopped tomato with a little basil**
It's important that if your fillings are substantial, they should be warm. There won't be time to cook them in the omelette.

Speed
Speed is of the essence; I wasn't exaggerating when I said 10

seconds. If the omelette cooks too slowly, it will be tough. Traditionally, commis-chefs learned to make an omelette on the back burner — with the front burner blazing under their wrists! That soon taught them.

THE CLASSIC OMELETTE
PER PERSON:
2 large fresh free-range eggs
pinch sea salt
a twist of the black pepper mill
a generous tsp butter
a tsp finely chopped herbs (parsley, thyme, basil, chervil, tarragon . . . as available), or fillings as described above, or both

— Have everything ready, and next to the stove. That includes a warmed plate. You've only got 10 seconds so you can't run around the kitchen looking for the spatula.

— In a bowl, mix the eggs with a fork until they're a uniform pale yellow. Don't beat in lots of air bubbles, which toughens the eggs. Add the salt and pepper.

— On a high heat, heat the frying pan (see above). Put in the tsp of butter; quickly swirl it about. It must scoot around the pan, sizzle and brown, *but must not burn*. If it does, wipe the pan with kitchen paper and start again. (Since the pan is most likely dark, your nose will tell you the butter's burning before your eyes see it happening.) The first couple of times you do this it may go wrong, but you will soon learn the right timing for your pan and your burners.

— The moment the butter covers the base of the pan, pour in the egg. By the time you're scraping the last of it out of the bowl, it should already be starting to set at the edges of the pan. If it isn't, the pan wasn't hot enough!

— Take the fork and pull some of the cooked edge in towards the centre of the pan. It will wrinkle, like gathered fabric. Runny egg will flow into the gap. Keep doing this around the edges of the pan, tilting it to let uncooked egg run on to the base. If big bubbles rise up, pierce them. If the omelette seems to be hardening too quickly, take the pan off the heat.

— When there are just a few slender patches of uncooked egg left on the top of the omelette, scatter the herbs and/or filling across it. With a spatula, lift the edge of the omelette. Fold over a third of it, then fold again — like folding a letter. Slide it onto the waiting plate, where it will land with a soft flop.

Phew! Done!

CHUNKY OMELETTES

Here are some variations on the omelette theme. These are quite different: chunkier, more substantial. The cooking method varies too, as you will see.

INDIAN OMELETTE

Chillies, tomatoes and onions for breakfast? Yes, please. Of course, it's good for lunch, brunch or supper too. (For best effect, use fresh coriander, but you can substitute chives or leave it out.) This is a large omelette which is cut into wedges and can serve 2–6, depending on what else is on offer.

2 medium onions
1 green chilli (to taste)
⅓ tsp whole cumin seeds
2 tbsp butter
1 large ripe tomato
6 large fresh free-range eggs
½ tsp fine sea salt
3 tbsp fresh coriander leaves

The pan: A well-seasoned or non-stick heavy frying pan, about 30 cm across the top/22 cm at the base.

Peel the onions, chop off the root and halve them. Lay them flat on the chopping board and slice them lengthways, not too finely. Slice the chilli (deseed it if you're not sure about how hot you like these things). Turn on the grill.

On a medium heat on the hob, toast the cumin seeds in the dry frying pan until they're just coloured and fragrant. Tip them out and crush them (with pestle and mortar, or with something heavy on a chopping board).

Heat the pan to hot. Add the butter, onions and chillies; fry briskly until the onions are lightly coloured but still a little crunchy. Meanwhile, halve the tomato. Squeeze out the seeds and discard them; chop the tomato flesh. Whisk the eggs and salt in a bowl. Add the tomato and coriander.

Pour the egg mix into the pan and reduce to a medium heat. When the egg starts to set on the base, pull it in from the pan's edges to open up channels into which the uncooked egg can flow. Once it has really thickened, sprinkle the top with the ground roasted cumin. Slide the pan under the hot grill to cook the last of the egg.

Cut into 6 wedges and serve.

AROMATIC CHEESE OMELETTE

Fresh cheeses marinated in flavoured oils are a superb store cupboard standby, and **Knockalara** is one of my favourites, available in delis and good cheese shops. A farm-made feta cheese from near Cappoquin, its marinade of herby olive oil is a bonus for cooking. If you can't find it, choose another oil-preserved cheese such as delicious balls of goats' **Boilie**.

SERVES 2
4 free-range eggs, beaten with salt and pepper
100 g Knockalara feta (about half a jar) or goats' Boilie
2 tbsp flavoured oil (from the jar)

Turn on the grill. Heat a well-seasoned or non-stick heavy frying pan (30 cm across the top) until it's hot. Add 1 tbsp flavoured oil from the jar of cheese. Reduce the heat to medium low, then pour in the eggs. Allow them to set a little, then, with a fork, pull the cooked egg from the edges towards the centre of the pan, as if you were gathering its skirts, allowing uncooked egg to flow into the gap.

When the egg is almost cooked, crumble the cheese over it, spoon another tbsp of the flavoured olive oil over the omelette, and slide it under the hot grill, just long enough to heat the cheese through. Serve with salad and crusty bread.

PEASANT OMELETTE

For breakfast, lunch, supper or tea, this is a meal in a pan. For 1 large omelette for 2-4 (in a pan 30 cm along the top), slice **100 g rindless streaky rashers** into pieces, then fry them in a hot, heavy or non-stick pan. (You may need some oil and you may need to mop up white, oozing goo, unless you have great rashers.)

Add **2 peeled boiled/steamed potatoes**, cut in chunks; fry till crusty (add extra oil if you need it). **Whisk 4–5 fresh free-range eggs**, pour them into the pan and season well with **salt, pepper** and some finely-chopped **chives** if you have them. Cook until the base is set and golden, then finish this chunky omelette by flipping it over onto a plate and sliding it back into the pan — or, if that unnerves you, by just putting the pan under a hot grill.

poach, scramble, fry

POACH

The thought of dropping a liquid raw egg into a bath of hot water in order to cook it seems improbable (how could it possibly work?), and if you've ever tried doing it with a less-than-fresh egg you'll have had your worst suspicions about this odd form of cooking confirmed, as the white drifts through the water in opaque little strings. But work it can, and a good poached egg is a lovely thing, like a gentler, more free-form boiled egg, with this great advantage over a boiled egg: you can prod it to test for doneness. So here's how.

— Use **fresh eggs**. Really, really fresh eggs. For successful poaching, your egg must be so fresh that when you crack it into a saucer, the white is still a thick jelly, clinging to the yolk. If the white is wet and watery and flat, your poached egg will be stringy.

This can pose a bit of a problem. So often, supermarkets sell eggs which are weeks old; the 'best before' date is 28 days after laying, so if the date you're looking at is 2 weeks away, your egg is already 2 weeks old. That's all right for baking, but it's hopeless for poached eggs. Let

the shop know you'd like your eggs fresh! Or buy eggs from a market or local shop, from someone who can be trusted to be telling you the truth about when the eggs were laid.

— Use **free-range eggs**, which have better structure and are less likely to break when cracked open.

— To the **hot water**. Bring a fairly deep frying pan full of water to a brisk simmer. Don't bother with salt and/or vinegar in the water — they don't really help.

...-law, sister-in-law, nieces, nephews, relatives and friends. Rest in peace. Removal from Daly's Mortuary Chapel, Francis St., this (Sunday) evening at 7.30, to Newmarket-on-Fergus Church. Funeral Mass tomorrow (Monday) at 11 o'c. Burial immediately afterwards in Quin Abbey.

DONOHOE, Teresa Bridget (Tess) (formerly of Castlepark, Ballinasloe, County Galway and of Wimbledon) — April 14 (Saturday) 2001, passed away (peacefully, aged 91 years); dearly loved aunt of Ann and Bernadette. R.I.P.

DOOGAN (Limerick) — April 21, 2001, (suddenly), at home, Daniel, 8 Derravaragh (Roxboro), Caherdavin Park, formerly Department of Agriculture, beloved husband of Lauretta, and dearly loved father of Grainne, Orla (O'Brien), Deirdre and John; sadly missed by his loving family, son-in-law Paul, grandchildren Conor and Rory, brothers John-Francis and James, brothers-in-law, sisters-in-law, nephews, other relatives and friends. Rest in peace. Removal from Thompson's Funeral Home, Thomas Street, to Christ the King Church, Caherdavin this (Sunday) evening at 7 o'c. Requiem Mass tomorrow (Monday) at 11.30 o'c. Funeral afterwards to Drumcliffe

McGRANE (nee ... Moydow, Co. Longford) — April 20, 2001, at her residence, Kathleen, beloved wife of the late Patrick, deeply regretted by her loving son James, daughters Theresa, Kathleen, Bernadette and Una, brothers, sisters, sons-in-law, daughter-in-law, sisters-in-law, nephews, nieces, grandchildren, great-grandchildren, relatives and friends. R.I.P. Removal leaving her residence this (Sunday) evening at 6.30 o'c. to Moydow Church. Funeral Mass tomorrow (Monday) at 12 o'c. Burial afterwards in local cemetery.

MEANEY (née Kelly, Bally... and formerly ...corick, Bally...) — April 4, 2001, at the residence, ... the late Ann and Tossy Meaney; deeply regretted by ..., brothers-in-law, sisters-in-law, aunts, uncles, nephews, nieces, relatives and friends. Reposing at remains ... Monday (Sunday) ... o'c. ... Requiem Mass ... at 11 o'c. Funeral afterwards to Lissycasey Cemetery.

MILNER (Walsh Island, Co. Offaly) — April 20, 2001 (suddenly), at his residence, Carmel, (Eneghan); Thomas; deeply regretted by his loving Michael, brother ... sister Ailish and Maureen ...

TINNELLY (Corglass, Kingscourt, Co. Cavan) — April 21, 2001, (peacefully), at the Mater Hospital, Dublin, Brian; sadly missed by his loving wife Kathleen, sons Terence and Joseph, daughters Mary and Bríd, mother, brothers, sister, aunts, nieces, nephews, relatives and friends. R.I.P. Reposing at his home. Removal this (Sunday) evening at 6.30 o'c. to The Church, The Immaculate Conception, Kingscourt, arriving at 11 o'c. Funeral on Monday after Mass to adjoining cemetery.

WATTERS (nee Gilmartin) (Cloonacrin, Grange, Co. Sligo) — April 21, 2001, Maura; deeply regretted by her loving husband Francie, daughter Mary, brothers Seamus, sister ...

Crack an egg into a saucer. (If the white's watery, change your plans now and fry or scramble the egg instead.) Slide the egg into a patch of water where you can see lots of little bubbles. If the white seems to be drifting all over the pan, you can use a spoon to gently coax it back towards the yolk. Keep the water just below simmering point for 3-4 minutes, or until the yolk is done to your liking.

— To **test the yolk**, just lift the egg out of the water with a large slotted spoon and prod it with your finger. When it's done, put the egg on kitchen paper or a clean tea towel to dry. And then eat it quickly, on hot buttered toast.

— You can **keep poached eggs warm** for a while in a pan full of warm (not hot) water.

SCRAMBLE

Simple.

— Break **2 eggs per person** into a bowl and gently whisk them with a fork to break them up; but don't whip in lots of air. When you're ready to cook, add a little **salt** and, if you like, some **pepper**.

— Melt a **big knob of butter** in a heavy-based saucepan over a medium heat. Add the eggs and turn the heat down. Stir with a wooden spoon. Make sure you scrape right into the edges and along the base of the pan.
— If you want the eggs pourable, stir a lot and vigorously. I prefer them tender but somewhat curdy, so I allow a brief moment for the heat to build up, then stir. Keep the heat low to medium, and keep a hawk-eye on the pan. Keep stirring.

— When the eggs look not quite ready, take them off the heat. (This is vital, as they'll go on cooking even as you scoop them out of the pot.) Quickly stir in **another knob of butter**, or **1 tbsp cream per egg**. Or both. And get them out of the pot right away.

Tip: The scrambled egg pot is hell to clean. A non-stick pot takes care of this problem, but look for one with a somewhat textured non-stick surface. Food needs to grip a surface to cook well. The ultra-slippy pots make the butter and eggs slither too much, and they just slide around the pan rather than scrambling properly.

Serve just as they are, with toast, or with **a few tsp chopped chives** stirred in, or a **few tbsp smoked salmon**, or both. If using the salmon, be sure to add the cream to the eggs.

FRY

A crispy frill at the edges, and a soft saffron sticky yolk to spear ... mmm.

— A **fresh egg** helps, though it's by no means as crucial as it is for poached eggs. I find the yolks of **free-range eggs** break less easily when the egg is cracked.

— **Use a well-seasoned heavy frying pan, or a heavy-based non-stick pan with a textured non-stick surface** (see the tip above). If you're using a well-seasoned pan, heat it to hot before adding fat (important). If using non-stick, heat it with the fat in it.

— Use **1 tbsp dripping, bacon fat, olive oil or sunflower oil per egg**, and have the heat on medium-high. Yes, eggs fried in olive oil are quite delicious.

— Unless you're a veteran egg fryer and maestro egg cracker, it's easier to crack the eggs one by one into a saucer first, then slip them into the hot fat. Again, if the eggs are fresh, the jellied whites will cling to the yolk and won't spread all over the pan. Once the eggs are in, lower the heat to medium.

— Using a tablespoon, baste the yolk with sizzling fat from time to time so it firms up a little. You can prod it gently to check how it's doing. If you want the yolk quite hard, turn the egg over and fry the other side as well.

— And that's that!

pasta

'The angels in paradise', the Duke of Bovino, Mayor of Naples, declared confidently in 1930, 'eat nothing but vermicelli with tomato sauce.'

What culinary chauvinism! Still, you couldn't really blame the man. The futurist poet Filippo Marinetti had launched a campaign to get rid of Italy's traditional food, and had unleashed a national furore; provocatively, he had denounced pasta: 'it is heavy, brutalising and gross,' he had claimed of his country's staple food; 'its nutritive qualities are deceptive; it induces scepticism, sloth and pessimism'.

(Do those words sound familiar? Almost identical sentiments were expressed time and again about the potato, by appalled English observers of Ireland's poor in the 18th and 19th centuries.)

Denouncing the monotonous, stomach-filling, allegedly brutalising diet of the masses comes easily to those who can enjoy the luxury of finer sensibilities.)

Marinetti's campaign was clearly at least partly tongue in cheek (his suggested alternative diet was full of such shockers as *salame* in a bath of black coffee and eau de Cologne). And yet, when it came to attitudes to pasta, he was certainly not alone. Even a great food writer like Elizabeth David, when she wrote her 1950s classic *Italian Food*, was sure that 'enlightened Italians' agreed with her: pasta was unsuitable for eating daily. American nutritionists were of the same mind. They worked hard to change the 'unhealthy' eating habits which Mediterranean immigrants were bringing to the US — too many carbohydrates, too many vegetables, too much olive oil!

Well, the pendulum has swung. Nowadays, we side with the angels once more, and pasta's back on the menu. Though, thank God, it's a bit more varied on earth than it is in heaven.

THE PASTA
Fresh or dried?
There's no need to scorn dried pasta. The Italians don't (and they ought to know). A curious snobbery favouring the 'fresh' stuff has emerged outside Italy lately. This is odd because it's actually easier to find good dried pasta here; most so-called 'fresh' pasta is pretty awful — it's stodgy, and when cooked has none of the light, supple slipperiness which makes good fresh pasta so divine.

The best dried pasta, on the other hand, cooks to a sprightly, resilient chewiness. It has a spring and a bounce to it. It actually has some flavour, it's not just a neutral vehicle for sauce.

If this doesn't sound like the pasta you've been eating all these years, the problem may well be the pasta, not your cooking. Many dried pastas go from undercooked crunch to overcooked sludge without passing through the intervening, delicious, 'al dente' stage. It all depends on the quality of the pasta, which depends on a few things — the flour, the water, and the way the pasta is cut and dried. The very best dried pastas are cut on old bronze dies which give them a slightly grainy texture, all the better to hold a sauce. And they are slow-dried, not speed-dried. There is a considerable difference in flavour (and texture).

Good dried pasta?
Head for the Italians. Non-Italian brands I've tasted are significantly inferior to good Italian ones. Of brands available in Ireland, I'd recommend Castiglione, de Cecco or Barilla (in that order).

Egg pastas
Not all dried pastas are supposed to cook to a firm, sprightly bounce. Some are made with eggs (most dried pasta is made only with durum wheat semolina and water), which gives them a more tender texture and slightly floppier feel when cooked. Indeed, considering the sad quality of most fresh pastas I've tasted in Ireland, a dried pasta made with eggs may well be a better alternative. Of brands available here, I like de Cecco, and some of the Irish-made Noodle House pastas.

How much to cook?
Most cookbooks specify paltry amounts. For generous main course pasta portions, allow 100–125 g dried pasta per person.

This is for real Italian-style pasta, where the pasta is the star, and the sauce is but an adornment which clings to it very lightly.

The pot of water
— It's important to have lots of water, or you'll get a starchy swamp. You need 1 litre of water for every 100 g dried pasta. Work this out and you'll probably find your largest pot is really too small if you cook pasta for 4 or more. (If you're looking for a pot, this is one time when lightweight is a good thing. It should also have two handles for easy pouring.)

— Salt the water properly: 1 tsp salt for every litre of water. If the pasta isn't salted while cooking, it will taste dull no matter how good the sauce.

— Oil in the water is unnecessary. It doesn't stop the pasta from sticking. Save it for anointing the finished dish.

Cooking the pasta
Boil the water. Add the salt. Add the pasta. Stir to separate it. Put the lid on the pot. When the water comes back to the boil, stir again, and leave the lid off.

How long?
Ignore packet instructions, they're nearly always wrong. Watch it closely, and taste it often. *Remember that pasta goes on cooking after you drain it.* Italian cook and teacher Marcella Hazan is typically caustic on the subject: 'Soft pasta is no more fit to eat than a soggy slice of bread. Do not be afraid to stop [cooking] too early. It is probably already overcooked.'

pasta

Draining the pasta

Now here's a crucial moment. Firstly: *before you drain the pasta, scoop out a mugful of the cooking water and keep it.* And secondly: when you drain the pasta, be sure not to overdo it. Pasta needs to be a bit wet. It should glisten and be slippery so the sauce can spread easily. If you dry it out too much, you'll have a tangled, stuck mess, and you'll need far too much sauce to moisten it again.

The reserved water? It's there to moisten the pasta if you realise you've overdrained it. (Using oil doesn't work — it just makes the pasta greasy.) It will also loosen sauces like pesto, and make the sauce for a carbonara. You'll find recipes for those on the next pages.

And finally . . .

— Always call people to the table before the pasta is done. Pasta waits for no one.

— Don't ruin pasta with the rancid stench of those brand-name ready-grated Parmesans in tubs. If you've never showered your pasta with just-grated fruity, sweet, tangy, grainy Parmesan you're in for a treat. If that's hard to find, or too pricey, Irish-made Regato is a reasonable alternative.

PASTA SAUCES

Here is a clutch of pasta recipes, all easy enough for everyday eating and good enough to serve to friends. Except for the first, long-simmered tomato sauce, all of them can be made in the time it takes the pasta to cook.

SIMPLEST SIMMERED TOMATO SAUCE

I can't say what the angels in paradise would think of this pomodoro, but down here it's a staple food in my house. Tinned tomatoes make a much better sauce than unripe fresh ones, but if you can get some red-ripe fresh tomatoes, chop them (skinned, if you're fussy) and stir into the sauce towards the end of cooking. It really lifts the flavour.

This makes enough for 6–8. It freezes brilliantly and is also a great sauce for vegetables.

1–2 tbsp butter
2 tbsp olive oil
3 onions, very finely chopped
2 cloves garlic, finely chopped
2 tins chopped tomatoes
salt, sugar and lemon juice
2 tbsp chopped fresh herbs, e.g. marjoram, basil or thyme (optional)

Melt the butter with the oil in a large saucepan over a low heat. Stir in the onions and the garlic. Cover with a lid and turn the heat down to the lowest possible. Allow the mix to seethe and melt gently for 20 minutes, checking to be sure it doesn't 'catch' and start to brown. The onions should look soft, glassy and creamy; their acrid onion smell will dissolve into a sweet, buttery aroma.

Add the tomatoes, 1 tsp salt and 1 tsp sugar. Simmer, uncovered, for 20 minutes, stirring occasionally. Towards the end, add a squeeze of lemon juice and taste to check the seasoning balance. Stir in the herbs. Serve on any kind of pasta, with freshly grated cheese.

If you freeze the sauce, hold back the fresh herbs and add just before serving.

QUICKER TOMATO SAUCE

There's nothing like the sweet flavour of the sauce above, but there are times when you just don't have 40 minutes to make it. So:

SERVES 3–4
1 onion
1 clove garlic
2 tbsp olive oil
1 tin chopped tomatoes

Chop the onion and garlic very finely. Heat the olive oil in a frying pan and sizzle the onion and garlic gently, enough to colour them but without letting them darken. Turn the heat up to maximum. Pour in the tomatoes and stand back as it spits and hisses. Stir before the onion bits burn. Simmer the sauce gently for as long as you can, 10–20 minutes, adding a little water if it dries out. If you have some rosemary to simmer with the sauce, so much the better. Simmer a sprig in the sauce for a few minutes, lifting it out before the needles fall off.

Season with salt and pepper, add any fresh herbs you may have, and serve.

Variation: To add instant flavour to the sauce, mash **1 anchovy fillet** and cook it with the onion before adding the tomatoes. The result is a savoury oomph — but not an anchovy flavour. Even my children love it.

NO-COOK FRESH TOMATO AND FRESH HERB SAUCE

This is fantastically fragrant and fruity, the essence of summer. It needs no cooking at all; the hot olive oil just sizzles on the fresh herbs and releases their freshest aromas and brightest colour. Use parsley or basil as a base, but try to get a variety of others. When last I made this, I used mostly parsley, but added 1 tsp each of coriander, marjoram, mint, sage and dill.

FOR 500 G PASTA, SERVING 4–6. BOTH CHUNKIER SHAPES AND SPAGHETTI WORK WELL.

500 g ripest, reddest, sweetest tomatoes, preferably cherry or vine

4 scallions

4 oil-packed sun-dried tomatoes

½ tsp dried chilli flakes or fresh chopped chilli (or more)

3–4 generous handfuls mixed fresh herbs (see above)

125 ml olive oil

sea salt and black pepper

While the water comes to the boil and the pasta cooks:

Cut the tomatoes into small chunks (quarter cherry tomatoes, cut others as appropriate). Chop the scallions; slice the sun-dried tomatoes very finely. Chop the herbs, again very finely — you should have a total of about 10 tbsp chopped herbs. Gently pile everything into a large, beautiful serving bowl, tomatoes first, herbs on top.

When the pasta's nearly done, heat the olive oil in a small saucepan until it's extremely hot. Pour it over the herbs and tomatoes.

Remember to remove a mugful of cooking water from the pasta pot. Toss the drained, slippery pasta with the sauce ingredients in the bowl. Season to taste, and add a little of the cooking water to moisten the mix if necessary.

Variations: You can add all sorts of things to the mix. **Chopped olives**, green or black; a teaspoon of **tapenade** (a Provençal black olive and anchovy paste); cubes of **feta cheese** . . . let your imagination take hold.

pasta

FRESH TOMATO PUTTANESCA

Here's another variation on the fresh tomato sauce theme, this time a more gutsy mix. It also happens to be rather low in fat — yet bursting with flavour.

FOR 500 G DRIED PASTA SHAPES SUCH AS BOWS OR TWISTS, ENOUGH FOR 4–6

1 onion
½ red chilli
2 cloves garlic
1 tightly packed handful parsley leaves (1–2 bunches)
3 celery stalks
1 heaped tbsp capers
3 anchovy fillets
20 black olives or 1 tbsp black olive paste
200 g very ripe tomatoes
1 tbsp olive oil
salt and freshly ground black pepper

While the water comes to the boil for the pasta, and while the pasta cooks, chop the onion, chilli, garlic, parsley, celery, capers, anchovies and olives (if using) into the tiniest dice you can manage, keeping each pile separate as you do. Chop the tomatoes roughly, saving every scrap of juice.

In a frying pan, heat the olive oil over medium heat, then sizzle the onion, garlic and chilli, stirring, until they are fragrant and golden. Add the parsley, stir for half a minute, then stir in the celery and take the pan off the heat. Stir in the capers, anchovies, olives (or olive paste) and tomatoes. Add plenty of freshly ground black pepper and a little salt to taste.

Quickly toss the glistening pasta with the sauce and serve right away. A little grated cheese is optional.

CLASSIC CARBONARA

Yes, this is a true Carbonara recipe, and no, there's no cream in it. The sauce coats the spaghetti with a satiny cream all the same: try it and see.

FOR 500 G DRIED SPAGHETTI OR LINGUINE, ENOUGH FOR 4–5

200 g smoked streaky rashers (or Italian pancetta if you can get it)
3 cloves garlic
2–3 tbsp olive oil
3 large fresh free-range eggs
100 g freshly grated Parmesan or Regato, plus extra for serving
freshly ground black pepper

Cut the rashers (or pancetta) into very slender little strips, and peel and halve the garlic cloves.

Heat a large frying pan and add the olive oil. Add the garlic; fry until golden; take it out and discard it. Fry the rashers in the flavoured oil until they start to crisp. Take the pan off the heat.

While the pasta cooks, beat the eggs in a bowl. Grate the cheese finely and stir it in to the eggs, with plenty of turns of the black pepper mill.

When the pasta is still a tiny bit underdone, turn the heat under the frying pan of rashers to low to reheat them. Scoop out a mugful of the pasta cooking water and keep it. Drain the pasta, leaving it glistening, and return it to its still-hot cooking pot, off the heat.

Add the egg and cheese mix, plus a little of the pasta water from the mug, to the pasta. Toss well, adding more pasta water if necessary (you'll need a total of 50–100 ml). The heat of the water and the pasta cooks the egg lightly. Reheat it if you must, but watch out, or the eggs will scramble.

Toss the rasher strips through the pasta, being sure to add the flavoured oil. Serve at once on hot plates with more cheese and with the pepper mill.

Note: As with all lightly cooked egg dishes, be sure to use the best, freshest, free-range eggs from a Quality Assured or salmonella-tested flock. See the note on p. 5.

STIR-FRIED COURGETTE SLIVERS AND PARSLEY

Use the smallest courgettes you can find; they have a nuttier flavour and ooze much less water.

FOR 500 G DRIED SPAGHETTI OR LINGUINE, SERVING 4–6

750 g courgettes
4 cloves garlic
½ red chilli
small handful parsley (or chives)
100 ml olive oil
salt and freshly ground black pepper

Slice the courgettes at a steep angle to get quite long slices. Stack these and cut them into narrow strips. Crush and chop the garlic. Deseed the chilli and chop very finely. Chop the herbs finely.

While the pasta cooks:
Put a very large frying pan or (better still) a wok on your hottest burner. When it's very hot, add the oil. Then add the garlic and chilli. Stir-fry for just 1 or 2 seconds, then add the courgettes. Stir-fry until they are softening but not quite cooked through. Taste; stir in the chopped herbs and turn off the heat.

Remember to reserve cooking water from the pasta. Toss the sauce into the slippery pasta, moistening it with a little cooking water. Serve with cheese.

PEAS, PROSCIUTTO AND CREAM

FOR 500 G DRIED PASTA, SERVING 4–6

whites of 1 bunch scallions
125 g Parma or Bayonne ham in one thick slice; or smoked rindless streaky rashers
50 g butter
250 ml cream or crème fraîche
250 g frozen petits pois
freshly ground black pepper
125 g Parmesan or Regato, freshly grated, plus extra for serving

Chop the scallion whites very finely and slice the ham or rashers very finely.

While the pasta cooks, heat the butter in a saucepan. Gently cook the scallion whites until soft. Turn up the heat; add the ham or rasher slivers; cook until aromatic and starting to crisp. Add the cream, frozen peas and pepper. Simmer to reduce just a little. Taste; add salt if necessary.

Remember to save a mugful of the cooking water to moisten the pasta later if necessary. Drain the pasta; toss with the sauce and cheese.

Don't forget the pestos . . .
Pesto is one of the best no-cook sauces for quickie pasta dinners. More than with any other sauce, though, it's imperative to have the pasta glistening and slippery, and to add a few tbsp hot cooking water per serving to loosen that dense green stuff. Remember pesto should barely season the pasta with little green flecks, not load it down with globs of oily goo as so many restaurants seem to think.

WONDERFUL PESTO

This pesto — wonderfully, unusually, heretically — includes mint. Ligurians would probably be horrified. The idea jumped out at me from Bernadette O'Shea's *Pizza Defined* — although where she uses a lot, I use just the merest touch for a lift in the flavour. Addictive.

75 g fresh basil leaves
5 g (2 tbsp) fresh mint leaves
25 g pine nuts
3 cloves garlic, crushed
50 g freshly grated Parmesan
25 g freshly grated Pecorino
40 g butter, at room temperature
salt and pepper
200 ml olive oil

Stuff all the ingredients except the olive oil into the bowl of a food processor. Blend to mix well. With the blade turning, pour in the olive oil until a well-blended pesto has formed.

Pesto tips
- If you can't get Pecorino, use all Parmesan. But keep looking for the Pecorino. It has a distinctive flavour (and it's cheaper than Parmesan).
- For a classic pesto, just use all basil.
- To store pesto: This is extremely difficult to contemplate doing, since it tastes so good. Don't keep it for more than a few days, or your pesto will start to taste of rotting vegetables. Cover it with a thin film of olive oil while storing it in the fridge.
- Come across a glut of basil? Make up the pesto, but leave out the cheeses and garlic (they tend to go rancid). Freeze. Add the rest after defrosting.
- **Coriander pesto** is a favourite. Use coriander instead of the basil.

WINTER PESTO

2 cloves garlic (smoked garlic is nice if you can find it)
50 g walnuts
a small handful fresh parsley (flat-leaf if possible)
30 g freshly grated Parmesan
salt and pepper
olive oil

Mush the garlic with the side of a knife or a garlic press, then add it with all the other ingredients except the oil to the food processor and grind to a paste. Add olive oil with the blades whirring until it's a sauce.

potatoes

The potato is a delicate thing. This may sound surprising, for we generally treat spuds with precious little consideration, heaving them into the boot of the car, tumbling them into the sink with a thunderous roll, and boiling the bejaysus out of them. We just don't think much about them (until we're left stranded without a decent one). But the fact of the matter is that this tender tuber needs a gentle hand — and none more so than the Irish potato.

Irish potatoes, you see, are different. A sumptuous Irish boiled potato, the stuff of our dreams, is a 'ball of flour'. Its taut jacket, just cracked, curls open to release the steam. Inside, it is parched, crying out thirstily for lashings of butter to melt into it, to moisten its fluffy centre and crown it with a salty deposit. The rest of the world, meanwhile, prefers its spuds rather more moist — 'soapy', as the Irish scathingly dismiss them. Even the English, who profess to enjoy a floury spud, have a different benchmark than we do: a potato like Cara, which by Irish standards is creamy, is described as floury in many English cookbooks.

boiled potatoes

Achieving perfect balls of flour is no mean feat. A floury potato is a temperamental creature, much harder to cook well than its waxier cousins. It is likely to explode, flinging its insides all over the pan, or to crack slowly, leaving you with a sullen hard centre coated in wet sludge. So how can you get sumptuous boiled spuds every time, spuds which are fluffy, steaming and dry?

In earlier days, they boiled them in sea water. 'There are old people in Co. Down today who talk of the "good old days" when this was done. No matter how "floury" the potatoes are, if boiled in sea water, the skin does not crack,' said cooking adviser Florence Irwin in her book *The Cookin' Woman* in the early nineteenth century. You can try this without heading for the shore by salting your fresh water until it tastes unpleasantly salty — several tbsp per pot. I've found it usually works . . . but not always!

Better again, and much more reliable? Don't boil your boiled potatoes at all. Steam them instead. If they crack, they go on cooking without becoming waterlogged. Steaming also means you can cook cut potatoes without any problems.

BEAUTIFUL 'BOILED' POTATOES

1. **Start with good, floury potatoes;** Golden Wonders and Records are the flouriest and Kerr's Pinks can also be good. Sadly, if they are overfertilised and have taken up too much water, they may be unpleasantly soapy; if you can't get these varieties from a good grower, you may be better off with Roosters.
2. **Carry them carefully!** Potatoes are prone to bruising; they should be carried as carefully as eggs. If you buy washed potatoes, buy in small quantities and keep them in a cool place (not the fridge) out of the light, or they will turn green.
3. **Scrub**, leaving the skins on. As far as possible choose potatoes of a similar size; cut them if necessary, but cut ones will never cook as floury as whole ones. Trim off any green parts.
4. **Don't boil them — steam them.** Steaming takes a minute or two longer than boiling but retains more flavour. Simplest of all for the job are inexpensive metal 'petal' steamers which fan out like a flower to fit any pan; well worth investing in.
5. **To test if they're done**, don't use a fork, which breaks them up. Slip the tip of a small sharp knife in; if it goes in easily, the potatoes are cooked.
6. **Dry them.** This is important. When they're done, fold up a clean tea towel, tuck it over the cooked potatoes, and replace the lid. Leave the pot off the heat for a few minutes. The tea towel absorbs steam from the potatoes and dries them.
7. **No steamer?** Boil the potatoes in water for most of their cooking time, keeping an eye on them. At the first sign of cracking, empty the pot of all but an inch of water, then continue to cook with the lid on. This is reasonably successful.

Finally: you'll find many recipes tell you to boil *peeled* potatoes before doing something else to them. Be wary: a floury Irish spud will parboil for 5 minutes or so, but then start to break up. As a rule you're better off steaming them in their jackets; then peel and proceed.

Waxy potatoes

If you have a truly waxy potato, such as a Pink Fir Apple, Nicola, Elvira, Charlotte or La Ratte, or another waxy European variety, you can boil these in plenty of salted water without any problems. However, for maximum flavour I'd still always recommend boiling in their skins, then peeling later.

For more on potato varieties, see p. 43.

Waxy Potatoes with Dill

When you have a good, waxy potato, or tasty 'baby' potatoes, seek out a bunch of dill and a few knobs of butter. Simmer the potatoes in their skins with the dill stalks. When done, drain the potatoes and remove the boiled dill stalks. Chop the dill fronds and toss with the hot potatoes and the butter, adding salt as well. Wonderful.

Perfect mash

1. This depends, first of all, on **perfectly steamed (or boiled) floury spuds**. Make sure the potatoes are a really floury variety, and that they are nicely dry, or your mash will be rather gluey.
2. **The implement.** I've never found a *potato masher* very satisfactory. Its holes are too

boiled potatoes

big; maybe this speaks of my laziness but it nearly always leaves me with lumpy mash. If you've ever tried using a *food processor* you'll have found that you get glue. Some cooks recommend a *mouli*. This inexpensive, low-tech French gizmo (basically a sieve with a handle, which you turn to push the food through) is great for puréeing and straining all sorts of vegetables, and I'd use it if I had nothing else, but it too tends to make the mash a little sticky rather than fluffy. If you have a *Kenwood with a 'K' beater*, you can make excellent mash in moments. Best of all, and strangely out of fashion, is a *potato ricer*. This gadget looks like an outsize garlic crusher, big enough for spuds. It creates slender strands of potato which need only a quick stir to become smooth and fluffy mash. (Potato ricers are available in good kitchen shops.)

3. Don't add anything (butter, milk, etc.) before mashing, to avoid lumps.
4. Heat the milk before you stir it in. And stir it in slowly, beating all the while.
5. Season mash/champ well; it needs it.

CHIVE CHAMP

Autumnal comfort food at its best. This version uses no butter in the mash itself; if you prefer it richer, leave out a little milk and stir in a knob of butter.

SERVES ABOUT 4

900 g floury potatoes
about 400 ml milk
25 g chives
salt
knob of butter

Steam or boil the potatoes in their skins; dry with a tea towel under the lid of the pot. Peel them while they're still hot enough to hurt. Mash with your chosen implement and return to the pan. Chop the chives very finely. Heat the milk; pour most of it onto the potatoes, adding the chives. Stir the potatoes vigorously over a low heat until you have fluffy mash; add the rest of the milk if you need it. Salt to taste. Serve in a heated dish, with the knob of butter melting in a dip in the centre.

Scallion champ: Substitute **1 small bunch scallions** for the chives (or use them in addition). Chop scallions finely and heat them with the milk for a minute, then proceed as above.

POTATO, HERB AND PARSNIP MASH

The parsnip flavour is delicate in this mash.

SERVES ABOUT 6

900 g floury potatoes
500 g parsnips
1 bunch parsley
1 bunch scallions
½ tsp thyme leaves
450 ml milk
salt
generous knob of butter, or more

Put the potatoes on to steam or boil, in their skins. While they cook, peel and quarter the parsnips and if they have hard cores, cut them out; simmer the parsnips in salted water until they're soft, about 10 minutes.

Chop the parsley leaves, scallions and thyme leaves quite finely. Put them in a saucepan with the milk, bring it to simmering point, and set aside to infuse.

Drain the parsnips when they are done and mash them. Peel the cooked potatoes while they're still hot enough to make you wince as you hold them. Mash them very well in a saucepan together with the parsnips, until there are no lumps (a potato ricer does this job best — see 'Perfect mash', p. 17); stir in the hot milk and herbs. Add salt to taste and heat it up if necessary. If you're feeling wicked, stir a great big lump of butter into the mash. Serve it in a big mound with the knob of butter melting in a pool in the centre.

Tip: Champ and mash are very obliging. They can be made in advance and reheated; just don't keep them warm for hours or you will get that revolting hospital mashed-potato smell. Reheat in a big ovenproof serving dish, covered with foil, on the lowest shelf in the oven for about 20–30 minutes while you cook the rest of the dinner.

POTATO CAKES

Potato cakes provide magnificent, soothing morning-after soakage and go well with everything from rashers to spicy corn salsa (for which recipe, see p. 93).

SERVES 4–6

Allow **500 g uncooked potatoes.** Steam them, skin them and mash them while hot (a potato ricer works best — see 'Perfect mash', p. 17). Melt in a **25 g knob of butter** and add **1 tsp salt** and **lots of freshly ground black pepper.** If you like the cakes quite firm and slim, add **100 g flour;** if you'd prefer them fluffier and fatter, add just **50 g flour.** Mix quickly; don't overmix or you'll make them gluey. Pat out the dough with your fingers (1 cm thick if you added 100 g flour, 2 cm if you added just
50 g flour). Cut into rounds or triangles, whichever you prefer. Set them aside now until you're ready to cook.

Potato cakes can be cooked in a non-stick frying pan or in the oven. I find the oven easier since there's usually enough going on in all the frying pans at breakfast time. Whichever way, don't rush the cooking or they will taste gluey and claggy — from the raw flour.

To cook in a non-stick pan: Heat the pan to medium. Lie the cakes in the ungreased pan and cook on a low heat for 15–20 minutes, turning as necessary; be sure they don't burn.
To cook in the oven: Heat the oven to 200C/400F/Gas 6, leaving a baking tray in it as it heats. Put the potato cakes in; bake for 20 minutes, turning once.

fried potatoes

The clammy grey pallor of last night's potatoes when you take them out of the fridge is so very unappealing — they look as if they really will taste like death warmed up. Yet give them a go in the frying pan, give them a long, slow fry, and they'll land golden and russet-flecked and crunchy on your plate, and their hot steam will burn your mouth as you bite into them impatiently. One always does.

Most books don't tell you how to fry potatoes; it's one of those skills which sounds too simple to be worth describing. It's easy to end up with a greasy mess though, especially when you're dealing with Irish floury potatoes and their explosive tendencies. But if you get the knack, the result is heaven. And what does heaven taste like? It might be flavoured simply with salt, or perhaps with some spicy, chewy chunks of Spanish chorizo sausage, or with a kaleidoscopic flavour-burst of whole Indian spices.

The potatoes
The best way is to start with potatoes you steamed or boiled yesterday. (Day-old cooked potatoes are firmer.)

But if you didn't steam extra last night, cut chunks of washed but unpeeled potatoes (see below for size). Steam for about 5–7 minutes. Stop cooking when the chunks aren't quite done, before the peel starts to come adrift at the corners. Spread out in a single layer to cool, for 20 minutes at least, preferably longer.

To peel or not to peel?
I don't, if the skin is thin and delicate. The fried skin is crunchy and tasty and helps the potatoes hold together and absorb less oil. But it's up to you.

The chunks
Slices are delicious — they make more crust — but they take up so much room in the pan. I prefer chunks, so I quarter small potatoes, and cut medium ones in six. For a good proportion of crusty crunch, the chunks should be about 2–3 cm.

The pan
It must be large enough to hold the potatoes in a single layer, otherwise they'll steam and won't crisp. (However, they don't have to be as well spaced out as meat needs to be when it's frying — potatoes don't contain as much moisture.)

The pan should be reasonably heavy so it can deliver a good slow heat. Best flavour comes from a well-seasoned heavy pan. A decent non-stick can do a good job, but only if it's one with a textured surface, so the potatoes can get enough of a grip to develop a good crust.

The fat
This makes a big difference. Best flavour? *Goose* and *duck fat*, especially fat saved from a roast bird. Every teaspoon is precious! (It keeps for months in the fridge or can be frozen.) *Dripping* may be dreadfully out of fashion but the flavour it produces never could be. *Olive oil* is excellent. Plain *vegetable oil*? Fine if using lots of spices.

The frying
— Good fried potatoes can't be rushed. Only time — about 15–20 minutes — at a moderate heat will build up a satisfying crust. Try to speed it up and they'll just burn.

— For cast-iron and other finishes, start by heating the *pan first* over a moderate to high heat. This is vital to prevent the potatoes from sticking when they fry. Hold your hand an inch or so above the pan; when you can feel strong heat, the pan is ready. Add the oil or other fat.

— If you have a non-stick pan, heat it with the oil or fat in it.

— When the oil is hot, add the cold cubed potatoes in an even layer. Do not touch! Allow the first crust to form.

— After a few minutes, turn the potatoes carefully using a pair of metal spoons, to coat them with the hot oil. Salt them now.

— Then turn down the heat to low-to-moderate, and leave them to cook uncovered. They should need to be turned only twice in the 15–20 minutes. The temptation is always to fiddle around with them far too much, turning them too often, breaking them up and interfering with the crust formation. Good fried potatoes should certainly be a touch scruffy; the wayward crunchy bits are scrumptious. But if the potatoes break up too much, there'll be no hot centres to provide steamy contrast.

— As they fry, listen! The sizzling and spitting sounds must be quite brisk. If the sound is a quiet seething one, you're in trouble: you'll get stewed oily spuds. Keep your nose alert for the smell of burning too. If black patches form, turn down the heat. There'll be no crust if they burn.

— And finally . . . sometimes you'll need to add more fat to the pan. (If you see black flecks on pale potatoes, and no golden crust forming, there's not enough fat.) The important thing is that the fat must be hot before it comes into contact with the potatoes, or they'll just soak it up. So . . . push the potatoes to one side. Move the empty side of the pan over the heat, holding it at a slight tilt. Pour in the extra oil, allow it to heat up, then continue frying.

BASIC FRIED POTATOES

SERVES 4, USING A LARGE FRYING PAN (ABOUT 23 CM ACROSS THE BASE)

about 1 kg boiled, cooled potatoes
2–3 tbsp olive oil, duck or goose fat, dripping, etc.
1½ tsp salt
garlic and/or parsley (optional)

Follow the method for frying them as it's described above. If you want to add garlic, chop it and add it nearly at the end of cooking or it'll burn. Chopped parsley should be added at the very last moment.

FRIED POTATOES WITH CHORIZO

This spicy Spanish garlic and paprika sausage contributes great aroma and colour to the potatoes.

Fry the **Basic Fried Potatoes** in olive oil. You'll also need a small, soft

chorizo sausage (not the salami-type for thin slicing), about **75 g.** Cut the sausage into quite thin slices, then cook gently in the oil. Once it has released its oil, remove the sausage and set aside. Turn the heat up under the oil, then add the potatoes and proceed as described for the basic method, not forgetting the salt. Near the end, add the chorizo again. **Garlic** is a delicious addition; **chopped coriander** is particularly good as well.

IRRESISTIBLY SPICED FRIED POTATOES

Salty, spicy, crunchy . . . mmm. The spices crackle and pop a little as they cook, like the occasional retort from a log fire, a most reassuring sound.

Serve with any kind of grilled or roasted meat, or with a fried egg, or just with a tomato salad for a light meal.

Use the quantities for **Basic Fried Potatoes** above. You'll need 3 tbsp sunflower or olive oil and the salt, but no garlic. In addition, prepare:

2 tsp black mustard seeds
2 tsp sesame seeds
1 scant tsp fennel seeds
1 tsp turmeric
½ tsp paprika

Place these all on a saucer, and have the potatoes ready. Heat the pan and then the oil; throw in the spices, stir once, then add the potatoes immediately, turning them so they're evenly coated with colour and flecked with seeds. Add the 1½ tsp salt, turn again, and fry slowly for 15–20 minutes.

roast potatoes

Getting the roasters right requires a generous eye, a little timing — and a rough hand. Generous, because everyone will always eat more of them than you have made. Timing, because when the roast potatoes are ready they just won't wait.

And rough? Rough, because that's the only way to end up with a perfect, scruffy roast spud. Crisp crusty crunch on the outside, hot steaming fluff within.

This is something the rest of the world, poor things, know nothing about. When it comes to the best roast potatoes, the cooking of these islands is king. Nothing, except certain desserts, is accompanied by so much sighing at the table: sighs of delight at the taste of the potatoes, sighs of dismay at how many of them have just been eaten.

Mind you, there are times when Mediterranean-style rosemary and olive oil potato wedges are by far the better option. They are speedier, wonderfully aromatic and much more forgiving. But they're never consumed with the same reckless abandon as the traditional floury roasters, and that says it all.

TRADITIONAL ROASTERS

Essential for great roasters is the roast: nothing else provides the fat which makes a good roast potato so delicious and so crunchy. Old-fashioned floury potatoes are crucial too. And you need to allow a total of at least $1\frac{1}{2}$ hours, for peeling, parboiling and finally roasting the potatoes.

The potatoes must be a floury variety. This can be difficult nowadays when potatoes are so often grown with too much fertiliser. It makes them take up too much water; a wet, soapy spud results. Seek tenaciously for a good source. Organic are often, though not always, better. See pp. 17 and 43 for details on varieties.

Large potatoes are essential, unless you want to spend half an hour at the sink . . .

How many? It depends entirely on appetites — and on the size of the roasting tin. Most recipes underestimate the passion for roast potatoes of nearly everyone I know. You need a basic of 500 g for every 2 people, more if some of your guests are very hungry. That's the unpeeled weight. (Have extra, in case you need to trim the potatoes.)

The tin. A reasonably heavy, large roasting tin is essential. It must be large enough so that the potatoes don't crowd each other out.

The oven temperature can be a bit of a problem if you're roasting meat too — roast potatoes need 220C/425F/Gas 7, whereas most roast meat does best at a lower temperature. If the oven is lower, make sure the potatoes go on the top shelf, then get them really crusty by finishing them at maximum heat while the meat rests.

Prepare the spuds by peeling them with a swivel potato peeler and cutting out any eyes which are left behind. Then cut them into chunks. A size that sits neatly into my cupped palm delivers the right ratio of crust to fluff, about the size of a large plum.

Boil the potatoes first. This is quite essential. (If you haven't time, make the Rosemary and Olive Oil Roast Potato Wedges instead.) Simmer the peeled chunks in salted water for 10 minutes, or until the edges start to give and you can smell cooking potato in the air.

The dripping . . . now here's a word we don't often hear. But the fat from roast meat does make the best roasters. Don't believe anyone who tells you that potatoes are fantastic roasted in sunflower oil. They're fine, but they'll never be wonderful.

However, you don't have to have potfuls of dripping stashed in the fridge. You can start with a little sunflower oil, then top it up with fat from the roast as it drips off. And if you ever roast a duck, or a goose, bless the mountain of fat that it sheds, and save every drop. (Freeze it in ice cube trays, then bag it, if you won't be using it soon.) It makes the best roast potatoes in the world.

How much oil/fat/dripping? Enough to have just a little covering the base of the tin, so it depends on the size of your tin.

Heat is important. The oven *must* be hot when the potatoes go in. Even before that, the fat in the tin must be seething with heat, so the potatoes sizzle energetically when they're added. Heat the tin, with the fat in it, on a low heat on the hob as you drain the potatoes.

Drain the parboiled potatoes well in a colander, then leave them for a moment to dry as you check the fat is really hot. Then . . .

Rough 'em up. Shake the potatoes about in the colander, or in the saucepan with the lid on. This forms the scruffy, fluffy outer layer which will turn crusty in the oven. Don't worry if you lose some in the process; it's unavoidable. If the potatoes disintegrate entirely, it'll be mash with this meal — and don't parboil them so long next time!

Put them in the roasting tin. Using a pair of spoons, turn each one to coat it in the sizzling fat. Scatter a little fine salt over them. Then put the tin in the oven. They will now need an hour, and should be turned twice during the roasting.

Remember to give them a blast at a higher heat right at the end if the oven was at a lower temperature.

When they're done, eat! They won't be as good 5 minutes later. This means juggling the timing of the roast to suit the potatoes, rather than the other way round. Remember, the roast will keep well in a warm place for up to 20 minutes or longer.

ROSEMARY AND OLIVE OIL ROAST POTATO WEDGES

These are probably the most important reason to have a rosemary plant in your garden or in a pot. They go with all kinds of foods, everything from a full roast dinner to a simple salad.

FOR 4–6
Allow about 1 kg potatoes
You will also need about:
3 tbsp gutsy virgin olive oil
2 tbsp fresh rosemary leaves, chopped
1 generous tsp Maldon sea salt flakes, or ½ tsp fine sea salt

The potatoes
Any size and variety will do. These are speediest made with pre-washed potatoes; all they'll need is a quick scrub since they taste best if you leave the skin on, though if it's very old and warty it's probably best to peel them.

To make them
Turn the oven on to 200C/400F/Gas 6. Wash the potatoes. Cut them in quarters lengthways, or in half if they're small. Put the potatoes into a roasting dish in which they're not too crowded. Add the olive oil and rosemary. With your hands, turn the potatoes in the oil to coat them all over. Wash and dry your hands, then scatter the salt flakes all over. Roast in the hot oven for 40–45 minutes, turning them once or twice during this time. They should be crispy on the unskinned sides when they're done. Eat soon.

SPICY POTATO WEDGES

Very tasty, and very quick indeed. My choice would be a fragrant Malaysian curry powder.

SERVES 4–6, OR MORE AS A NIBBLE
2 tbsp sunflower oil
1 kg potatoes
2 rounded tsp curry powder
1 tsp coarse sea salt
extra chilli flakes (optional)

Heat the oven to 200C/400F/Gas 6. Wash the potatoes, but don't peel them unless they're very rough. Cut them

into wedges lengthways: cut quarters or eighths, depending on the size of the potato.

Put the oil, curry powder and salt (and chilli flakes, if you want an extra kick) in a roasting tin or dish; toss the potato wedges in this, coating them well. It's easiest to do it with your hands. Bake for about half an hour, until golden, turning once.

Serve with a **Simple Dip**: plain **yoghurt**, with **chopped fresh chilli** and **chopped fresh coriander** stirred in.

PARCHMENT-BAKED NEW POTATOES

This delightful recipe was the first I ever cooked from Deborah Madison's *The Greens Cookbook* and it got me hooked. This is excellent with all kinds of roast or grilled meats, or with a well-ripened goats' cheese and a green salad.

SERVES 4–6
greaseproof paper
1 kg very small new potatoes
20 large fresh cloves garlic, unpeeled
small branch fresh rosemary, or several of thyme
4 tbsp extra virgin olive oil
salt and pepper

Heat the oven to 200C/400F/Gas 6. Fold a very large sheet of greaseproof paper in half to make a crease; then open out and lay the potatoes on the lower half. Add all the other ingredients. Bring the top of the paper over and roll up the edges tightly, pressing firmly on them, to form a pouch.

Bake for half an hour on a baking sheet. Serve immediately, while the paper's still puffed up high.

potato gratins

Potato gratins are a guaranteed pleasure-giver — to both cook and eaters. In the oven, something magical happens to those stacked potato slices. They soften into the creamy milk, releasing some of their starch. It thickens the hot juices. The result is a tender, oozy, velvet-sauced meld which dissolves on your tongue like fondant.

All cooks love gratins because they're such a doddle to prepare: assemble the dish, and you can forget about it — no last-minute timings to worry about. They can be cooked at just about any temperature. They can be kept warm for ages — and can even be reheated, which is more than you can say for their competitors in the irresistible-potato stakes, the roast potato.

By far the best gratins, the most succulent, melting textures, are achieved with waxy spuds. I don't mean just the less floury Irish types, I mean truly waxy potatoes. Look for European varieties, ones which are quite sticky when boiled. Mind you, although a gratin won't be as velvety with a floury spud, it will still be irresistible. See p. 43 for more on potato varieties.

Oh, and finally — a word about the thickness of the potato slices. I'm not generally one for requiring the use of a ruler in the kitchen, but there's a case to be made for it here. I like the slices to be just over $\frac{1}{2}$ cm. They shouldn't be wafer-thin, or the gratin will be too gluey, nor should they be much thicker, or it'll be clumpy. This is one of those jobs which it's really worth using the food processor or a mandolin for.

GRATIN DAUPHINOIS

Believe it or not, this simple dish is a hotbed of controversy. What should a true Gratin Dauphinois be made with? All cream? All milk? Creamy milk? Eggs? Cheese?

Does it matter a damn? Not really. I love this version, because it's simple. Not too rich, yet still very creamy. And I add cheese only when I'm going to eat it on its own, as a simple supper dish. See below.

SERVES 4–6

a little soft butter
1 kg potatoes
2 cloves very fresh garlic
salt and pepper
200 ml cream or crème fraîche
250 ml milk

You need a heavy gratin dish, about 20 x 28 cm. Earthenware or stoneware work best; heavy enamelled cast-iron is also good.

Turn the oven on to 200C/400F/Gas 6. Smear a little butter on the base and sides of the dish. Peel and slice the potatoes. Crush the garlic, which *must* be very fresh (no shrivelled yellowing, sprouting cloves, or the rancid whiff will permeate the cooked dish).

Lay half the potato slices on the base of the dish, in overlapping slices if you have the patience. Add plenty of salt and some pepper as well as the garlic. Cover with the rest of the potatoes. Pour over the milk and the cream and dot the top with a little butter.

Put the dish in the oven and cover it (with a lid, flat baking tray or foil) for 15 minutes. This allows the potatoes to steam a little first and stops the top layer from going hard and leathery. Take off the cover and continue to bake for another 35–45 minutes, until the potatoes are cooked through and the top is well coloured.

It will hold at a low temperature for a while, or can be cooled and reheated. (To reheat, add a few tbsp milk and cover it; reheat at 200C/400F/Gas 6 for about 20 minutes.)

Gratin Dauphinois for 6–8: Use 1.5 kg potatoes, 3 cloves garlic, 300 ml cream and 375 ml milk, in a dish about 24 x 32 cm.

CHEESE GRATINS

Cheese is rather good inside a potato gratin. Use a handful of grated cheese or squished nuggets scattered in with the salt, pepper and garlic. Some favourites? Slices of rindless Milleens, or soft goats' cheese, grated Gruyère, soft Cashel Blue … let your imagination run free!

POMMES BOULANGÈRE

When the waistline dictates that cream is off the menu, this is a good substitute. I can't pretend it's as beguiling as the creamy version, but it is very nice. You can substitute the wine with stock if you prefer.

SERVES 4–6

a little butter
1 kg potatoes
salt and pepper
1 tsp chopped fresh chives
½ tsp fresh thyme leaves
300 ml real stock
100 ml white wine

Make and bake as described for the Dauphinois, scattering the herbs between the potato layers and substituting stock and wine for the milk and cream.

JANSSONS TEMPTATION

This Swedish classic is one of the all-time greats. Some people become terribly agitated at the thought of anchovies, and I used to be one of them, but this is one of the dishes which converted me from anchovyphobe to anchovy-adorer. The fishy flavour is very mild — the anchovies melt into the spuds and creamy milk, yet provide a little salty savour to balance the rich effect of the rest. This makes a good supper dish on its own, with a green salad. Or serve with fish, or with roast lamb with rosemary.

A SUPPER DISH FOR 4–6, DEPENDING ON WHAT ELSE IS BEING SERVED, OR AN ACCOMPANIMENT FOR 6–8

a little butter
1.5 kg potatoes
2 onions, thinly sliced
1–2 x 50 g tins anchovy fillets (10–20 fillets)
a little salt
plenty of pepper
375 ml milk
300 ml cream

Make and bake as described for the Dauphinois, using a 24 x 32 cm dish and using onions and anchovies in place of garlic. The Swedish classic method is to cut the potato slices once again, into matchsticks, and to sauté the onions gently in a little butter before adding them to the centre of the gratin with the anchovies. You can, however, get away without either of these refinements if you're in a rush.

Bake for about an hour.

rice

How do you cook rice? With trepidation? To a sludge? Not at all?

You are not alone. It is odd that something as simple as plain old rice should have been turned into an impossible task, but it has. Ludicrous instructions on rice packs are the prime offenders — follow most, and you'll get slop. (Have they never tested their own instructions?) Meanwhile, recipes galore repeat those instructions. Or they suggest you boil rice like the spuds, in lots and lots of water. With rice, this just sends most of the flavour down the sink.

And yet . . . cooking rice really is terribly simple. 'Even a boiled egg requires more finesse,' declares Indonesian food writer Sri Owen, and she's right. All you need is the right proportion of water to rice. The rice absorbs the water and swells up, and in the final stage of cooking it steams gently in its own heat to fluffy grains.

THE RICE

Which rice you use has a significant effect on your results. The rice we're dealing with here is all called **long-grain rice** (as opposed to stubby, rotund little short-grain rices, which are used for risottos, paellas, sushi and puddings). **Standard long-grain** is cheap and there's nothing wrong with it — but it doesn't really have any flavour either. **Thai jasmine** rice is appearing a little more these days. It has a distinctive aroma and is sometimes called **fragrant** rice — somewhat strangely, since it's not nearly as aromatic as basmati. It cooks to a slightly moister stickiness than other long-grain rices, and it's delicious.

Meanwhile, **basmati** is the undisputed queen of rices. It's so elegant it actually triples in length as it cooks (other rices grow fatter). It is grown in the highlands of the Himalayan foothills, it has an instantly recognisable scent which fills the house as it cooks, and a wonderful, delicate, nutty flavour.

Basmati is incredibly expensive in little supermarket packs — and very bad value at that, since many are inferior in quality and flavour. Head for an Asian food store where large packs of excellent Tilda basmati and jasmine rice are often cheaper than ordinary long-grain at the supermarket.

TO COOK PLAIN, DELICIOUS RICE:

— **The pan:** Use a good-quality, heavy-based saucepan with a tight-fitting lid. If the pan is clattery and tinny, the rice will stick and probably burn.

— **The quantities:** Measure the rice and water *by volume*. 250 ml rice makes enough for 2–3. Handiest of all is to find a cup or small mug of that volume. Then you always know to use 1 cup of rice for every 2–3 people. For 4–6, use 2 cups, or 500 ml rice.

— **The rinsing:** Give the rice a rinse in one or two changes of water to rid it of some of its surface starch. (Use the pot you will cook the rice in and a sieve to do this.) Swirl the rice gently in the water with your fingers — it's fragile. Drain it and tip it into the pot.

— **How much water?** Here's your mantra: 1⅓:1 water:rice. Add 1⅓ cups water for every cup of rice (rice packets mostly advise 2 cups water to 1 cup rice, which explains the dire results). Add some salt.

For 2–3 people: 1 cup rice (250 ml) and 1⅓ cups water (330 ml)
For 4–6 people: 2 cups rice (500 ml) and 2⅔ cups water (660 ml)

As you get to know your favourite brand of rice and your storage conditions (the drier your rice the more water you'll use),

you may find you want to vary the amount of water a little.

— **The boiling:** Bring the water to a boil. Then turn the heat down to an absolute minimum — ideally, put the pot on a heat diffuser. If you cook on an electric hob, take the pot off the heat until the temperature is right down. Jam a tight-fitting lid on the pot. If there are gaps and lots of steam is leaking out, lay a sheet of foil between the pot and the lid.

— **The steaming:** Leave the rice to cook for 15 minutes. Take it off the heat and leave it undisturbed for another 5 minutes to steam. It's ready now, but will keep warm for 20–30 minutes.

A variation for basmati rice: If you have time, basmati will be even more beautiful if you let it soak in the last change of water for 20–30 minutes before cooking it. The grains swell more elegantly, the result is more delicate and separate. If you do this, reduce the water quantity to *equal parts water to rice* (rather than the 1⅓:1 which the non-soak method calls for).

Easiest of all . . . is to buy a rice cooker. In Asia, no home would be without one, just as we wouldn't consider life without a kettle. They cook rice perfectly, they switch themselves off when the rice is ready, and they keep it warm while you finish cooking the dinner. Just put rice and water in to the proportions described above and switch it on. I've had mine for 15 years and would feel bereft without it.

UTTERLY SIMPLE SPICED RICE, THREE DIFFERENT WAYS:

A: Cook plain steamed rice as described above. To the cooking water, add a **bay leaf**, a **piece of cinnamon stick** and **1–2 whole cloves** as well as the salt.

B: **Coconut rice.** Cook rice by the method above, but substitute tinned coconut milk for half the water. Don't shake the tin or stir the milk too energetically — you want fairly thin milk. If you like, add the spices in (A) above as well.

C: When you are ready to serve rice, heat **3 tbsp oil** (for up to 4 people) in a small saucepan until it's pretty hot. Add **1 tbsp black mustard seeds** with **1 tbsp chopped green chilli**, or **2 tsp whole cumin seeds**. Once the seeds pop and are fragrant, immediately tip them and the oil over the rice. Make sure everyone gets some of the topping as you serve.

rice

SIMPLE SPICED BASMATI RICE FOR 4 (OR 6)

You'll find that most cookbooks allow this kind of quantity for 6. The cooks' acquaintances must have daintier appetites than the people I know; I find it's just right for 4.

500 ml basmati rice
1 small onion
1 hefty tbsp butter
½ bay leaf
thumbnail-size piece of cinnamon stick
½ tsp salt

Rinse the rice gently in a couple of changes of water, then leave it to soak in plenty of water for 20–30 minutes.

Peel and halve the onion, then slice it into the finest possible slices. In a heavy-based pan large enough for rice and water, melt the butter. Cook the onion in this on a minimal heat until it's very wilted. While it cooks, tip the rice into a sieve and allow it to drain.

Add the bay leaf and cinnamon to the onion and cook for a minute to release their fragrance. Add the rice, salt and 500 ml water. Turn the heat up to full and bring the water up to the boil. Immediately put the lid on tight and cook, preferably on a heat diffuser, on the lowest possible heat for 15 minutes. Take it off the heat and leave it to rest undisturbed for another 10 minutes.

Inspect the rice. If it seems wetter underneath than on top, turn it gently with a fork and leave it to rest, lid on, for another 5 minutes.

FRIED RICE

Fried rice should be in everyone's repertoire. It's one of the easiest, homeliest, happiest dinners there is.

It will taste much better than a takeaway (and it'll probably arrive quicker). It's a one-wok meal, so there's hardly any washing up. All you have to do is cook extra rice one day. Keep it in the fridge or freezer, ready for an evening when you feel like steamy-hot comforting food, and you don't much feel like cooking.

This is the beauty of it. The cooked rice is ready in the fridge (or you took it out of the freezer earlier.) You chop and grate, you slice an onion. You quickly stir up a Thai-style dip for spooning over the finished dish. Then you stand at the wok, adding one ingredient after another. First they sizzle and spit at you. Once you add the rice, it all steams and heats through. And dinner is done, in minutes.

Fried rice tips

- Be sure the rice is cold, and the wok (or frying pan) is hot. Otherwise the rice will go soggy and soak up too much oil.
- Wet your hands, then rub the clumps of cold cooked rice to separate the grains.

SIMPLEST FRIED RICE WITH ONIONS, GINGER AND PEAS

SERVES 2 AS A LIGHT SUPPER, 4 AS AN ACCOMPANIMENT

500 g cooked rice
2 onions, halved and sliced lengthways into slivers
2 tsp grated root ginger
2 tbsp oil
100 g frozen peas

Heat a wok or large frying pan. Wet your hands and loosen the cold rice clumps into grains; prepare the onions and ginger. Add the oil to the extremely hot wok/pan, then add the onions and ginger and sizzle till they're

really aromatic and have blackened somewhat. Keep the heat *very* high and add the rice and (still-frozen) peas. Continue to fry until the rice has picked up plenty of colour and is fragrant. Add salt if it's needed and serve right away.

Some things to add:
Chorizo sausage (the softer kind, not salami), chopped and fried with the onions gives great colour and flavour to the dish.
Egg strips: Before you fry the onions, whisk 2 eggs and add a splash of fish sauce or soy. Heat the wok, add 1 tbsp oil, add the egg and swirl it round till it's a thin sheet, like a pancake. It will cook in seconds. Tip it out, roll it up and cut into slivers. Proceed with the recipe, adding the egg strips towards the end.

THAI DIP

4 tbsp Thai fish sauce (nam pla)
1–3 sliced red chillies
1 clove garlic, crushed
½ tsp sugar
juice of 1–2 limes

Mix all the ingredients, using as much chilli as you would like. Add enough lime juice to create a pleasing salty-sour balance. (If you're making it for vegetarians, use soy diluted with water in place of the fish sauce.)

quick grains

Couscous and bulgar are two intriguing foods. They're staples of eastern Mediterranean and north African tables, as important as our potatoes, Italy's pasta, Asia's rice. We know little enough about them and use them rarely. And yet couscous and bulgar are quicker, easier and more forgiving to cook than any of those other starchy staples. They're ready in 10 minutes; they can be kept warm for ages, even prepared in advance and reheated. It makes them perfect quick supper and large party food. You can even skip the saucepan and prepare them straight in the serving dish.

I wouldn't be without them in my kitchen — they're the quickest, no-hassle accompaniment to stews, meats, vegetables, curries and more besides (and they also make great salads). But what exactly are they?

BULGAR

When a bowlful of bulgar is ready, a sweet, wheaty, nutty scent rises from it. Bulgar (also called burghul or spelled many similar-sounding ways) is a parboiled, cracked wheat with a nutty flavour and slightly chewy texture. It comes in various grades; most common here are quite coarse and very fine, though they're rarely labelled, unfortunately. Bulgar needs only to be soaked in water (for serving cold), or simmered briefly (for serving hot), and it's ready.

COUSCOUS

Couscous, meanwhile, although it looks like a tiny round grain, is actually semolina flour rolled with water: like the teensiest pasta balls imaginable. When soaked in hot water (it doesn't even need simmering), it swells up to become tender and fluffy, delicious with soupy stews. (Which is why it has given its name to all those glorious north African spicy creations.) It is, incidentally, brilliant baby food: easy to eat and, importantly for parents, easier to prepare.

Note: You may have more luck finding these in a deli or health food shop than in the supermarket.

10-MINUTE COUSCOUS

This is the easiest 'grain' in the world to prepare, and the very best one for large gatherings, since it reheats perfectly in the oven.

SERVES 4

350 g couscous
1 level tsp salt
boiling water (see below)

Fill a large heatproof serving bowl with a first kettleful of hot water, then put the kettle on again. When it boils, empty the hot water out of the bowl and put in the couscous and salt. Pour in 500 ml boiling water and stir well. Cover the bowl with a lid and leave the couscous to swell. After about 10 minutes the couscous will have absorbed all the water. Fluff it up with a fork, then serve right away, or put the bowl, covered with a close-fitting lid or foil, in a low oven to keep warm until you're ready to eat.

For more separate grains: When the couscous has absorbed all its water, pour 2 tbsp melted butter or sunflower oil or olive oil over it. Fluff the couscous with a fork until it's a little

cooler, then rub the grains with your fingertips and palms to distribute the butter or oil right through. Cover the bowl with a close-fitting lid or foil, and put it in a low oven to heat through again.

*If you're preparing couscous in advance for reheating later, you needn't bother heating the bowl first, but it's best to add the step above for more separate grains.

As an optional garnish for the couscous, or for the bulgar below, use one, two or all of the following:

- **Almond flakes:** Turn 4 tbsp almond flakes in 1 tsp butter, in a small frying pan over a very gentle heat, until the almonds are lightly coloured. Cool on kitchen paper.
- **Sultanas:** Soak 4 tbsp sultanas in warm water until they have plumped up (about half an hour), then drain.
- **Pine nuts:** Turn a few tbsp pine nuts in a little butter in a pan, as for the almonds above.

15-MINUTE BULGAR

SERVES 4

300 g coarse bulgar
1 tsp salt
600 ml water or stock (cube won't do)
garnishes, as above, or 4 tbsp chopped fresh parsley or coriander (optional)

Put the bulgar, salt and water or stock in a large pan. Bring to a simmer, partially cover and simmer for 7 minutes, until the water is absorbed and the bulgar's nearly tender. Stir it with a fork and leave to stand, partially covered, for 5–7 minutes to steam. Serve right away, with some of the above garnishes if you like, or stir in the fresh parsley or coriander.

quick grains

COUSCOUS AND HERB SALAD

This is a pyramid of herbs, tomato dice and mozzarella. Find a gorgeous shallow bowl and don't toss the salad until everyone has seen it.

SERVES 4–6 IF SERVED WITH OTHER SALADS, OR ABOUT 3 AS A MAIN COURSE

200 g instant couscous
½ tsp salt
250 ml boiling water
1 small handful fresh dill leaves
1 small handful fresh tarragon leaves
1 small handful fresh mint leaves
4 ripe tomatoes
4 lettuce leaves
1 small handful rocket
2 balls water-packed mozzarella (preferably buffalo)
1 large red chilli
2 large lemons
salt and pepper
4 tbsp fine extra virgin olive oil, plus extra to serve

Put the couscous and salt into a heatproof bowl and pour on the boiling water. Leave it to swell for 10 minutes. Tip it into a large, shallow serving bowl, fluff it with a fork and leave it to cool a little longer. If you like, you can do the step for more separate grains (see above).

Chop the dill, tarragon and mint finely, mix and pile high in the centre of the couscous. Chop the tomatoes quite finely and pile on top of the herbs with all their juices. Tear the lettuce leaves and rocket into smallish pieces and lay around the edge of the bowl; slice the mozzarella finely and lay on the lettuce. Deseed the chilli and chop finely; sprinkle it on the cheese. Pour the juice of 1 lemon all over, and season with salt and pepper.

Pour 4 tbsp olive oil on the cheese. Toss at table, before serving with extra olive oil in a jug and some lemon wedges.

Variations: Serve it with any seared, sliced meat instead of the cheese (sirloin beef, duck breast, chicken breast, loin of lamb . . .). Or use feta instead of mozzarella. Or leave out the meat or cheese altogether and serve it as a side salad. And so on . . .

TABBOULEH

Real tabbouleh is actually a chopped parsley salad speckled with the odd beige fleck of bulgar. The flavour of all the herbs is quite intense. It's perfect for large gatherings. I prefer coarse bulgar for its chewiness, but fine bulgar is the one which is traditionally used.

ENOUGH FOR UP TO 10, DEPENDING ON WHAT ELSE IS TO BE SERVED

250 g bulgar
150 ml lemon juice (3–4 lemons)
1 tsp salt
6 ripe tomatoes, chopped
60 g fresh parsley leaves (about 5 tight handfuls)
30 g fresh mint leaves (about 2 tight handfuls)
1 bunch scallions
75–100 ml olive oil

Put the bulgar in a large beautiful bowl (blue looks especially good for this salad) and cover with boiling water. Leave to soak for 10 minutes, then drain. The bulgar will still be fairly tough. Add the lemon juice, salt and tomatoes and leave the bulgar to soften further and absorb all the juices. Allow up to an hour for this.

Chop the parsley, mint and scallions very finely. Toss all the greenery with the bulgar and add enough olive oil to flavour the salad. This can be served right away but it also keeps very well, for 1 or 2 days.

SALT AND PEPPER

I often specify Maldon salt in recipes. It's my favourite salt. It's unlike any other I know, a sea salt harvested naturally from Essex, which comes in a shower of tender crystalline flakes, some of them perfect little pyramids. They add not just flavour but a delicate crunch as well when used to finish a dish — just right for a final flourish on a focaccia, or salads, or roasted vegetables, or just about anything else. The flakes are tender enough to be crushed between your fingers, which makes Maldon the perfect salt to have on the table, in little bowls. Maldon salt is available in good delis and some supermarkets. For stirring into sauces, stews and other wet things, however, I use finely ground sea salt.

As for pepper . . . there's simply no comparison. When black peppercorns are crushed, they release their fragrance. Within minutes, the ephemeral, volatile aromas have gone. Don't waste your money on buying ground pepper (unless you have a use for sneezing powder). If you want pepper's flavour in your food, you need peppercorns and a pepper mill.

fried fish

How about a sweet fillet of plaice, speckled with salty, buttery gold on the outside, its leaves of tender flesh just-set within?

There's certainly no quicker dinner. (Allow about 3 minutes. Maybe 4. Well, to be honest, allow 20, because that's how long it takes to cook the potatoes, but you can't blame the fish for that.) If you finish the fish on the plate with a squeeze of lemon and a shake of fluffy parsley from the hot buttery pan, you'll be humming with pleasure.

Fish is perfect when it's curdy: moist and quivering, like a just-set custard. If it's cooked beyond that point it will seize up, start to harden and then go gritty. Don't worry; you'll do better next time.

The one catch with fish is that you only have a minute or so to nab it at its tender best. Most cooks in Ireland overcook it. Fish is delicate, infinitely more so than meat, and needs to be handled with a little bit of respect. Just think. People have risked their lives to haul it in from the sea for us.

The other catch, when frying fish, is turning the damn things. The fish will break up if you do this too much. So remember to turn it as little as possible. Here's how . . .

fried fish

FRYING A WONDERFUL FILLET OF FISH

— *Buy fresh fish* (stale fish is never nice, but the rank odour of slightly stale fish in a frying pan is just disgusting . . .)
— *Keep it really cold*, so it stays fresh. Get it home quickly. Every minute fish spends off ice hastens the demise of its fresh flavour. Lay it on a bag full of ice at the bottom of your fridge; but if at all possible, eat it the same day. Alternatively, see if your fishmonger can vacuum-pack it for you.
— *Wash it* thoroughly but quickly under cold running water.
— *Dry it* carefully with plenty of kitchen paper.

TO FRY A FILLET OF PLAICE:

Have flour, butter, lemon wedges, chopped parsley and hot plates ready.

— *The flour.* Put a few tbsp plain flour on a large plate. With your fingers, mix in a little salt and freshly ground pepper.
— *Shake it.* Turn each fillet of plaice in the flour. Shake off any extra. The merest whisper should cling to the surface, like a delicately powdered cheek. Fry them soon, or the flour will sink in.
— *The frying pan.* The pan must be big enough to fit the fillets without crowding, or they will stew rather than fry. This usually means you will need 2 pans if you're cooking for more than 2 people.
— *The frying.* Heat a couple of tbsp of butter in the pan(s) over a medium heat. As soon as it foams, add the floured fillets — *flesh-side down, so the skin is looking up at you.* This feels wrong; one instinctively lays them the other way round. But if you lay them flesh-side down, you'll only have to turn them once.
— *How long?* Fry just 2 minutes, then turn the fish. Fry another 1–3 minutes, depending on their thickness. (Are they done? See the panel.) As soon as they're ready, lift onto hot plates.
— *Butter and parsley.* (If the butter burned in the frying, wipe the pan clean now.) Add a knob of butter, swirl till it foams, add the parsley and fry for a few seconds, then scatter it over the fish.

And finish with a squirt of lemon.

*This works with any fillets of flat fish, such as sole, dab, John Dory, etc. And also for all flat fish on the bone; allow a little longer to fry.

TO FRY A FILLET OF SALMON, MACKEREL, TROUT OR SEA TROUT:

(or any other fish fillet up to 2½ cm at its thickest point, with the skin on)

This method is even simpler and is a particular favourite of mine: the fish fries on one side only. The total frying time is 10–15 minutes. The result is extra-crispy skin and the most quiveringly delicate flesh imaginable. Plus you never even have to move the fish until it's time to put it on the plate!

— *Check for bones.* There may be 'pin' bones in the centre of the fillet and it's best to remove these with a tweezers.
— *The pan* must be big enough for the fish to fit without crowding.
— *Heat the pan*, then add a teaspoon of olive oil.
— *Lay the fillets skin-side* down in the pan (yes — the opposite to when you're cooking a floured, flat fillet).
— *Fry over medium heat* for 5–7 minutes. The fillets should now be opaque about halfway up.
— *Don't move the fish* — just put a lid on the pan. Continue frying, for another 5–7 minutes. Telling whether this is done is even easier

---

BUT IS IT DONE?

This worry is one of the main reasons why people get uneasy about cooking fish. Honest, it's simple. All you need is a small knife and decent lighting in the kitchen. (Don't use a fork, as books often advise; you're likely to damage the flesh too much.)

Take the pan off the heat. Approach the thickest part of the fish with the point of the knife. Watch which way the flakes lie, and try to lift one. Where the fish is cooked, it will have turned opaque and the flakes will separate easily. If it isn't done yet, it will still have the translucent look of raw fish and will still hold together.

If the fish isn't done . . . just put it back and keep cooking. If it's cooked, and the rest of the meal isn't ready, whip the fish out of the pan and keep it warm in a low oven or under a very low grill. It's never as perfect when it has been kept warm, but it's a hell of a lot better than overcooked, gritty flesh.

— since the fillet cooks from the bottom up, the very top is the last to be done. When the top is opaque, serve immediately — the well-crisped skin should be savoured, and it will go soggy if you wait.

SOME 2-MINUTE FLAVOURINGS FOR FISH

Streaky Rashers with White Fish

Their salty savour is a brilliant partner to sweet white fish. Before frying the fish, finely chop a few streaky **rashers**, then heat them in the dry pan until they crisp up and release their fat. (Unless you have great rashers, you will have to mop up white goo with kitchen paper as they fry.) Add a little extra **butter** to the pan; when it foams, fry the fish as described above for the fillet of plaice, finishing with **parsley** and **lemon juice** as well.

Quickest Coriander and Lemon Fish

Fry a fillet of fish. Any fish. Or some squid rings, or some prawns. When it's done, squeeze some **lemon juice** over it. Scatter with some **fresh coriander leaves** and **sea salt** (preferably Maldon flakes). Serve.

Salsas and Relishes

These make very quick accompaniments, especially good with salmon and mackerel. See the recipes on pp. 92–4. Recommended:
- Ripe Tomato Salsa
- Zesty Green Coriander and Lime Salsa
- Red and Yellow Salsa
- Quickest Corn Salsa
- Thai Dipping Relish with Lime, Garlic and Chilli
- Thai Tomato Dressing
- Spicy Yoghurt Relish with Mint and Coriander

ROASTED RED RELISH

This is done in moments if you have the peppers ready-roasted.

SERVES 4

2 large fresh red peppers or 2–3 large roasted, peeled peppers (home-roasted, bottled or tinned)
2–4 anchovy fillets (optional)
1–2 cloves garlic, crushed
1 tbsp olive oil
1 tbsp wine vinegar
½ tsp sugar

Roasting peppers
If you have time, roast fresh peppers in the oven at 200C/400F/Gas 6 for about 20–30 minutes until fairly blackened (see the roast vegetable section, pp. 74–5 for more). If you're in a rush, quarter them and deseed, then trim so they can lie flat, skin-side up under the grill; grill them until they blister and blacken. Either way, steam the peppers by putting them in a bowl and covering with cling film until they're cool enough to handle. Peel off the skins and remove seeds if you've roasted them whole.

Make the sauce
Finely chop the roasted, peeled peppers and the anchovies; mix with the rest of the ingredients. If you roasted the peppers whole, there'll be lots of luscious, syrupy pepper juice left in the bottom of the bowl which you can add to the sauce.

COUNTRY BUTTER SAUCE FOR FISH

They don't come simpler than this 1-minute sauce, which is usually called black butter. That's rather misleading, since muted burgundy and luscious gold are its colours. I use country butter here, where the flavour really shines through — though it is very good made with ordinary creamery butter too. It's such a pleasure to make, with its succession of smells — salty roasting butter, then hot sharp vinegar.

The classic accompaniment for this sauce is poached skate, with its succulent tendrils of flesh, but it's good for plaice and other sweet, fresh white fish. Just pan-fry or grill them, then make the sauce.

SAUCE FOR 4

100 g country butter (or ordinary butter)
3 tbsp good red wine vinegar
1 tbsp well-rinsed capers (optional)
4 tbsp finely chopped parsley

When the fish is cooked, keep it warm while you make the sauce. Heat a large, heavy-based frying pan over a high heat until it's hot. Add the butter and swirl it round as it sizzles. It will spit and splutter first; when melted the foam will rise and the butter will go ominously silent. Stir through the foam to peer at the colour of the butter solids: the second they have turned a nutty brown, add the vinegar.

Once the sauce has bubbled fiercely for a couple of seconds, stir in the capers if you are using them, then pour it over the fish without delay. Return the pan to the heat, add the parsley, stir to turn it bright green, scoop it over the fish and serve right away.

steamed fish

Steamed fish is so elegant, so pure, so uncompromisingly simple — and so very different from the extra-exuberant style of cooking which we tend to favour these days.

But there are times in cooking, just as in art, when less is more and when simplest is the most beautiful of all. Steamed fish is one of those times. Sitting in an all-enveloping bath of steam, the fish sets in minutes to perfect curdy moistness. Its flavour is exquisitely delicate. Better again, as if by magic, a clear, intensely flavoured sauce appears on the steaming plate. And that's your dinner, done in under a quarter of an hour.

The steaming gear

Before you rush out to buy a fish, check your equipment. You'll need to be able to put a large dinner plate into a steamer — and to lift it out again afterwards without losing the precious sauce which collects during cooking.

— The plate must be heatproof — as a guide, I've found dishwasher-proof plates safe.
— A 'petal'-type folding steamer will do only if it has no central spoke. Most steamers which fit over saucepans are too small.
— At Asian suppliers, large bamboo steamers are cheap — about a fiver. Mine are 30 cm in diameter, just right for a small fish, or a few fillets, on a large plate.
— If you have no large steamer, put a trivet in your wok or large pot and simply stand the plate on that. (You'll then need a lid for the wok or pot you're using.)
I do love bamboo steamers. You simply sit them into a wok over simmering water (no rack needed). You can stack several over each other. The elegant woven basket lid absorbs condensation, to stop water from dripping onto the dinner. And the hot wet smell of the bamboo plus the inevitable slight scorching of the basket edges are mouthwatering signs that dinner is nearly done.

Next, to the fish

Only really fresh fish will do. Buy fish for steaming from someone who can be believed when they claim 'it's fresh'. This is, after all, a cooking method which the Chinese would save for a fish which was still swimming when they bought it.

Best and most beautiful for steaming? A whole fish. Yes, head, tail, bones and all. (But minus the guts.) Still, if you can't find a whole fish, then boneless, skinless fillets will do well too.

The varieties I've had most success with are sweet, fairly dense-fleshed fish: sole, sea trout, trout, salmon, sea bass, hake, plaice. Not forgetting scallops, which are possibly the best of all.

Whole fish: Be sure to know your steamer's size or bring it with you when shopping, so the fish will fit (remembering that once it's gutted and the flesh has been slashed ready for steaming, it'll bend quite easily). A fish with a cleaned weight of about 450 g will serve 2–4, depending on what else is for dinner; fish with a cleaned weight of about 700 g still fits in my steamer, and serves 4 or more.

Fillets: 150–200 g per person. If you want to steam dinner for 4 on one plate, choose thick, narrow centre-cut fillets rather than the wider, flatter pieces from the tail end.

The aromatics

I've tried many ways of steaming fish, and I keep coming back to the Asian ones for their perfect simplicity.

Just as with the fish, the aromatics must be fresh, even the soy sauce:

— If your soy has been on the shelf for months (or even years) it will have evaporated and coarsened in flavour; treat yourself to a new bottle, and make it Kikkoman, which is significantly better than the rest.
— Be sure your Thai fish sauce is fresh too.
— Finally, look for young, juicy root ginger. No wrinkled specimens with hard skin.

CLEAR-STEAMED FISH WITH GINGER THREADS

FOR 1 WHOLE FISH, OR 2–4 FILLETS, OR A PLATE OF SCALLOPS:

a small bunch of scallions

1 scant tbsp Shaohsing rice wine (or very good dry sherry)

1 scant tsp Kikkoman soy

a knob of young root ginger

If the fish is whole, rinse it well, cleaning away any traces of blood around the backbone or gills (they'd taint the sauce). Dry with kitchen paper. Make several deep cuts from backbone to belly on the diagonal (at about 2 cm intervals, not quite reaching down to the bone); this helps it to cook evenly.

If you have fillets, just rinse them carefully and dry well.

Trim the scallions well. Cut off the white and pale green sections and lay them on the steaming plate. Add the rice wine/sherry and soy to the plate. Lay the fish on the scallions.

Peel the ginger, slice it thinly and cut it into the finest 'threads' you can manage. Scatter these over the fish.

Steam the fish for 8–15 minutes, until done. Slender fish take about 8 minutes; fat centre fillets about 12–15; whole fish about 15. It's easy to check: just wiggle a knife in between the flakes and see if the fish is opaque all the way through.

Scallops will take 5–8 minutes, depending on their plumpness. To check them, squeeze their midriffs gently: they should have a little give to them, but not feel flabby like raw ones.

Serve with plain rice and some vegetables.

CLEAR-STEAMED FISH WITH GINGER THREADS, THAI-STYLE

More exuberant flavourings with this one.

Cook the fish as above, but add 1 clove chopped garlic to the steaming plate.

Dressing

3 tbsp chopped scallion greens	
red chilli to taste, about 1–2 tsp very finely chopped	
3 tbsp lime juice	
1½ tsp caster sugar	
3 tsp fish sauce	

to garnish: 2 tbsp coriander leaves

Stir together all dressing ingredients until the sugar dissolves. Taste to check for balance. When the fish is done, spoon some of the dressing over it and its liquid, and serve the rest of the dressing separately.

mussels

Mussels don't let you forget they're from the sea. There's a sweet seashore whiff when you open a bagful of the clattery indigo shells. There's a rumbling roar as you swirl them in a sinkful of water to clean them, like the suck of waves on a pebble beach. And, like any great day at the beach, there are also the less pleasant aspects to contend with. Barnacles. Grit. Sand everywhere.

And oh it is worth it. Working your way through a big plate of mussels is rather like negotiating a rocky shoreline: a bit like hard work, but exhilarating all the same, with that wonderful salty scent of the sea and smelly wet weed in your nostrils.

The first basic about mussels? They're the cheapest seafood you can lay your hands on. Oysters may have more cachet, but mussels are sweeter and more tender. At a pound for a huge plateful, you can't have a cheaper pleasure. Even a glass of Guinness costs more.

The second basic about mussels? They're so damn beautiful. Who would think that those charcoal dark shells would ease open to reveal lustrous pearly interiors, and surrender that vivid orange, ridiculously suggestive, moist flesh?

And yet . . . an awful lot of people are terrified of them. For some people of course the problem is precisely that moist, wobbly flesh. I'm afraid I can't do anything about that. For others, though, it's the thought of all that scrubbing, and all those tales of what needs to be done.

Discarding them if open, then discarding them if closed. It's all a bit confusing.

Don't be put off. To do mussels, all you need is a big pot, a stiff brush and a keen sense of anticipation. Here goes:

1. If you're not in the mood for wrestling with barnacle-crusted bivalves, buy farmed mussels. Their shells are smooth and they really need no more than a good rinse.

   (Farmed mussels aren't fed anything different, they're just put out on ropes and left in the sea to get on with the business of growing.)

2. You may be tempted to collect mussels from the shore. Remember: they're filter-feeders, used by scientists as a gauge for toxins and pollutants. Be very sure that there's no sewage or other undesirable stuff entering the water within a wide range. At least you know that mussels from fishmongers come from pristine waters or have been purified.

3. When buying mussels, look for ones which are shut tight. Gaping shells mean that they're too warm.

4. Forget anything you've read about plumping them up in buckets of water with oatmeal. Mussels will die in fresh water. Don't keep them at all, preferably; but if you need to, store in the fridge in its coldest spot.

5. Barnacled, gnarled mussels? You need a good stiff brush.

Wash all mussels in several changes of water, rumbling and rumbling them round, then scrubbing if necessary, until there's no more sandy grit falling to the bottom of the sink. Pull out the little tufty 'beards' if there are any.

6. Which mussels to discard? It's quite simple. The idea is to avoid dead ones, since dead shellfish goes off quickly.

   — If they're gaping wide open before being cooked, they may not be alive. If in doubt, rap the shell firmly on the work surface. If the two shells move, even slowly, the mussel's alive.

   — When the mussels are cooked, the shells will open. It's considered best to throw away those which haven't opened during cooking, in case they're dodgy.

7. Above all, for mussel pleasure . . . *don't overcook them*. If you do, they'll seize up, then go gritty and dark, and eventually go hard. It's quite astounding (and pretty unforgivable) how often mussels are served in this condition in restaurants.

8. If you don't want to miss the magic moment, you need to stir and turn the mussels in the pot at least once a minute. It's not too onerous since they only take 3–4 minutes to cook. As soon as the shells have opened enough for you to see the nuggets of wobbly, just-set orange flesh, they're done. Whip them off the heat . . . and serve at once.

9. Some recipes call for mussels to be taken out of the shell. Personally, I think this is missing the point. The excuse to eat with your fingers. To probe that sharp-edged shell, to feel the tug as it creaks open, to pull the mussel from inside, to lick the salt off your sticky fingers. And the fantastic display that a plateful of those shells makes. However, if you insist . . . cover the nuggets in their briny broth or another sauce immediately. This will preserve their moistness reasonably well.

10. And finally . . . *never* add salt. Mussels' brine is intensely salty already.

MOULES MARINIÈRE

2 kg mussels (a starter for 4, main course for 2)

1 onion, chopped very fine

2 cloves garlic, chopped very fine

a knob of butter

about 200 ml dry white wine

Scrub and rinse the mussels well. In a pot large enough to hold all the mussels, cook the onion and garlic very gently in the butter. When they start to sizzle, add the wine. Pour in the mussels. Put on the lid. After a minute, stir and turn them, and cover

again. Keep doing this until they just start to ease open. While this has been going on you will have poured yourself a glass of the wine and will be enjoying the evening more already. But don't let it distract you from checking for the magic moment. When the mussels are done, serve them right away, in great big piles in bowls, with lots of crusty bread.

*Mussel quantities:

Allow 500 g per person in the shell for a generous starter, 1 kg per person for a generous main course.

THE GRIT TIP

Sometimes you just can't get rid of all the grit, especially if the mussels are very barnacled. If the liquid looks rather grey, strain it through a fine sieve, leave it to stand for a minute, then, as you pour it, keep back the last few gritty tablespoonfuls.

MUSSELS WITH THAI GREEN CURRY SAUCE AND FRESH HERBS

An almost soup-like, fragrant brew of Thai aromatics and herbs. Serve with lots of fragrant rice (Thai jasmine or basmati) to make a filling meal of it.

SERVES 3–4 AS A MAIN COURSE, 6–8 AS A STARTER

3 kg mussels
6 cloves garlic, well mashed
1 tbsp grated root ginger
1 green chilli, finely chopped
2 tbsp Thai green curry paste
1 tbsp oil
1 x 400 ml tin coconut milk
1 tbsp Thai fish sauce (nam pla)
2 tsp light muscovado sugar
1 lime, zest grated finely
handful fresh basil or coriander

Scrub the mussels well and wash in several changes of water. Heat a pot or wok large enough to hold all the mussels. Have the garlic, ginger, chillies and curry paste at the ready. Add the oil to the wok, fry the garlic, ginger and chilli until they smell good (just a second or two if the wok was hot), then add the curry paste and fry again, stirring, until a good aroma rises — a minute or two.

Add the coconut milk, fish sauce and sugar and stir; add the mussels and stir again. Put the lid on the wok. Stir the mussels frequently. When they begin to open, add the lime zest and juice from half the lime. The sauce may need more lime juice or more sugar to balance the mussels' saltiness. Scatter with basil or coriander leaves and serve.

squid

Real, whole squid, fresh on the fishmonger's ice, seems to induce unease. Maybe it's those Medusa-like wet twisty tentacles. Maybe it's just the name. 'Squid' sounds uncomfortably similar to squeamish and squelch, and there is, it's true, a rather sucky sound when you clean them, sliding your fingers into the slithery sac. Perhaps that's why we tend to prefer to find squid in restaurants, preferably deep-fried, preferably in light crunchy batter, and preferably called Calamari.

But go on — give it a try. Squid is one of the most underrated fishy things we have. Of course, it isn't really a fish at all. It's a cephalopod, related to cuttlefish and octopus, and like a poor man's scallop, it has a sweet, shellfish-like flesh.

If you're really wary you can buy it already cleaned, when it lies flattened out and denuded on the ice. (But if you do, you won't be able to stuff it, and you won't be able to cut it into rings, and you won't have those pretty twisted tentacles to decorate your dish.) Still, it really doesn't take long to clean; see below. Once you know what needs doing, you can always get your fishmonger to do it for you.

The fun of squid is not just in the eating, it's also in the cooking: squid is done in half a moment. It's ready as soon as it's opaque, and if you cook it much longer, it'll toughen. That makes it perfect for quick, flash-in-the-pan suppers, grills and stir-fries.

And what of its rubbery reputation? Sometimes this is due to overcooking — I'm not kidding when I say it's done in seconds. Sometimes, as with any creature, you just get one that's a bit on the chewy side. Bear in mind, though, that if you want a long-simmered dish, squid is perfect too — after 30–40 minutes, it becomes tender once more.

When buying squid . . .
Fishmongers always seem to be keen on offering us enormous ones. Take no notice. It's the tiny ones you want; they're much more tender, and if they're really small, you can cook them whole. However, if you're planning on stuffing squid, be sure they're at least 15 cm long, or you'll find it a rather frustrating experience.

Tip: Unlike most fish and shellfish, squid freezes very well. You can even freeze it whole (yes, head, innards and all) and take care of the cleaning after it has defrosted. This is great news, since supplies can be rather erratic.

To prepare squid . . .

Grab the tentacles with one hand and hold the body with the other. Pull them apart gently but firmly. The insides will slither out, attached to the head and tentacles, with a bit of a squelch. Chop off the bunch of tentacles above the eyes and discard the rest. If there's a pointy bit stuck in the centre of the tentacle ring, discard that too. From the body, pull out the clear 'pen' (its cartilage-like backbone — it was actually once the animal's shell).

Rinse the body well, using your fingers to check there's no more goo lurking inside (it's really not that yucky, and it's not a major problem if a little gets left behind, either). Books usually recommend cleaning off all the purply, veil-like coating, but I like to leave it on — the colour it adds to the cooked dish is very pretty.

You can now stuff the squid, or cut it into rings. And don't forget the tentacles — their comical, tight curls once cooked are part of the fun of eating squid. Nicest of all is to leave them in one piece; when cooked, they'll look like a whacky cartoon coronet.

Alternatively, you can cut the body open and make little 'barrels' — this is also your best bet if you've bought pre-cleaned, flat squid pieces. Lightly cut very close lines all over the body very finely with a sharp knife, but don't cut through. Then cut lines at right angles to these, so the whole thing is finely cross-hatched. Finally, cut the squid into 4 cm squares. As they cook, they will curl up into little hedgehog barrels.

QUICK-FRIED SQUID WITH OLIVE OIL, BASIL AND CHERRY TOMATOES

SERVES 3–4

about 500 g squid (uncleaned weight; about 350 g cleaned)
2 cloves garlic
fresh red chilli, to taste
12 cherry tomatoes
2 tbsp fresh basil leaves
3 tbsp olive oil
salt and pepper

Clean the squid as described above. Keep the tentacles in one piece and cut the body into rings (if you've bought cleaned squid, slice it into strips or cross-hatch it and cut into squares). Smash the garlic with the flat of a knife, then chop it roughly. Chop red chilli to taste (about 1 tsp from a finger-long chilli would be right for me). Halve the tomatoes, and chop the basil.

Heat a large frying pan or wok over maximum heat until very hot, then add 2 tbsp olive oil. Toss in the garlic and chilli, stir once, then add the squid. Cook until it's opaque. Tip it onto a hot serving dish and keep warm. Add 1 tbsp olive oil. Heat the pan to very hot again. Toss in the cherry tomatoes and sear them until they're just hot through. Add the basil, turn it once, then add the tomatoes to the squid. Add salt and pepper to taste, and serve right away.

SQUID A LA PLANCHA

Squid is excellent simply seared on a char-grill pan, or *a la plancha* as the Spanish would say. All it then needs is a drizzle of olive oil and a scatter of chilli, or perhaps a salsa or relish. See p. 67 for how to do it.

CHILLIES

There are scores of varieties of chillies and their heat levels vary a great deal too. Since they are rarely sold with varietal labelling here, it can be hard to know exactly what you're dealing with. It's also worth knowing that the same variety can vary a great deal depending on where and how it was grown — even a different position on the same bush can make a difference to heat levels. One guiding principle: the smaller the chilli, the hotter they tend to be (though this is not infallible).

When cooking with chillies, always test their heat level first, either by smelling a cut surface, or by touching it carefully on the tip of your tongue. The seeds and the pale seed-bearing ribs are the hottest, so you can cut these out if you prefer. All chilli quantities in any recipe are entirely optional — vary them to your own taste. In my recipes they have been based on the most widely available, finger-length green and red chillies.

Always wash your hands scrupulously after handling chillies, before touching any sensitive membranes on your body — eyes, nose and elsewhere. You'll know about it for many hours if you forget!

steaks and chops

Getting the steak just right was something that bedevilled me in my early cooking years. In theory, a wonderful, richly flavoured steak or chop would be a big treat: caramelised and crusty outside, juicily tender within.

The problem was, it never quite seemed to work. Sometimes the pork chop was succulent; other times, it might seize up and be tough. One minute, the steak seemed bloody, then suddenly it was overdone and no longer juicy. How would I know? How could I tell?

It is possible to give frying times for a piece of meat, and plenty of cookbooks do. But just consider the variables. How thick is the steak? How hot the pan? Is the chop at room temperature, or have you just taken it out of the fridge?

Frying times can only be a rough guide. To be sure of what you're doing, you need to learn the prod-test. But first, the meat . . .

The meat
For meat that's guaranteed to be succulent, **lamb** is your most reliable bet.

Pork can be wonderful, if you are lucky enough to have found a good free-range or organic pork supplier. Most pork these days comes from pigs that have been bred to be utterly lean and are kept in extremely intensive conditions; it is also processed too quickly by factories. The result is that a loin chop is almost inevitably tough — it's not your cooking, it's the meat. Ask for better. We deserve it (and so do the pigs).

Steak? For the best flavour, you need one which has been hung long enough, 14 days at least, to develop true, rich, minerally flavours. Ideally, it should be from a traditional Hereford cross or Aberdeen Angus, not a 'continental' breed; the traditionals have delicate marbling within the meat to make it succulent, so ask your butcher. **Sirloin** and **striploin** have much more flavour than fillet.

Meanwhile, the **thickness** of your chop or steak really does matter — there's no excuse whatsoever for the poor butchery we see all too often. If it's cut unevenly, it will cook unevenly. A steak in particular should be thick, at least 2 cm, so that it can develop a crust yet still be juicy inside. If you don't see a steak like this on display, have it cut specially for you.

The pan
A non-stick pan just won't give the best caramelised, crusty flavours. You need a heavy frying pan, one which can be heated when dry to very high temperatures.

The cooking
1. Take the meat out of the fridge, if possible half an hour before cooking.
2. Don't cut off any fat yet. Cook with it, and trim later. The flavour's in the fat.
3. Preheat a warming oven or grill, and plates.
4. Start heating the pan. Dry. No oil, no matter what the recipe says. The pan needs about 4–5 minutes on a medium heat, until it's shimmering

hot when you hold your hand a few centimetres over it. Like a hot pavement, in another country, on a very hot day.

5. Smear the meat with olive oil. If you like, press some roughly cracked pepper into it, but don't salt it.
6. Lay the meat on the hot pan. Leave it. It will stick if you try and move it before it's ready.
7. After 3–4 minutes, turn the meat with a spatula or a tongs. Do not pierce it with a fork! If it sticks, leave it for another minute. When enough of a crust has formed, it will move easily.
8. As the second side fries, learn the prod-test. Press the meat with your fingers (gently). When still rare, it has a soft give, like the flabby feel of raw meat. When well done, it feels pretty hard. If it's springy, but not hard yet, it's medium. Simple! After a few goes, you will have mastered it.
9. When the meat is done, it has to have a little rest. This allows the hot juices to cool down from boiling point, so they stay in the meat when you cut it, rather than bubbling out all over the plate. So put the meat on a rack over a plate in a warm oven for 3–5 minutes.
10. Serve it, with one of the following sauces . . .

QUICK WINE SAUCE

The main requirement for this sauce is not to have burned the pan while you were frying the meat. If you haven't, you can proceed:

- While the meat rests, return the pan to the heat. Add **a glass of red or white wine**. Bubble it fiercely to allow it to reduce by half.
- Add **half a glass of stock** and simmer again for a minute. Now get the resting meat and add any juices which have seeped from it to the sauce.
- Finally, whisk in a **knob of cold butter** in little pieces to give the sauce a glossy finish.

And serve, right away.

2-MINUTE GREEN PEPPERCORN SAUCE FOR BEEF, DUCK OR PORK

SERVES 4

200 ml crème fraîche
1 scant tsp green peppercorns in brine
1–2 level tsp Dijon mustard

Simmer all ingredients until thickened a little. Taste and season if necessary.

FLAVOURED BUTTERS

One of the quickest ways to zip up a steak or chop is to mash some herbs into slightly softened butter, then put a spoonful on the meat and watch it melt. Best bets: parsley and garlic; chives; thyme; tarragon; or basil. Then put the butter on a length of foil or greaseproof paper, and roll it up into a log. Keep it in the freezer, well sealed, and slice rounds as you need them.

DERRY CLARKE'S CAFÉ DE PARIS BUTTER

This scrumptious, vivid, speckled savoury butter is superb with any pan-fried or grilled meat. It is from Derry Clarke of Dublin's L'Écrivain restaurant.

MAKES ABOUT 250 G, ENOUGH FOR 10–15 SERVINGS

1 large shallot, finely chopped
½ glass red wine
1 clove garlic, mashed
225 g butter at room temperature
2 soft sun-dried tomatoes, finely chopped
1 tsp rinsed capers, finely chopped
½ tsp turmeric
½ tsp wholegrain mustard
pepper

Simmer the shallot with the red wine until the pan is dry, but stop before it burns. Allow to cool, then with a wooden spoon beat together with all the other ingredients. Spread in a line onto a length of greaseproof paper, then roll it up and shape into a log. Keep in the freezer and cut slices as you need them.

1-MINUTE LEMON AND CHILLI SAUCE

A 1-minute sauce for steaks and chops. It's one of my favourites. For anchovyphobes: the anchovies dissolve, mingle with the meaty pan juices and the lemon juice, and disappear, leaving only a wonderful savoury sauce, with no fishy aftertaste. Go on, try it!

SERVES 4

60 g butter
2–4 anchovy fillets, mashed
1 clove garlic, crushed
2 tbsp chopped fresh parsley
chopped fresh red chilli, to taste
juice of ½ lemon
lots of freshly ground black pepper

Fry 4 chops or steaks. Sear them well but be sure not to burn the juices in the pan. When done, put them in a warm oven to rest.

If there's extra fat in the pan, spoon most off — but don't wash the pan. Gently melt the butter and mix it with the frying juices. Stir in the rest of the ingredients and cook briefly, mashing the anchovies if they don't dissolve. Just before serving, add in any juices the meat has released while resting. Spoon over the meat, and serve with steamed or fried potatoes.

ORANGE AND ONION SAUCE

Really this is a superior sort of onion gravy, and it doesn't even need real stock. It goes particularly well with pork, and would be good also with chicken (especially juicier, darker thighs) or lamb.

THIS QUANTITY SERVES 4, though if you use it as a vegetable, 2 people will find it all disappears without any difficulty whatsoever

4 onions
2 cloves garlic
2 tbsp olive oil
1 heaped tbsp marmalade
juice of 1 large or 2 small oranges
200 ml stock (cube is fine, see p. 91)
salt

Halve the onions, then cut lengthways into slivers. Chop the garlic. In a frying pan, fry onions and garlic in the oil until they have softened and coloured, but stop before they smell acrid. Once the onions look soft and are shiny again, add the rest of the ingredients and simmer until reduced to a sauce consistency. Check for seasoning before serving.

steaks and chops

If you'd prefer fresh, zippy or herby flavours, you'll find these in the 'Salsas and Relishes' section:

WITH STEAK: Ripe Tomato Salsa, Zesty Green Coriander and Lime Salsa, Red and Yellow Salsa, Thai Tomato Dressing, Salsa Verde.

WITH PORK: Ripe Tomato Salsa, Zesty Green Coriander and Lime Salsa, Red and Yellow Salsa, Quickest Corn Salsa, Pineapple and Lime Salsa, Thai Dipping Relish with Lime, Garlic and Chilli, Thai Tomato Dressing, Salsa Verde, Spicy Yoghurt Relish with Mint and Coriander.

WITH LAMB: Ripe Tomato Salsa, Zesty Green Coriander and Lime Salsa, Salsa Verde, Spicy Yoghurt Relish with Mint and Coriander.

CIDER-APPLE SAUCE FOR PORK (OR CHICKEN)

SERVES 4

4 shallots or 1–2 onions
2 tart, crisp eating apples
2 knobs butter
300 ml dry cider
salt and pepper

While the chops are frying, peel the shallots; peel and core the apples. Slice the shallots thinly and the apples thickly. In a small pan, gently cook the apples with one of the knobs of butter until they're translucent; keep them warm in a low oven.

When the chops are done, lay them on a serving dish and keep them warm too. Add the other knob of butter to the chop pan and gently cook the shallots; when they're soft, add the cider and turn up the heat. Simmer briskly until the sauce has reduced by half. Taste it and season it.

Add the apples and their sweet buttery juices to the chops on the serving dish and pour the sauce and shallots over them all. Serve with a Chive Champ or a Potato, Herb and Parsnip Mash (see p. 18–19).

HOW TO CHOP AN ONION

Do it this way, and perfect little onion cubes will tumble onto the chopping board. Use a sharp knife.

The basic principle is to leave the root attached while you cut, so the onion's layers can't slide away from under your knife.

— Peel the onion, leaving the root attached, then cut it in half through the root. Stand one half up on the chopping board, holding it by the cut side and resting it on its root end, and slice twice downwards, parallel to the cut side – but don't slice right through. The half must still hold together.

— Lie the onion on its flat side on the chopping board, with the root end at 12 o'clock. Make about six parallel cuts with the knife tip pointing towards the root end, still cutting short of the root end so it continues to hold the piece together.

— Finally, turn the root to 9 o'clock (presuming you're right-handed). Cut down, at right angles to the cuts you've just made. Perfect cubes will fall from your knife, their size dependent on how wide apart you made your previous cuts.

ALL ABOUT SPUDS

Although we're eating lots of pasta and rice these days, the Irish love affair with the potato continues, as does the concomitant distress when the spuds fail to measure up to expectations. Disappointing potatoes spoil a meal profoundly for most people, far more than vile vegetables or other wretched cooking ever could.

Here are some tips for potato heaven; don't forget to have a look at the various potato sections for more.

Why are potatoes so often disappointing?

You may not be choosing the right varieties for you, so read on about floury versus 'soapy' and waxy spuds. That factor aside, lots of potatoes are awful these days because they are grown in dead, flavourless soil and are over-fertilised, which makes them take up too much water. Too much water is a double problem, firstly because it reduces flavour, and secondly because it makes the spuds rather slimy-textured when cooked.

The quality of potatoes depends largely on who has grown them and how they have done it. Look for the grower's name if you find good potatoes, and try to track them down again. It's also worth trying organic or fertiliser-free potatoes; if grown in good soil these may taste better.

Great balls of flour

Here's the nub of the issue. Irish people love great balls of flour, the fluffiest, driest potatoes imaginable. As a result, all classic Irish potatoes are floury — yes, new potatoes as well, and even those we might call creamy or soapy. Some, however, are more floury than others; knowing the differences will help you to find perfect potatoes. Figuring out which category any potato falls into is much easier than trying to learn those impossible-to-remember 'good for roasting/boiling/chipping/baking, etc. lists.

Extra Floury

These Irish classics should be truly fluffy and dry: **Golden Wonder, Record, Kerr's Pinks, Rooster**. Rooster is the most recent variety, a bit bland but very reliable. The others need to be grown well to taste really good. All are 'maincrop' spuds, available from autumn to late spring.

Home Guard and **British Queens** are also floury; these 'new' varieties come in early and mid-summer.

Perfect for: Steaming in their skins (better than boiling); fluffiest mash; fluffiest, crunchiest traditional roasties (handle with care when parboiling); baking; soup.

Still Floury, But Less So

You'll either prefer these ones because they're 'creamy' or you'll hate their more moist, 'soapy' quality. Either way, they're still a floury potato: **Pentland Dell**, **Maris Piper**, **Cara** (all maincrop – autumn to late spring) and **Wilja** (a second early: mid/late summer).

Perfect for: You can use these just as Extra Floury spuds, though they're less dry; if you prefer a 'creamier' spud you'll like them more. However, mash won't be quite as light. When roasting, I prefer these roast as wedges (with rosemary or spiced) rather than traditionally. They are marginally better for gratins than the Extra Flouries.

Really, Truly Waxy

When they're good, they can be delicious: dense-fleshed, intensely flavoured, and slightly sticky. Yum. Love them or hate them, truly waxy potato varieties are becoming easier to find in Ireland now. They are the perfect salad potato. Those new potatoes from Italy, Cyprus and Egypt can occasionally fit the bill (though they're often disappointingly watery and tasteless; picking out the smaller ones sometimes helps). Better again is to look for named varieties, such as: **Nicola**, **Elvira**, **Charlotte**, **La Ratte**, **Pink Fir Apple**.

Perfect for: Salads — they don't fall apart and they absorb much, much less dressing; frying; sliced in potato gratins; simmered in stews and curries, where they'll keep their shape. If you like their fudgy texture, they're also delicious simply boiled or roast.

'New' Potatoes

This is a minefield! The joy of new potatoes (i.e. any potato early in its growing season, but specially in early summer) is their wispy curls of thin skin and fresh flavour. However, beware. Outside Ireland, new potatoes are always waxy, so recipes reflect this. Remember that classic Irish new varieties, Home Guard and Queens, are very floury, so these may not be right at all. For example, they're terrible for potato salads (use baby potatoes or truly waxy ones).

roast chicken

It does look unpromising, a pale, pimply, clammy-skinned chook. Who would think that a simple roasting could transform it so? First there's a bit of noisy sputtering from the oven. Then there's the agonising smell that drifts through the house, making it quite impossible to concentrate on anything. And finally, out comes that crisped skin of coppery crackling, the hot moist flesh, the sticky bits of intense flavour in the roasting tin. Roasting a chicken is, in theory, the simplest of operations, yet

when I look back on early days in the kitchen there are few things which gave me more grief. Eventually, I figured out that it wasn't the chicken's fault; it was the gravy, stuffing and three veg bringing up the rear. The finale was a nightmare of coordination which never quite came together. The skin was perfect? The bird was underdone. The gravy was ready? The crisp skin had gone flabby. The bird was just right? But the veg weren't cooked yet! These days, I go for a simpler approach. To go with the roast

chicken: some roast potatoes (either traditional or rosemary-roast — see pp. 22–3), plus a green salad dressed simply. And that's it. I don't even make gravy: the buttery roasting juices, done this way, are just perfect on their own (and the salad leaves are lovely with a little savoury roasting juice mingled in).

Will they moan, 'But where's the carrots?' They may. But not when they've finished eating, they won't.

THE CHICKEN

Buy a real free-range bird. This kind of roast chicken is not a midweek supper, it's a glorious, fortnightly treat. A bird that has had some exercise and has reached a decent age will taste so much better. It deserves as much respect as any other roast.

SERVES 4–6

1.8–2 kg chicken

30 g butter at room temperature

fine sea salt and freshly ground black pepper

1 lemon

a branch of fresh rosemary, or a bunch of fresh thyme

water or white wine (see recipe below)

1. **Wash the chicken:** *Set the oven to 230C/450F/Gas 8.* Wash the bird well, inside and out, in cold water. Pull out and cut away any fat deposits in the cavity. Dry the chicken well with kitchen paper.

2. **Slather it in butter:** Put the chicken in a deepish roasting tin, one which contains it quite neatly so its juices won't burn. Turn it so the drumsticks are pointing at you. Gently lift the breast skin up from the breast meat without breaking it, and poke the soft butter between skin and flesh. It doesn't need to be very evenly spread. Smear the last streaks from your fingers on the surface of the breast. Wash your hands and scatter plenty of salt and pepper all over the chicken, inside and out.

3. **Stuff its cavity:** Slash all over the skin of half the lemon and put it inside the chicken's cavity. Squash the rosemary or thyme in too.

4. **When the oven's hot,** put the chicken in.

5. **Roast it:** *After 15 minutes,* add a wineglass of water or white wine to the tin. Turn the oven down to *190C/375F/Gas 5.* The chicken will need *about another 50–55 minutes* (that makes the *total roasting time about 1 hour 5 minutes–1 hour 10 minutes*).

6. **Darkening too quickly?** If the skin looks as if it might burn, lay a sheet of foil on top. But don't wrap the whole chicken in it, or you'll be steaming the bird. And keep an eye on the juices in the tin. If they're in danger of burning, add more water or white wine to cover the base.

7. **Is the chicken done?** The skin should look, well, like crisp roast chicken. The smell should be heavenly. Then get a sharp knife and a large tablespoon ready. Cut the skin between leg and breast and bend the leg away from the chicken's body. Spear the chicken in the thickest part of its inside thigh (but not next to the bone) with the tip of the knife, holding the spoon underneath the cut to catch the juices which run out. If they are clear, the chook is done. If they are tinged or streaked with pink, the bird needs a little longer in the oven.

   Or: use a meat thermometer. The inner thigh should be 78 °C, rising to 80 °C during resting time.

8. **When the chicken's done,** pour off the juices in the tin (and tip the bird to include those which always lurk in the cavity) into a smallish bowl. Leave the bird to rest in a warm place for 10 minutes *(that makes the total time, roasting plus resting, 1 hour 15 minutes–1 hour 20 minutes).* Above my hot oven in a warm kitchen is warm enough; you'll get to know the best place in yours. I don't like to cover the bird with foil — it steams the skin. Heat plates until they're very hot now.

9. **The resting time** gives you a chance to get organised. Turn the oven up full blast to finish the potatoes. Toss the salad, lay the table . . .

10. **The 'gravy'.** With a spoon, scoop off any fat which has risen to the top of the roasting juices (throw it away, or save it for roasting potatoes another day). Add juice from the leftover half-lemon to taste, and salt and pepper if it's needed. This makes a light but intensely flavoured sauce. If you feel you must thicken it up, see the 'Gravy' section, pp. 52–3, but I much prefer it as it is.

Reheat the sauce if it's cooled down too much. And remember, as you carve the bird, to add any juices to the sauce bowl as well.

And then serve. That's all there is to it.

SOME VEGETABLES

If you feel you really can't do without some carrots or parsnips or cabbage to go with the bird, have a look at recipes in the vegetable sections (see ''Brassicas', pp. 80–81, and 'Roots', pp. 82–3). Simplest of all? Roast vegetables, all done in the same dish as the potatoes. See pp. 74–5.

more roast chicken

SPICED-UP CHICKENS

There's more than one way to roast a chicken, that's for sure. In the winter months I rather like the full shebang: the large, buttery, coppery-crackling-coated bird, sitting breast-up, plump and high in the tin, its drumsticks pointing out, ready for a flourish of the carving knife.

Come summer, though, and the urge for the formality of a big roast seems to have evaporated. I want more spices, I want brighter flavours, and I want to wiggle them all into every nook and cranny of the bird. I want to eat with my fingers, sitting in the garden. Come to think of it, I want to barbeque the chick long and slow on a charcoal-scented grill while I pour the drinks out in the garden, and I want the sun to shine all day long.

Well, whatever about that last bit, at least the urge for flavour can definitely be fulfilled in this country. To get zippy flavour into your chick, you need to mush together a spice paste or marinade of some sort. And to get the marinade to wiggle into every nook and cranny of the bird, you need to lay it out flat.

THE FLATTENED BIRD

It's a great way to roast a chicken, because when the bird lies flat, it cooks faster and the breast stays moister. To do it, you need to cut out the backbone. This is easier done than said.

Here's how

Arm yourself with a large heavy knife, or a cleaver, or some poultry shears, or just get your butcher, poulterer or supermarket to do it for you.

To do it yourself: Identify the backbone. It's about 2 cm wide and runs the length of the flat, non-breast side of the bird. Put the bird on the chopping board, breast-up, with the cavity and the drumsticks facing you. Start by cutting both sides of the little fatty triangular tail-bit which lies at the base of the cavity (which some people call the priest's nose; others attribute the same anatomical item to the parson); then stand the bird up on its end and just keep cutting all the way down. The little riblets attached to the backbone are very thin and can be cut through pretty easily by simply leaning hard on the knife.

When you've removed the backbone (*of course* you will remember to bag it and label it, and put it in the freezer for stock . . . won't you?), lay the chicken on the chopping board, skin-side up. Press down on the breast so it cracks a little and lies flat. Now you can marinate the bird easily, and stuff flavourings under the skin and all over.

— *To roast a flat chicken:* Simply lie it skin-side up in a roasting tin in which it fits quite neatly. Roast for 15 minutes at 220C/425F/Gas 7, then for another 35–50 minutes (depending on size) at 190C/375F/Gas 5. If you add a little water, stock or wine from time to time, just enough to cover the base of the tin, the juices won't burn and you will more than likely find you've instant gravy when the chicken's done.

— *To barbeque:* I would advise roasting first, then finishing the bird over the hot coals (preferably on a barbeque with a lid) for the last 15 minutes of its cooking time.

The following pastes and marinades can also be used for a whole, unflattened chicken, or for chicken pieces, with the skin on, and preferably with the bone in too. Use 6 large pieces (breasts) or 8 smaller ones (e.g. thighs).

SRI LANKAN ROAST BUTTER CHICKEN

FOR A 1.4–1.8 KG CHICKEN (APPROX.) SERVING ABOUT 4–6

3 cloves garlic, well crushed
1 heaped tbsp grated root ginger
1 tsp salt
½ tsp black pepper
½ tsp ground cinnamon
½ tsp turmeric
5 whole cloves, smashed fine with pestle and mortar (or with something heavy), or
½ tsp ground cloves
3 tbsp red or white wine vinegar
60 g butter at room temperature

Mush everything together. Smear the spiced butter under the skin all over, and smear the rest on the skin. Leave it to stand for up to an hour to allow the flavours to penetrate, then roast it. Add a little water to the roasting tin and keep an eye on it — top it up so there's always a shallow layer of liquid in the tin.

After the chicken has rested, there should be ample buttery, spicy juices in the tin and no extra gravy should be needed. Pour the juices into a bowl, scoop off the extra fat, and serve as a spicy gravy.

FIVE-SPICE CHICKEN

FOR A 1.4–1.8 KG CHICKEN (APPROX.), SERVING ABOUT 4–6

2 tbsp soy sauce, preferably Kikkoman

1 tbsp Chinese Shaohsing rice wine, or dry sherry

1 rounded tsp Chinese five-spice powder

½ tsp black pepper

½ tsp salt

1 tsp light muscovado sugar

2 cloves garlic, crushed

Mix the marinade ingredients and rub them all over the chicken in the roasting tin. Set it aside to marinate for about an hour, turning it once or twice. Then roast the bird as described above.

To serve

iceberg or cos lettuce — whole leaves

fresh mint and coriander leaves

Thai Dipping Relish with Lime, Garlic and Chilli (p. 93)

Each diner pulls chicken slivers from their meat portion, then wraps them in the lettuce with a few herb leaves, then dips in the relish.

Or

steamed rice, *or*

Rosemary and Olive Oil Roast Potato Wedges (p. 23).

ROAST CHICKEN WITH LEMON GRASS AND LIME

THAI-STYLE, FOR A CHICKEN OF 1.4 KG–2 KG, SERVING ABOUT 4–6

4 cloves garlic

3 stalks lemon grass

2 shallots

rind of 2 limes, grated or pared with a zester

1 tbsp finely grated root ginger

1 fresh red chilli (or more)

1 heaped tbsp light muscovado sugar

2 tbsp Thai fish sauce (nam pla)

2 tsp vegetable oil

Mash the garlic. Trim and peel the lemon grass stalks to half a finger length of tender, inner stalk and slice these. Peel and quarter the shallots. Put everything in a food processor or large pestle and mortar and pound to a paste. Use most of the paste on a smaller chicken, all of it on a large one, poking it under the skin and into corners. Leave it to permeate the bird with flavour for an hour, or 3 if you have time, then roast as described above.

SESAME GARLIC ROAST CHICKEN WITH SWEET CHILLI DIPPING SAUCE

FOR A 1.4–1.8 KG CHICKEN (APPROX.), SERVING ABOUT 4–6

Sesame garlic marinade

4 cloves garlic, crushed

1–3 tsp chopped fresh red chilli (to taste)

1 tbsp chopped slender fresh coriander stalks

1 tsp ground black pepper

1 tbsp Thai fish sauce (nam pla)

1 tsp soft brown sugar

2 tbsp sesame oil

Mix all ingredients and smear all over the backbone-free, flattened chicken, under the skin and over it. Leave it for about an hour or so, then roast.

SWEET CHILLI DIPPING SAUCE

5 cloves garlic

1–2 long fresh red chillies

2 tbsp chopped slender fresh coriander stalks

1 tsp salt

150 ml rice vinegar (or white wine vinegar)

125 g golden caster sugar

2 tbsp chopped fresh coriander leaves

juice of about 1 lime

Peel the garlic; chop the stems off the chillies. Pound them to a mush with pestle and mortar along with the coriander stalks and salt (or use a

blender or grinder which can do small quantities). Put that in a saucepan with the vinegar and sugar and simmer briskly for 10 minutes. It should have a glossy sheen to it when done. Set it aside to cool. When it's cold, stir in the coriander leaves and as much lime juice as you like to balance the flavouring. If it reduced too much and is rather sticky, gently stir in a few tsp of water.

THE 40-MINUTE ROAST CHICK DINNER

Even when a bird is flattened, roasting takes time. Here's how to get the flavours of a real roast chick dinner in just 40 minutes . . . roast some quail. Here is my version of Fergus Henderson's delightful recipe in *Nose to Tail Eating*: **Roast Quail with Balsamic Vinegar and Rosemary Potatoes.**

1–2 potatoes per person

a little fresh rosemary

olive oil

sea salt

ground black pepper

2 quail per person

balsamic vinegar

Turn the oven on to 230C/450F/Gas 8. Find 1–2 large roasting dishes in which there will be room for all the potatoes and the quail. Toss potato quarters (cut lengthways) in a little olive oil and add some rosemary, salt and pepper. Give them a 20-minute head-start in the oven.

Meanwhile, season the quail well with salt and pepper. In a heavy, hot frying pan, with just a little olive oil, brown the quail all over. When they are well coloured, add them to the roasting potatoes in the oven. Roast for another 20 minutes. They should be well done, at which time the potatoes will be ready too.

Splash on a few drops of balsamic vinegar and serve right away.

roasting meat

Roasting meat is as close as you can get to not cooking at all.

You put it in the oven, you go away, it smells wonderful, you take it out of the oven, and really isn't that all there is to it? If you want to get fancy about it you can rub in some herbs or poke in some spices, but the truth is that the simplest of roast meat will always taste good (as long as it's not too overcooked). In fact, it's such a straightforward kitchen job you might agree it hardly even deserves to be in this book.

But how could I leave it out? The results can be so splendid. There's the grand, celebratory effect of a large roast, as it is carried to the table and everyone beams and sits up straight in their chairs with anticipation — it's one of the most enjoyable moments a cook can create. And of course there's such pleasure in the eating, whether you love tender roast lamb, pink and pretty, or a moist, thick slice of a roast rib of beef, or thick strips of crunchy pork crackling, with its sticky layer underneath, where the fat hasn't quite dissolved.

Well. Having said that roasting is the quintessence of simplicity, there are a couple of crucial points, moments which can make all the difference between a good roast and a great roast. Funnily enough, neither of them has anything much to do with the roasting itself.

The first moment comes long before the meat goes in the oven — it's at the butcher's counter. Where will you buy, which meat

will you buy, which cut shall it be, and can it be trusted to be good?

And the second moment comes when the roasting is over — the moment at which you decide to take the meat out of the oven. But is it the right moment? Is the meat medium, or rare, or what, and how can you find out?

But before we get into all that nitty-gritty, let's start with some simple roast lamb.

ROAST LAMB WITH A CRUSHED CORIANDER CRUST

The orange-peel spicy smell of coriander goes so well with lamb.

SERVES 6–8

1 leg of lamb
olive oil
2 tbsp coriander seeds
salt and pepper
some dry white wine (optional)

When you're buying the lamb, ask the butcher to remove the parchment-like covering on the skin, and to cut out the 'H' bone (which will make it easier to carve). If the knuckle end is sawed through and the strip of 'lap' is tied around the leg, cut them off (save for stock). Weigh the lamb.

Preheat the oven to 200C/400F/Gas 6. Rub a little olive oil all over the lamb. Grind the coriander seeds finely in a spice or coffee grinder, then pat them all over the surface of the lamb. Add a generous scattering of salt and a good grinding of black pepper.

Put the lamb into a roasting tin into which it fits quite neatly. Roast for 20 minutes, then turn it down to 180C/350F/Gas 4. Roast for another 15 minutes per 500 g for rare; add 15–20 minutes over for medium.

(I really can't recommend eating it well done, but if you must, add 30 minutes over.) If you're not too sure how to check for doneness, you'll find out on the next pages.

If you like, you can add some white wine to the tin when you turn the oven down and add more during roasting if it's threatening to dry out. This will make an instant gravy — all you'll need to do when the roasting's finished is scoop the fat off the top (see the 'Gravy' section, pp. 52–3).

2 OTHER FLAVOURINGS FOR LAMB ROASTS

Rosemary and garlic are a classic. Chop 1 tbsp rosemary with ½ tbsp garlic and mix with salt and pepper. Make deep slits into the meat and poke the mixture in.

Anchovy is, surprisingly, another excellent, traditional Mediterranean addition. The sweet lamb doesn't taste strongly of anchovy afterwards, it just acquires a satisfying, savoury balance. Chop a few fillets in with the rosemary and garlic mix above.

Buying lamb

Lamb is the most reliable meat for tenderness and good eating — it's almost always 'free-range' in Ireland. It's also, joy of joys, still a seasonal meat: it's pale and rather namby-pamby in early spring, and sweetest and at its best in summer (the lambs have been out, feeding on grass by then).

In winter, roast it longer and slower, and maybe with more spices. It's still delicious, but it will be more chewy. After Christmas, it's best poached, braised or stewed. See Tender Simmered

Lamb with Green Parsley and Caper Sauce, p. 57. Or slow-roast a long-cooking cut such as the shoulder.

ROAST SHOULDER OF LAMB BOULANGÈRE

The meat on a lamb shoulder is the sweetest of all. And this way of cooking yields a crisped top, succulent meat, with tender, stock-flavoured potatoes underneath: a dinner in one roasting dish.

SERVES 3–6, depending on the size of the shoulder — which can vary a great deal depending on the butcher and what part of the country you're in

1 shoulder of lamb on the bone, about 1.5 kg

olive oil

1–2 onions

4 large cloves garlic

6 medium–large potatoes

2 tsp fresh marjoram, thyme or oregano

salt and pepper

500 ml real stock or water (don't use stock cubes)

Turn the oven on to 180C/350F/ Gas 4. Trim the lamb of any excess surface fat. In a large, flameproof, shallow roasting dish, on a medium heat, slowly fry the meat on all sides to brown it (about 10–15 minutes). Meanwhile, peel and slice the onions, chop the garlic, and peel and slice the potatoes.

Take the lamb out of the dish. Add the onions, garlic, potatoes, herbs and plenty of salt and pepper and turn them in the oil in the dish. Add the stock or water, then put the meat on top, skin-side down. Roast in the oven for an hour, then turn it skin-side up and roast for a further hour, or until the meat is well done and very tender.

If you'd like to know some more about shoulder of lamb, read on.

The thrill of cheaper cuts: in praise of shoulder of lamb and neck of pork

Recipes for roasting cheaper cuts, the ones which need slower cooking, are rare; they tend to be relegated to stews and braises. But I love cheap cuts, most especially shoulder of lamb and neck of pork. They can taste superb, and are actually easier to roast to moist perfection than expensive loins and legs.

This does seem hard to believe, I know. But it's all a question of how you cook it. With prime cuts, relatively quick cooking is important, or the meat will dry out. That's why these cuts taste better when rare or medium than when well done. That's also why recipes look for 'marbled' meat, and when they don't have it, they douse lean roasts in olive oil, smear them with butter, bard them with lard, wrap them in lacy caul fat, or drape them with streaky rashers.

But cheaper cuts are different. They need long, slow cooking, which gradually tenderises their gelatinous and connective tissues. The result is meat which is well done, but which is still fantastically moist. And after all that internal basting, the flavour of the meat is sweet and intense. Yes, there can be more fat. Just cut it away and savour the flavour of the lean.

Shoulder of lamb

This meat is sweetest succulence, when you roast it till the fat has rendered out. Shoulders of lamb vary around the country. In Dublin, you often get just a little square which may serve no more than 3. In Connemara, they give you half the sheep.

The carving is a little fiddly on a shoulder compared to the leg, since it has funny-shaped bones which seem to point every which way, so many people prefer it boned and rolled. Myself, I find the carving more tricky with a rolled shoulder — all that string!

Neck end of pork

This is also a shoulder cut, the one used for collar of bacon; it may be called gigot. (Because it's used for bacon you may well need to order it in advance from your butcher.) It's boneless, pretty lean and absolutely gorgeous. This moist cut makes the best of intensive pork if you can't get free-range or organic.

ITALIAN HERB ROAST PORK

Once you've tasted this you'll be reluctant ever to return to dry old loin again. It gets a long, slow roast, and it's worth doing a large piece to be sure of plenty of leftovers, so you won't have to cook the next day. Get some string from the butcher.

SERVES ABOUT 10

2 kg neck end pork

3 tbsp chopped fresh rosemary

2 tbsp chopped fresh sage

2 tbsp chopped garlic

3 tbsp olive oil

2 tbsp Maldon sea salt

2 tsp freshly ground black pepper

2 tbsp fennel seeds

250 ml dry white wine

roasting meat

Make deep cuts all over the meaty side of the piece. Mix together the rosemary, sage and garlic and stuff it into the cuts. Rub the meat with the oil. Then mix the salt, pepper and fennel seeds and strew all over the meat. Cover loosely and leave in the fridge overnight. Bring back to room temperature before roasting.

To roast: Heat the oven to 160C/325F/Gas 3. Tie the meat up just to make it a little neater and rounder. Put it in a roasting tin into which it just fits. Add the wine. Roast for about 2½ hours, until well done (no more pink juices; skewer hot; thermometer 70–75 °C). Rest 15–30 minutes before carving.

SOME ROASTING TIPS

— For a plain roast with no other ingredients, your **roasting tin** shouldn't be much larger than the meat, or precious juices will burn. It should be heavy, flameproof and scratchproof, so you can make the gravy right in it. A heavy enamel tin is good; so are some stainless steel and anodised aluminium. Enamelled cast-iron dishes work well too.

— **Have the meat at room temperature** going into the oven. Ideally, allow 2 hours out of the fridge for a large roast.

— **Weigh the roast oven-ready** (including any stuffing).

— **Don't burn!** Keep an eye on the tin. If the roasting juices are drying out, add a glass of water or wine.

— **Resting:** Meat must 'rest' after roasting, so it will lose fewer juices when sliced. Give it 15–30 minutes, and don't forget to add this into your roasting time calculations. Keep in a warm place; if it's in the turned-off oven, be sure it's not too hot. I prefer not to cover the roast, or the crisp skin will soften.

Buying pork

Pork is so often tough and nearly tasteless. If you can only get standard intensively reared pork, I'd strongly recommend you roast the neck end rather than the loin.

Why is pork such poor quality now? Because we are obsessed with producing and buying cheap meat. To achieve this, pigs are kept in highly stressful intensive conditions, are fed antibiotics to keep them 'healthy', and have been bred for such leanness and fast growth that they suffer pain and heart problems. To compound these ill effects, pork is often poorly processed in the large factories and it is almost invariably sent out without hanging. The end result is meat that's cheap, all right, but it just doesn't taste as good as it should, so what's the use in that? Unfortunately, it's becoming increasingly difficult to find butchers who have produced pork with care. The small abattoirs from which this higher-quality meat came have all too often folded under excessive bureaucratic pressure.

Do look for and keep asking for free-range or organic pork. And then be prepared to pay the little bit extra for it. Not only should it taste better, but there's the comfort of knowing you're supporting more civilised and safer farming and food.

GREAT ROAST BEEF

I have two favourite cuts of beef for roasting.

- A **rib roast,** preferably on the bone, is succulent, buttery-textured and best-flavoured of all.

For perfection, ask for the sirloin (striploin) end of the rib (more tender). Look for a butcher who has rib roasts from a Hereford cross or Aberdeen Angus, and who hangs it for at least 2 weeks (closer to 3 is better). Rib roasts from these smaller animals are neat — the meat's about the size of a saucer.

- If your butcher's rib roasts are the width of Finn MacCool's thighs, he's getting them from large 'Continental' animals. They're too big to roast really well. In that case, I'd use **striploin** instead.

**Rib of beef on the bone:
a 2 kg joint will feed 6–7 people;
allow 3 kg for 8–10
or Striploin:
1.2 kg boneless will feed 6; 2 kg
will do 10
olive oil
coarse-ground black pepper**

— Leave the meat at room temperature for a couple of hours. Preheat the oven to 200C/400F/Gas 6. Rub 1–2 tbsp olive oil into the surface of the meat. Grind plenty of black pepper over the top.

— **Rib:** Roast the meat in the fully preheated oven for 20 minutes. Then turn the heat down to 180C/350F/Gas 4. Roast for 15 minutes per 500 g. This should be rare. Add 20 minutes to this time for medium beef; add 30 minutes to the time for well done.

Striploin: Roast for 45–55 minutes: 20 minutes at 200C/400F/Gas 6, then 25–35 minutes at 180C/350F/Gas 4.

— Rest the meat for at least 20 minutes in a warm place to allow the juices to stop seething before you carve.

Serve it with:
Salsa Verde
or **Coriander Salsa Verde**
or **Ripe Tomato Salsa**
(see pp. 92, 94)
or a **classic gravy** (see pp. 52–3)

or:

HORSERADISH HERB CREAM

300 ml crème fraîche
about 2 tbsp horseradish (to taste)
1 tsp Dijon mustard
4–6 tbsp chopped fresh herbs, e.g.
parsley and chives

a small clove of garlic, crushed
salt and lots of freshly ground
pepper

Stir it all together and taste to check for seasoning.

Buying beef

We're lucky in Ireland: our beef is generally produced outdoors, and grass-fed, which can make for very good meat indeed, from a careful producer. But you need well-hung, well-treated beef from well-reared animals to get the best results. Butchers should know all about the farm the animal has come from, and ideally about the rearing, finishing, age and breed. Two to three weeks' hanging or maturing time is essential.

Unfortunately I don't have room here to go into more detail about buying good beef, lamb and pork in Ireland, but if you'd like to know more, see my book, *Good Enough to Eat*.

IS IT DONE?

This is the crucial question. How can you tell? Start by working out the time per 500 g; see the recipe, or the list which follows for some timings. But the one thing I can guarantee you is that your oven cooks differently from mine. *Timings are not gospel, and never can be.* You have to check the meat.

The skewer

This is the low-tech answer: an ordinary, thin metal skewer.

Slide it into the thickest part of the meat (not near a bone) and leave it in for 10 seconds. Lay it on the inside of your wrist.

If it feels . . .
cold, the meat is raw
warm, the meat is rare
pretty hot, the meat is medium
burning hot, the meat is well done.

Try it once or twice, then observe how the meat is when you carve. It works. Honest!

The quick-read thermometer

Alternatively, try an **instant-read digital meat thermometer**. I love mine and find it infinitely more reliable than those ones with a dial like a clock. I can't understand why they're not widely available. (I got it from Sweeney O'Rourke kitchen suppliers for about £15; 34 Pearse Street, Dublin 2, (01) 6777212)

Insert the thermometer's probe — again, to the thickest part, not near a bone.

Beef and lamb

Rare 60 °C
Medium 70 °C
Well done 80 °C
Take these out when they are 5 °C below this and allow to rise to the temperature during resting time.

Pork

Cook until it registers 70 °C, rising to 75 °C during resting.

Poultry

Cook until 75–8 °C, rising to 80 °C during resting.

Always double-check by touching the thermometer probe on your inner wrist in case of a false reading.

SOME ROASTING TIMES

Ribs of beef, legs of lamb, and other large prime roasts:
— 20 minutes at 200C/400F/Gas 6 first.

— Turn down to 180C/350F/Gas 4; now calculate 15 minutes per 500 g, for rare.
— Add another 20 minutes after that time has elapsed for medium.
— If you must cook the meat well done (it will be rather dry if you do), add 30–35 minutes after the calculated time has elapsed.

A **striploin (sirloin) of beef**, from 1.2 kg–2.2 kg (to serve 6–12), takes the same time whatever the weight. Roast for 45–55 minutes:
— 20 minutes at 200C/400F/Gas 6
— 25–35 minutes at 180C/350F/Gas 4.

By the same token, a **loin or rack of pork**, any weight, takes 1¼–1½ hours at 180C/350F/Gas 4.

A **rack of lamb** cooks quickly, but varies with the seasons, since it's larger in autumn than at Easter. On average allow
— 10 minutes at 230C/450F/Gas 8, then
— 10–15 minutes at 180C/350F/Gas 4.

To roast a **shoulder of lamb** or **neck of pork**, roast in a preheated 160–180C/325–350F/Gas 3–4 oven for about 2–2½ hours, depending on its size, until medium to well done.

gravy

Everyone seems to get into an awful state making gravy. Relax. Gravy is easy. But there is one twist to the tale: a gravy recipe won't make the same gravy every time. Every roast is different. Still, if you learn to taste, you can have a good gravy no matter what happens.

The tin

Use a heavy roasting tin which can go directly on the hob. That way you can make the gravy in it once the roast is done, picking up every scrap of caramelised-meat-juice-flavour (and saving on washing up).

The roasting

Making good gravy starts with roasting the meat.

1. *Make sure the roasting juices don't burn*, or you'll have no flavour base for your gravy. If they look as if they're scorching during roasting, add a glass of water or, better again, stock or wine.

2. *Roast with onions.* Peel them (leaving the root on) and quarter them lengthways so the root holds each quarter together. These are utterly delicious roasted in the meat fat and juices. The outside layers are crisp and perhaps a touch charred, the inner ones soft and melting . . . you have a no-trouble vegetable for the meal, and added savour for the gravy.

Stock, giblets and all that . . .

Great gravy needs good stock. But if you haven't any home-made stock (see pp. 88–91), don't worry. For once, you have the time to make some. Throw a few bits in a pot, the stock will simmer while the meat roasts, and it will be ready in time for gravy-making.

For the stock, buy or beg a handful or two of chicken giblets, wings or meat bones when you're getting your meat or bird. (Remember that bag of bits which you used to find inside a chicken? Such an unpromising collection, that fleshy phallic neck, the split gizzard, the tiny heart and little liver. I suspect it usually went to the cat, but it was a bag of gold for great stock.) Rinse them, put them in a pan with a quartered onion, a chopped carrot and a stick of celery, as well as a bay leaf and some parsley stalks and/or thyme branches. Cover with cold water and simmer while the roast sizzles. Skim any scum from time to time, and check the pot doesn't go dry — but do allow the stock to reduce and concentrate in flavour. Strain the stock, then get ready for gravy-making.

When the meat is done . . .

The gravy jug

Heat it up with the plates. I always forget to do this.

The oven gloves

Find sturdy oven gloves. Folded tea towels will do but they're a bit fiddly when handling a hot roasting tin on the hob.

Rest the meat

Lift the roast out of the tin and put it on a plate to 'rest'. *Lifting the meat:* It's big and hot. You can spear it with forks if you like, though you'll lose extra juices. The easiest way? Pick it up wearing your (clean!) oven gloves. They're washable, after all.

Where to rest the meat: On its serving plate in a warm part of the kitchen, or in a warm oven. If you're leaving it in the turned-off oven, watch the temperature — some ovens retain a lot of heat. Don't cover the roast with foil if you want the skin crispy.

Rest yourself!

You have plenty of time, so take it easy. A large roast holds heat well — at least a quarter of an hour for a chicken, up to half an hour for a large joint, longer for a large turkey.

Remove any roast vegetables from the tin too — but keep them warm separately from the meat (you'll see why later). Put them in a serving dish and cover them. Make sure the dinner plates are getting hot by now.

Removing the fat

Pour the contents of the roasting tin into a bowl (not too small). When the juices have 'settled' (the fat has risen to the top), spoon the fat off. Keep it for delectable roast potatoes. You may be left with just a tablespoon of juices, you may have much more. Return them to the pan.

Making the gravy

The purest, most delicious gravy is simply made from good roasting juices and good stock. On a good day, that's all you need. Put the roasting tin on a very low heat. Whisk with a wire whisk to incorporate the sticky bits, and add a cup of stock for smaller roasts, 2 cups for larger ones.

Simmer, whisk, taste, and whisk some more. Simmer some more and allow the gravy to reduce. Is it delicious? If so, you're having a good day, and you can move on to the next stage.

If not . . . add some of these flavourings, simmer, whisk and taste again:

— 1 tsp redcurrant jelly or cranberry sauce, for a sweeter flavour
— 1 glass of wine (or 1 tsp balsamic vinegar or 2 tsp lemon juice) for a lift in the flavour
— a small knob of butter whisked in vigorously, for a smoother glossier gravy
— a sliver of stock cube (but go easy, or it'll taste like Bisto), if the flavour lacks depth

A favourite combination of mine is 1 tsp redcurrant jelly or cranberry sauce plus 1 glass wine.

Simmer well to evaporate the alcohol in the wine.

Remember: add flavourings one at a time, simmer, whisk, and taste, taste, taste. You'll get the balance right.

A vital tip
Before you finish, add the juices which have seeped from the roast. (This is why you didn't want anything else on the platter.) Tip the dish, holding on to the meat, so the juices run into the tin.

To thicken or not?
The purest gravies have no thickening. But if this is too austere for you, there are two ways to thicken a gravy.

1. If you have **roux** (see p. 96) whisk it in; if you have none, mash a nugget of butter to a paste with the same amount of flour, then whisk scraps of this in as the gravy simmers.

(see p. 96)

IF YOU CAN'T BE BOTHERED . . .
There is a quicker way. As the meat or bird roasts, keep a 1 cm layer of liquid in the base of the tin. Do this by adding a glass or two of wine, water or stock from time to time, making sure the edges never burn. At the end, just remove the fat from this as described on the previous page. It'll be delicious, instant gravy.

2. Dissolve 1 tsp **arrowroot** (for a clear gravy) or **cornstarch** in a little cold water, then whisk in this by the *teaspoon* as the gravy simmers.

Be very wary of all thickeners. One minute you've got a thin liquid, next minute there's glue in the tin.

Finally, taste again, season, and pour into the hot gravy jug.

poached chicken

This, where the canon of basic cooking skills is concerned, is an unusual one; it sounds like the stuff of Victorian invalid trays, not food for the 21st century. Nobody poaches anything any more — these days, even asparagus comes char-grilled. Roast a chicken? Sure. But poach one? Why?

Here's why. It's brilliant. It's easy. It requires almost no attention. It can be done in advance. And it leaves you with two for the price of one: a supremely tender, succulent fowl, plus the bonus of a potful of tasty chicken stock

without hours of boiling. The stock alone is almost reason enough to give it a go.

The chicken

Don't even *think* of trying to do this with an intensively reared fowl (unless, perhaps, you're going to make the rather spicy Bon Bon sauce, the recipe for which you'll find later). An honest-to-goodness slow-grown free-range chicken is what you want. The kind which you buy in a market, or from a good butcher or poulterer. The kind, ideally, where you can be told the name of the

person who reared it. If, when you ask where it came from, they look vague and say 'Monaghan', you're likely to be disappointed. Most chicks in the supermarket labelled 'free-range' which come from large-scale producers won't really do. They are birds from fast-growing breeds, and they just don't have the flavour. However, some well-reared birds are beginning to become available in supermarkets too. Look for organic chickens, or those whose label states they have been reared for at least 80 days.

and lamb

The pot
You need a heavy pan into which the chicken just fits snugly, with a tight-fitting lid. My large Le Creuset oval casserole does all chickens, up to nearly 2 kg.

The poaching
Rinse the chicken very well in several changes of water, then put it in the pot. Add 2 peeled and quartered onions, 3 bay leaves, 1 tbsp grated root ginger and 1 tsp salt. Add enough cold water to cover the chicken completely, then quickly bring it to a simmer. Simmer gently, with the lid on, for 30–40 minutes. Skim off any scum which floats to the surface. Check it's done in the usual way: lift it out of the poaching liquid, poke a knife tip into the inner thigh and catch the juices which run out in a spoon to check they are clear; or use a meat thermometer (see p. 51). Simmer another few minutes if needed; otherwise just leave it in a cold place to cool down in the stock, refrigerating it as soon as it's cool enough.

Strip the meat off the bones
Put on an apron, roll up your sleeves and prepare to get your fingers sticky. Take the chicken out of the pot and put it on a large plate. Pull off and throw away all the skin and fat. Remove the meat from the bones and set it aside. Put the bones back in the pot.

Simmer the stock
Do this for another hour if you've time, or at least another half-hour to extract the flavour from the bones. Then strain through a fine sieve.

Storing the chicken
If you have more meat than you need, or you don't want to serve it until tomorrow, put the meat in a bowl, cover it with stock and keep it in the fridge. The beauty of this is that the chicken remains perfectly moist.

Storing the stock
Store in the fridge or freezer. Best way to freeze stock? Simmer it to reduce it to rich brown concentrated flavour, then freeze it in ice cube trays. Instant, real stock cubes are then to hand . . .

Now you're ready — to make chicken salad one day, wonderful quick soup the next.

Take a look at the soup section for ideas. The Thai-style Hot and Sour Soup (pp. 86–7) is perfect: you already have stock and chicken ready for an instant meal.

SALSA VERDE
Probably the very best of all possible accompaniments to some poached chicken is a zippy, herby salsa verde. It's excellent with just-poached, warm chicken, and also goes well with cooled-down chicken meat.

For two salsa verde recipes, see p. 94.

VIETNAMESE CHICKEN SALAD
Supremely light and laced with herbs.

SERVES 4 AS A MAIN COURSE, OR MANY MORE AS A STARTER OR AS PART OF A LARGER MEAL OR BUFFET

2 red onions
½ large poached chicken (about 350 g boneless cooked meat)
½ large cos or other crispy lettuce, or 3–4 handfuls mixed salad greens
2 carrots
small handful fresh mint leaves
small handful fresh coriander leaves

Dressing
1–3 red or green chillies (or to taste), seeded and chopped
2 tbsp sugar
2 tbsp rice or cider vinegar
6 tbsp lime juice
4 tbsp Thai fish sauce (nam pla)
black pepper

Halve the onions, then slice them finely lengthways and soak them in several changes of cold water. Strip the chicken from its bones and tear into small shreds.

Stir all the dressing ingredients together until the sugar has dissolved. Marinate the chicken in half the dressing for half an hour.

To serve, chop the lettuce into shreds; peel and grate the carrots. Drain the onion slices well. Toss the lettuce, carrots and onion with the chicken, mint and coriander, and as much of the rest of the dressing as you need to coat it all; serve immediately.

To serve with noodles: Cook thread noodles (transparent or egg) as directed on the pack, then season with fish sauce, lime juice and black pepper.

poached chicken

MARINATED CHICKEN SALAD

This comes from chef Martin Webb (in Richard Whittington's *Quaglino's: The Restaurant*, Conran Octopus). It's one of those mysterious recipes: a slow developer. When just made, it's pretty dull. Next day, it's yummy. Serve just with crusty bread, or turn it into a main course with mixed salad leaves and/or tomatoes, and tender little boiled potatoes.

SERVES 4–8, DEPENDING ON THE SIZE OF THE CHICKEN AND WHETHER IT'S A STARTER OR MAIN COURSE

1 poached chicken, 1.4–1.8 kg approx.

3 tbsp pine nuts

3 whole cloves

2 bay leaves

3 tbsp sultanas

½ tsp dried chilli flakes

175 ml extra virgin olive oil

2 tbsp red wine vinegar

juice of 1 lemon

1 tbsp caster sugar

salt and pepper

Remove the flesh from the chicken, leaving the pieces large. In a dry frying pan, carefully and slowly toast the pine nuts gently until coloured. Mix all ingredients together in a large bowl and turn the chicken in them. Refrigerate overnight. Remove from the fridge several hours before eating, and pick out the bay leaves and cloves before serving.

CHICKEN MAYONNAISE

The best mayo for dressing a scrummy home-made chicken salad is a light one which can coat the meat easily. Try the Very Slightly Lighter Mayonnaise or the Herb Mayonnaise for Shellfish (or Chicken or Vegetables), p. 100.

POACHED CHICKEN WITH GINGER AND SCALLION DIPPING SAUCE

This Cantonese classic is a celebration of the simple purity of flavour of poached chicken, contrasting it with the zesty dip. Save it for the very best of free-range chickens. Serve as a main course with stir-fried greens and rice, or as a starter for many (in which case you will need to double the sauce quantity).

1 poached chicken

2 cm cube ginger

1½ bunches scallions (about 9), very finely chopped

75 ml sunflower or peanut oil

1 tsp salt

chilli oil and light soy, to serve

Remove the meat from the chicken, tear into smaller pieces and pile high attractively on a serving dish. Peel, slice and shred the ginger as finely as possible. Place the scallions in a small heatproof bowl. Heat the oil in a pan. Add ginger and salt. When the ginger starts to colour, throw the lot over the scallions and let them sizzle and spit. Serve with the chicken, with the chilli oil and light soy sauce on the side as well.

BON BON CHICKEN

This nutty, garlicky, sweet-and-hot Chinese sauce for a cold chicken salad also doubles well as a satay sauce. It's rather addictive.

½ poached chicken (about 350 g boneless meat)

1 cucumber, halved lengthways and sliced finely on the diagonal

Sauce

50 g crunchy peanut butter

50 g tahini (sesame seed paste)

2–3 cloves garlic, crushed

1 tbsp sesame oil

2 tbsp light muscovado (soft brown) sugar

2½ tbsp light soy

1 tbsp rice, white wine or cider vinegar

1 tsp dried chilli flakes

1 heaped tbsp fresh coriander, chopped

50–100 ml light stock

generous pinch roast and ground Szechuan peppercorns (if available)

Stir all the sauce ingredients, adding them one by one. Add enough stock to make a pourable dressing. Use to pour sparingly over the chicken, which you have stripped off the bones, torn into shreds and piled high on a plate over the cucumber slices. Serve the rest of the sauce separately, diluted with a little more stock if it's too sticky.

and lamb

LAMB

Chicken isn't the only thing worth simmering gently. Go on, try this. It's excellent.

TENDER SIMMERED LAMB WITH GREEN PARSLEY AND CAPER SAUCE

I think this is one of the highlights of traditional Irish cooking; it's a mystery to me that this succulent, flavoursome dish has vanished so completely from most people's imaginations. Of course the word 'boiled' has come to represent the worst sins of Irish cooking past, and since this meat was once known as Boiled Mutton with Caper Sauce it clearly had an image problem to contend with. But I needn't tell you that you don't actually boil the meat, you give it a long, slow, delicate simmer with herbs and aromatics. The result? Exquisitely tender lamb which you could cut with a fork, lamb which has absorbed flavours from the pot and which is then covered in a pretty, green-speckled parsley-laden, light sauce. It's just lovely.

The other bonus of this kind of cooking is its convenience. When the lamb is done, it will hold happily in its poaching liquid for an hour or more. If you want to keep it for longer, take it out and reheat it in the liquid later, when you're ready to eat. And finally, there's the poaching liquid: delicious broth for soup.

It's just the thing to do with winter's well-flavoured lamb (hogget, really) which is available before all that namby-pamby spring lamb is sprung on us for Easter.

P.S. Be sure not to leave out the cloves. They're essential.

SERVES 4–6

1 leg, shank or shoulder of mature lamb
2 onions
2 carrots
2 sticks celery
2 bay leaves
2 large sprigs fresh rosemary
stalks from the parsley (see below)
1 tsp whole peppercorns
2 whole cloves
1 tsp salt

Sauce

2 tbsp butter
2 tbsp plain flour
2 tsp smooth Dijon mustard
300 ml milk
300 ml lamb broth (see recipe below)
salt and pepper
30 g chopped fresh parsley leaves
50 g capers, rinsed and chopped

Before you buy the lamb, check the size of your pot. If you're doing a whole leg, you may need to ask the butcher to saw the shank bone higher than usual so it will fit.

Chop the onion, carrots and celery into large chunks. Put the meat and veg in the pot and add the bay leaves, rosemary, parsley stalks, peppercorns, cloves and salt. Cover with water, bring to the boil and simmer *very* gently, covered, until the meat is really, really tender. Scoop off any thick froth from time to time. The meat should take about $3\frac{1}{2}$–4 hours, depending on its age.

To make the sauce:
Melt the butter in a saucepan, add the flour and cook, stirring, for 2 minutes. Whisk in the mustard, milk and broth from the lamb pot. Cook for a few minutes, stirring constantly. Season well and add the parsley. Just before serving, add the capers and whizz the sauce (in a blender or food processor, or with a hand-held blending stick) for a lovely delicate green, speckledy effect.

Serve by carving the meat into thick juicy slices, laying them on a warm platter and spooning some sauce over. Serve the rest of the sauce separately, with lots of very floury steamed potatoes, preferably Records or Golden Wonders.

Of course, if it's St Patrick's Day, there must be some carrots as well.

stew

'An exquisite scent of olives and oil and juice rose from the great brown dish as Marthe, with a little flourish, took the cover off.

The cook had spent three days over that dish. And she must take great care, Mrs Ramsay thought, diving into the soft mass, to choose a specially tender piece for William Bankes. And she peered into the dish, with its shiny walls and its confusion of savoury brown and yellow meats, and its bay leaves and its wine, and thought, 'This will celebrate the occasion' . . .

'It is a triumph,' said Mr Bankes, laying his knife down for a moment.

He had eaten attentively. It was rich; it was tender. It was perfectly cooked . . . She was a wonderful woman. All his love, all his reverence had returned; and she knew it.'

Such is the seductive power of a beef stew, as described by Virginia Woolf in *To the Lighthouse*. Mr Bankes (a botanist, a childless widower who smelled of soap and who was scrupulous, careful and clean) considered dinner a waste of time which could better be spent working. And yet even he succumbed to the aromatic enticement and tender delicacies offered up by a long, slow simmer.

A good stew is soul food. It soothes, calms and coddles. It does need a little time (though three days' preparation, as Mrs Ramsay's cook had done, is not essential), but there's very little effort in it. The stew bubbles while the cook does just exactly what he or she pleases, pausing occasionally to lift the lid, give it a stir and smell the good smells. A good stew is a very satisfying thing.

BEEF OR LAMB DAUBE PROVENÇAL

This is aromatic with orange peel and thyme and salty black olives, and plenty of long-simmered flavour.

SERVES 6–8

1.3 kg well-trimmed stewing beef or lamb (in 1 or 2 large pieces — see The Stewing Basics below)
1 tsp coriander seeds
1 tsp peppercorns
2 bay leaves
2 cloves
500 ml robust red wine
olive oil
4 onions
6 cloves garlic
200 g smoked bacon, in one piece if possible, rind-on
2 tsp fresh thyme
1 tin chopped tomatoes
zest of ½ orange, pared in wide strips
salt and pepper
750 g carrots
200 g black olives, stoned
a handful of parsley

The night before cooking:
Trim any remaining fat or membrane from the meat if the butcher didn't do it for you. Cut it into large pieces (about the size of a small fillet steak, and 2 cm thick). Tie up the coriander, peppercorns, bay leaves and cloves in a muslin square (or a square of a new J-cloth blanched with boiling water) with a piece of string. Put the meat and the bag of spices in a large bowl and cover with the wine. Marinate in the fridge overnight.

At least 3–4 hours (or indeed 1 or 2 days) before eating, prepare the stew:
Lift the meat out of the marinade and dry it very well on plenty of kitchen paper. Gently heat a large heavy casserole dish and add a thin film of olive oil; fry the meat in 2–3 batches until it's nicely browned on both sides; be careful not to burn the base of the pot, though plenty of dark brown caramelising is fine.

While the meat fries, halve the onions and cut lengthways into thin slivers; crush the garlic. Cut the rind off the bacon and keep it; cut the bacon into thick little cubes.

When all the meat is done, add a little more olive oil and fry the onions, garlic, bacon cubes and thyme. Do this slowly until the onions soften and collapse, which will take about 15–20 minutes.

Add the beef and any juices which have seeped from it, plus the bacon rind, tomatoes, orange peel, 1 tsp salt and some ground black pepper. Add enough water barely to cover the meat and partly cover with the lid. Simmer very gently until the meat is really tender and the juices have reduced to a rich, aromatic sauce. (Take the lid off towards the end of cooking if necessary.) Allow 2 hours for lamb, 3 for beef.

Half an hour before the end of cooking, slice the carrots thickly and add them to the stew. If the sauce needs thickening, see the tip below. It may need 1 tsp of sugar to balance the flavour.

Finally, lift out the orange and bacon rind and stir in the olives. Check for seasoning, then finish the stew with plenty of finely chopped parsley. Serve with boiled potatoes or a pasta such as fresh tagliatelle, or dried tagliatelle made with eggs.

THE STEWING BASICS
Which cut of meat?

Spending more on your meat won't make a better stew. For some incomprehensible reason, butchers keep trying to sell round steak as glamorous stewing meat these days. Don't take it — it'll dry out with long cooking. The cuts to choose:

Beef: **shin** (my favourite), or **rib**, **flank** or **brisket**
Lamb or pork: **neck** or **shoulder**
Chicken: **thighs**
These cuts have all-important gelatinous material; during long, slow cooking it dissolves to keep the meat magnificently succulent.

'Stewing meat'?

Pass on pre-cut stewing meat. Buy a whole piece from the butcher instead, from one of the cuts listed above, ask him or her to trim it well, then cut it yourself at home. Here's why:

— Most pre-cut stewing meat mixes are a mix of various cuts. These will cook unevenly.

— The size of the meat pieces makes a considerable difference. Cookbooks and butchers seem to favour little itty-bitty cubes. But if you cut the meat into largish pieces, it will seem more substantial when it's later on the plate — and as long as they're not too thick, they won't take longer to cook. Aim for pieces about the size of a small fillet steak, and 2 cm thick.

stew

Fat . . .
Oh yes, this thorny subject again. Some cuts *are* leaner than others, such as shin beef, or neck of pork or lamb. If your butcher's good, any cut should be properly trimmed anyway. But don't get too obsessed with lean meat — a little fat's good for flavour, and it's easily removed after cooking.

— If you chill the stew, the fat hardens on top and can be lifted off easily.

— If there's no time for chilling, then let the stew sit for a minute when it's done. Scoop off any visible fat with a spoon, then lay a sheet of kitchen paper on its surface for just a second. It will soak up any fat. Whip it out and throw it away, and do it again until the glistening globules have disappeared.

The frying
The most troublesome part of a stew is the initial frying, and recipes say to do this in small batches until the meat is all browned, which can take ages. It's so tempting to skip that advice and pile the whole lot into the pan in one go. Don't. If the pan is crowded, there won't be enough heat for the meat to sizzle. It will just ooze brothy juices instead,

---

WHEN YOUR STEW'S A CURRY, YOU NEED TO USE YOUR NOSE

One of the crucial steps in a curry is the frying of the spices. Whether those spices come in a paste, or whole, or ground, they need to be fried to release their aromas and bring them to life. Be guided by your nose rather than frying times: stand over the pan and sniff!

---

and you won't get all those yummy caramelised flavours.

Frying the meat well spaced in the pot, at a pretty high heat, in several batches, takes longer — but it's essential for flavour.

The cooking
You can simmer a stew on the hob, or cook it in a low oven. On the hob, it's easier to keep an eye on — a diffuser mat will help to impart the gentlest of all possible heat and reduce the risk of burning. Wherever you cook it, use a pot with a thick base, and don't forget to check the stew once or twice. It may be bubbling too fiercely, or need a little more liquid (just add water). If it's on the hob, it will need stirring so it doesn't stick.

The time
Don't rush it. For flavours to emerge, time is required. Most stews will taste better tomorrow anyway.

Is the stew too watery?
This does happen sometimes.
— If the meat and vegetables aren't fully tender yet, just simmer the stew with the lid off.
— If the stew is ready and you don't want to overcook it, scoop the juices out with a ladle into another pot; boil them briskly to reduce to the consistency and flavour intensity you'd like, then return them to the pot.
— If you don't want to reduce the amount of liquid, you can thicken it. Mash 1 tsp soft butter to a paste with 1 tsp flour; add to the stew in little bits, stirring them in well while it simmers so no lumps form, and simmer for a few minutes to thicken. Repeat if necessary.

The finishing
A final flourish makes a big difference. Some recipes add lightly cooked veg at the end; easiest of all are sparky fresh green herbs. A big generous handful of chopped **parsley**, **coriander** or even finely chopped **scallion greens** will give the stew a lively, fresh lift.

CHICKEN (OR LAMB) IN A CREAMY CARDAMOM, YOGHURT AND BLACK PEPPER SAUCE

This is a spicy dish of wonderful delicacy. Hot with black pepper, not with chillies. Rich with yoghurt, not with cream — not that you'd guess from the flavour. And it tastes even better several hours or even a day after cooking. Is it better with chicken or lamb? I can't decide.

SERVES 4
2 onions
sunflower oil, for frying
4 large cloves garlic
large knob root ginger
$\frac{1}{2}$ tsp cardamom pods
1 tsp black peppercorns
40 g ground almonds
250 ml tub Greek-style yoghurt
225 ml hot water
about 900 g skinless, boneless chicken (preferably well-trimmed thighs)
1 tsp salt

Peel and halve the onions, then cut into very fine slices. In your largest frying pan, fry them gently in 2 tbsp oil, stirring from time to time.

While the onions fill the kitchen with their aroma, put the kettle on to boil. Peel and chop the garlic, then peel and grate enough ginger to heap onto a tablespoon. Release the black seeds from the cardamom pods: lie a large knife blade flat on the cardamom, lean heavily on the knife, and the pod will spring open. Grind the cardamom seeds and peppercorns in a spice or coffee grinder. Don't forget about the onions while you're doing all this. Take them off the heat once they are dark golden and smell savoury.

Add the garlic, ginger and almonds to the pan. Fry gently until they start to smell cooked; then add the ground spices and fry for just long enough to release their heady fragrance.

Transfer the contents of the pan to the food processor or blender and whizz; add the yoghurt and whizz again. Measure 225 ml hot water from the kettle and pour it into the frying pan to pick up all the tasty stuck bits. Add to the mix and whizz one more time.

Dry the pan, turn up the heat, then fry the chicken in 1 tbsp oil for just long enough to colour on both sides; you may need to do this in 2 batches.

Add the sauce to the chicken. Add salt to taste, then simmer slowly for about half an hour. If the sauce isn't thick and creamy, remove the chicken to a warm place, then reduce the sauce over a higher heat.

With lamb:

Use 900 g boneless lean lamb. This can be from the leg, or you can use shoulder, which is a good deal cheaper and tastes so good; it just needs careful trimming. Make it exactly as above, simply substituting slices of lamb for the chicken pieces. When simmering, cover the dish and cook for 1½–2 hours, depending on the cut of meat. You'll probably need more water so it doesn't stick while cooking. Uncover for the last half-hour to allow the sauce to reduce and thicken slightly.

BEEF TAGINE

A sweet-spiced, richly flavoured stew, Moroccan-style. (It has to be called a tagine — doesn't Beef Stew with Prunes sound dire?) Rich, nearly gamey flavours emerge from the long, slow simmer. The prunes melt away, just adding body to the sauce — even prunophobes are amazed at the transformation. Don't try to rush this, as the best flavours emerge with time. Start it on a winter weekend morning for eating that night, or cook it the day before.

SERVES 6

1 kg piece of beef: shin, flank or well-trimmed rib
2 tbsp olive oil
500 g onions
2 tbsp butter
2 tsp ground coriander
1 tsp ground ginger
½ tsp ground allspice
½ tsp cayenne pepper or chilli flakes
pinch saffron strands
1 bay leaf
1–2 tsp salt
½ tsp freshly ground black pepper
3 tbsp honey
½ stock cube (or some stock — see recipe)
500 g stoned prunes
some fresh orange or lemon juice (optional)

Cut the beef into 6 or more thick slices (much nicer to eat than itty-bitty cubes). In a large, flameproof casserole, fry it at a fairly high heat in 2 or 3 batches in the olive oil until it has coloured nicely. As each batch is done, set it aside on a plate.

While the beef fries, peel, halve and finely slice the onions. When the beef is done, add the butter to the pot. When it bubbles, add the coriander, ginger, allspice, cayenne pepper or chilli, saffron and bay leaf. Stir, then add the onions, salt and pepper. Cook very gently until soft. Return the beef and its juices to the pot; add the honey and stock cube (if using it). Pour in enough water (or stock) until the meat is covered. Bring the liquid up to a bare simmer, then cook over a very, very low heat, covered, for 1–2 hours, until the meat is nearly done (shin will take longer; rib is quicker).

At this stage the stew will be very watery, which is just right (add water if it isn't). Drop the prunes into the pot. Simmer the stew gently (uncovered this time) for about half an hour, or until the prunes are starting to fall apart and are thickening, darkening and enriching the sauce. Taste and adjust the seasoning. Set aside in a cold place to cool down and serve later, reheated, when the flavours will have melded beautifully.

If you feel the flavour's too rich, pep it up with some juice from a lemon or an orange.

To serve: I might serve this with a lot of very finely chopped scallion stirred through at the last moment; or perhaps some fresh coriander instead. It's good with bulgar, couscous, spiced rice, mashed potato . . .

Tip: This kind of stew is perfect for small children and weaning babies, who love the sweet flavours. Leave out the chilli and add it to adult portions at the end.

stir-fry

The essential ingredients for a stir-fry are a hot wok and a cool head. (The beansprouts are strictly optional.) This means that those of us used to the rhythms of European-style cooking have to think again. With cooking the way we learned it, there's time, in mid-recipe, to crush a clove of garlic, to rummage for an ingredient, to mull over the recipe once more. Not so if you're stir-frying. Stir-frying is the fastest of all: a burst of heat and intense activity. It's the 100 metres of cooking. If you're not totally focused at the starting blocks, you'll be left behind wondering what happened.

The result of all this frantic action, though, is quick, fantastic flavour. The wok is hot as dragon's breath. The food sizzles mercilessly in it. The smell —

unmistakable — is called 'wok fragrance' by the Chinese. And the taste? A barbecued, smoky aura envelops the squeaky freshness of the ingredients.

Can you do this at home? You can. The thought of dragon's breath in the kitchen sounds alarming all right. But the intense activity is limited to a mere 3–4 minutes. The preparation is done at your leisure. This makes it not only a speedy way of cooking but a beautifully flexible one.

The heat
Gas is essential for really good stir-fried effects in a wok. Electric hobs just don't pump out as much heat in the right places. (If you have electric, use a large, heavy, heat-retaining frying pan or heavy flat-based wok instead.)

The wok
You don't *have* to have a wok to stir-fry — a very large frying pan will do. But a wok works best, allowing for great heat and tossing of ingredients.

Stir-frying has become such a buzzword that woks are now available in all sorts of materials. Most of them are pretty useless. — *Non-stick*: you won't get the flavour because you can't get the heat without destroying the pan. — *Cast-iron*, *stainless steel*, *Calphalon* and others: These are not as good as, and are infinitely more expensive than, a traditional Chinese one. So if you have gas, don't bother. If you have an electric hob, try a very heavy wok, but the effects will never be quite the same. — A traditional wok is made of *carbon steel*. I used to have one which lived a rusty existence under the sink. Once in a while, I took it out, scrubbed it clean, cooked in it, and swore at it because the food stuck. That was because I didn't know how to season it. A seasoned wok is a naturally non-stick wok. So read the section below. It's easy; and once you've done it, you'll have one of the best pans in your kitchen.

Buy a thin, large carbon-steel wok. They're cheapest at Asian suppliers, about £10. Alternatively, branded ones are available in kitchen shops and department stores.

The seasoned wok

It has a soft, black sheen. This is its naturally non-stick surface. Discard any notions you might have of sparkling clean pots. A good wok is black!

To season your carbon steel wok

You need to do this only once, when you bring the wok home from the shop. Using a cream cleaner such as Jif, scrub off the protective machine oils. Rinse well and dry. Put the wok on a burner at high heat and allow it to get very hot. Slowly and firmly rub 2 tbsp vegetable oil all over the inside of the wok with a big wad of kitchen paper. The oil should smoke and the centre of the wok should blacken, as should the kitchen paper. Don't burn your fingers! Remove the wok from the heat. Repeat this entire heating and oiling process every 5 minutes for about 20 minutes, until the kitchen paper comes away fairly clean when you rub it on the hot wok.

Your wok is now ready to stir-fry in. With use, this special non-stick surface will build up and the entire interior of the wok will blacken in time.

Never clean a seasoned wok with abrasive cleaners or even washing-up liquid; just use hot water and a plastic washing-up brush. If you do this while the wok is still hot from cooking, the wash-up is easy. Store the wok so it can't be scratched on the inside — hanging it is best. If it rusts or bubbles, or if a helpful friend has scrubbed the sheen off for you, just take a deep breath and repeat the seasoning process.

STIR-FRYING

The cool head

For this cooking sprint, have everything ready. And that means everything. There's no time to lay the table or heat the plates once cooking has started. Prepare all the ingredients too. This is the only time you need to behave like a TV cook, with everything arranged next to the cooker in a series of bowls. Finally, read through the recipe and visualise all the steps mentally. You won't have time to figure it out while the food splutters frenetically at you.

The hot wok

And now for the frying. To create that dragon's-breath heat:

— Preheat your wok as you would an oven. It will need a full 2–5 minutes on your hottest burner, *before* you add the oil. Look for a light haze of smoke rising from it.
— Swirl oil in the wok to cover its surface up to halfway.

— Test the wok's heat with 1 piece of whatever will go in first: a sliver of meat, or a little garlic. It should sizzle and crackle vigorously, but not burn instantly.
— Ignore timings given in recipes. These are only the merest guides. How long each step takes depends entirely on how hot you manage to get your wok. Your guides: how the food smells, sounds and looks.

GOING AGAINST THE GRAIN

'Slice the meat against the grain.' This standard stir-fry speak gave me a great deal of grief when I was teaching myself to cook. What was the grain, and how could you go against it?

Slicing the meat against the grain means that you are cutting through the fibres which run within a piece of meat. As a result, the meat will be tender when quick-cooked. It's important for **beef**, **pork** and **lamb** — but doesn't matter at all for chicken, which is tender enough already.

To find that 'grain' . . . you need to cut 1 first slice and look at it. Are fibres running along the length of the slice? Then you have sliced with the grain. Turn the meat 90°; cut at right angles to your first cut. This should yield a piece of meat which is covered with a criss-cross effect and which, when pulled, stretches easily both ways, a good sign that you have cut against the grain.

Remember that some meat (e.g. large chops or beef rib slices) may have several different sections, each with the grain facing a different way. If your meat looks like this, separate out the sections before starting to slice.

stir-fry

Tip: For that dragon's-breath, stir-fried effect, *don't* stir. With the inadequate heat of many domestic cookers, if you stir constantly you just end up with stewed food. So when the food hits the hot pan, leave it to sizzle until it browns and becomes fragrant. Then stir.

Tip: If your food sticks, the most likely reason is that the wok wasn't hot enough.

STIR-FRIED GINGERY PORK WITH SQUEAKY GREENS

This is gingery and vivid. Use the freshest greens you can find. Try one of the following: French beans; mangetout; sugar snap peas; young runner beans, cut in chunks; celery, cut in fine slices; York (spring) cabbage, finely shredded; or Chinese pak choi, choi sum or Chinese green 'long beans'.

SERVES 4

4 x 125 g boneless pork loin chops
250 g greens (see above)

Marinade

1 tbsp sesame oil
1 tbsp Chinese Shaohsing rice wine or dry sherry
1 tsp cornflour
pinch salt

Sauce

1–2 tbsp root ginger, grated finely
1 tsp Chinese chilli bean sauce or chilli sauce
1 tsp black bean sauce
1 tbsp light soy sauce
1 tbsp Chinese Shaohsing rice wine or dry sherry
1 tsp sugar
150 ml chicken stock
sunflower or peanut oil

Slice the pork finely against the grain. In a bowl, mix it well with the marinade ingredients. Set it aside while you prepare the rest.

Prepare greens as necessary: string beans; slice celery finely, etc. Remove any stringy hairs from the grated ginger. Spoon chilli and black bean sauces into one bowl; spoon the soy, rice wine or sherry, sugar and stock into another.

On a burner at maximum heat, heat the wok. When hot, add 2 tbsp oil; swirl it halfway up the wok. Test with a piece of the marinated meat, which should sizzle and spit. Add the meat; stir-fry until nearly cooked through. Tip the meat and any juice onto a plate. Reheat the wok on maximum heat. Add 1 tbsp oil. Add the ginger; stir-fry to crisp a little. Add chilli and black bean sauces; stir-fry until aromatic; add the greens; stir-fry until hot through. Add the meat as well as the contents of the second bowl of seasonings. Cook until the mix bubbles vigorously. Taste to check seasoning, then serve immediately.

Variation: Make this with **beef**, adding **1 tsp Chinese five-spice powder** to the marinade.

LAMB WITH CELERY AND CORIANDER

This is a favourite: delicate, easy and quick. If you can get dried shiitake (delis and some supermarkets have them, as well as Asian stores), they add a lovely musky depth to the dish.

SERVES 3–4

2 dried Chinese (shiitake) mushrooms (or a few tbsp stock; see recipe)
450 g boneless, lean, tender lamb
2–3 cloves garlic (crushed)
2 tsp caster sugar
1 tbsp sesame oil
2 tsp cornflour
plenty of freshly ground black pepper
½ head celery
4 medium scallions
a small bunch fresh coriander
3 tbsp sunflower or peanut oil
2 tbsp Chinese Shaohsing rice wine or dry sherry
1 tbsp light soy
salt

Soak the mushrooms, if you have them, in hot water for 25 minutes. Cut the lamb across the grain into very slender ribbons. Mix it with the garlic, sugar, sesame oil, cornflour and black pepper and set aside for 15 minutes.

Prepare the vegetables:

Slice the celery finely at an angle and the scallions into 3 cm lengths. Trim the coriander: discard thick stalks, pull off the leaves and chop slender stalks finely. If you are using the mushrooms, lift them out of their soaking water (keep the water), cut out and discard their tough stalks and slice the mushroom caps very finely.

To stir-fry:

Heat the wok until it's roasting hot. Add 1 tbsp oil and swirl it round. Fry half the lamb, allowing it to crisp and colour without overcooking it. Tip it out onto a plate, then repeat the process with another tbsp of oil and the rest of the lamb. Add this to the first batch.

Add the final tbsp of oil to the pan. Stir-fry the celery, scallions and mushrooms (if using), until the celery is just starting to become translucent. Add the sherry, soy and meat. Add 1–2 tbsp mushroom-soaking water or stock to make a little sauce. Taste it and add salt if necessary. Stir in the coriander stalks and bubble one last time.

Top with the coriander leaves and eat right away. (See also pp. 78–9.)

char-grill

In the seventies you were nobody if you didn't have a fondue dish of boiling oil to dunk raw meat into. The eighties brought the wok; the early ones rusted under the sink. Then came the char-grill pan. Are you all still using it? Or have you given up in frustration: burned food, raw food, food that sticks?

You are not alone. And yet I think the char-grill pan will avoid being consigned to the shed, because once you learn to read its mind, it can be persuaded to deliver that intense, close-to-burning flavour we have all become addicted to. It sears stripes on food which look good and taste better. And it's a great way to deal with that quintessentially Irish summer event, the barbeque-moved-indoors.

What-grilling?

Before we go any further, let's clarify what we're talking about here. The 'char-grill' pan is not something you slide under the grill to burn the toast. It is a flat cast-iron pan with ridges on its base. It should be very heavy, and it goes on the hob. Its effect is a cross between frying and barbequeing. It may be called a *grill pan*, or a *cast-iron grill pan*, or a *ridged grill pan* — all the same thing.

If a cookbook says grill, it usually still means the slide-it-under-the-heat mode, though some are now using 'grill' for this pan. If speaking American, 'grill' means barbeque (they say 'broil' for grilling). 'Char-grill' is used interchangeably on both sides of the Atlantic to mean barbequeing or ridged-cast-iron-grill-pan

grilling. All clear? Never mind, let's move on.

To fry or to grill?

Do you need this pan at all? I'm sure one of the reasons for its runaway success is that we can describe fried food as 'grilled'. In truth, meat can be seared in a good, heavy frying pan nearly as well and with just as little fat. But you won't get the stripes, nor the same intensity of charred flavour without burning the food altogether.

One bonus of the grill pan is that the meat sits on those ridges, so doesn't soak up fat released during cooking. However, the frying pan has one benefit: in a grill pan, you can't make sauce.

No sauce?

In most cases, this isn't a problem, since the food you're cooking is likely to rely on new-style sauces. That means salsas and vinaigrettes galore, and more (see pp. 70–72 and 92–4 for those). Still, if it's a creamy pepper sauce for your steak you're after, stick to the old-fashioned frying pan.

The pan

If you haven't got one yet, measure your cooker. Look for a long grill pan which fits across two burners. Most (mine included) are just the right length to get halfway to the second burner. This means that you have to keep moving it around to try to get an even heat. Most irritating.

Heat it up

Just as with a wok, you must heat the grill pan until it is searingly hot. Everything will stick if you

don't. Think of preheating it just like the oven. Heat it dry on a medium heat for 5–10 minutes (not on high, which will damage the pan). Move it around if necessary to heat it evenly.

Oil it

Recipes tell you to brush oil onto the hot pan. Don't. If your pan is hot, the brush will melt. Rub a little oil onto the meat/fish/veg you are about to cook. Or lightly oil the pan with an oiled wad of kitchen paper (mind your fingers!).

Sear it

Lay the food on the smoking hot pan. It should do more than sizzle, it should spit and crackle frighteningly. (If it didn't, the pan wasn't hot enough and you're in trouble. Remove the food, wipe off the pan, heat some more and start again.)

Turn the heat to high now to compensate for heat loss as the cold food arrives, but remember to turn it down again soon in case things start to burn. This cooking method is a good test of your smoke alarm.

Leave it

Just as we learned when frying a steak (p. 40), don't fiddle around with the food. Leave it to char until half-done, or at least until it moves easily. (If it's stuck, it means either that you need to leave it longer, or that the pan wasn't hot enough in the first place.)

Above all, don't keep moving it around, or you'll lose the striped effect. Best of all, turn it once only. (If you want criss-cross markings, turn the meat 90° and continue grilling.)

char-grill

Cover it?

A large, domed lid, such as a wok lid, can help to keep heat in when the food is charred outside but still needs to cook through. Lower the heat a little and put on the lid, but make sure the food doesn't steam and stew in there.

Don't fill up the pan

It will lose heat, cease to sizzle and make sad steamy sounds. Most pans can handle only 2 large or 4 small portions.

What's cooking?

The char-grill pan is not a subtle cooking medium. Forget delicate fish fillets. Chops and steaks are perfect. Chicken tastes fantastic (indeed this is one of the best ways to cook tasteless supermarket chicks); but stick to boneless meat. Bone-in, it takes forever to cook. Moist, juicy thighs work so much better than breasts, which tend to dry out.

Be prepared for the clean-up

It's messy. To clean the pan, allow it to cool before putting it in water or it may crack; then give it a good soak in lukewarm water. Scrub well with a brush, but don't use abrasives or cream cleaners, or the finish on the pan will be destroyed. (And don't forget to turn the smoke alarm back on.)

2 GREAT MARINADES FOR CHAR-GRILLED CHICKEN

Marinade + char-grilling = lots of flavour, which is badly needed with run-of-the-mill supermarket chickens. Of course, if you have a lovely free-range bird, so much the better.

EACH OF THESE DOES 6–8 BONED THIGHS, OR ABOUT 4 BREASTS, TO SERVE 3–4

Ginger and Soy

This is the best way to get flavour in a hurry, and the ginger then crisps on the pan — mmm.

| 1 tbsp light soy sauce |
| 1 tbsp Thai fish sauce (nam pla) |
| 2 tbsp Chinese Shaohsing rice wine or dry sherry |
| 1 tbsp finely grated root ginger |
| 1 tsp sesame oil |

Mix with the chicken and marinate for ½–1 hour before char-grilling — no longer, or the flavour will be too strong.

Variation: For a change, add ½ tsp Chinese five-spice powder to the mix.

Olive Oil and Herbs

This is more subtle and needs a few hours' (or overnight) marinating.

| 1 small lemon |
| 4 tbsp olive oil |
| 2 cloves garlic, crushed |
| 1 onion, chopped |
| generous sprig of fresh marjoram (or rosemary or thyme) |
| sea salt and black pepper |

Peel the rind from the lemon in wide strips with a vegetable peeler, then squeeze its juice. Mix rind and juice with all the other ingredients and marinate with the chicken overnight before char-grilling.

THAI BEEF SALAD

I make no claims for authenticity here: it's my own favourite version as it has evolved over the years.

SERVES 4–6 AS A STARTER, OR 2 HUNGRY PEOPLE AS DINNER WITH RICE OR ROAST POTATO WEDGES

| 350 g well-hung beef sirloin |
| 50 ml Thai fish sauce (nam pla) |
| 1 tsp vegetable oil |
| 2 red onions |
| 1 cucumber |
| salt |
| 2–3 tbsp fresh mint leaves |
| 2–3 tbsp fresh coriander leaves |
| 6 tbsp lime juice (2–3 limes) |
| 3 tbsp Thai fish sauce (nam pla) |
| 2–4 tbsp finely chopped fresh red chilli |
| mixed salad leaves |

Marinate the beef in the fish sauce for ½ hour–2 hours, turning it occasionally. Heat the grill pan (or have the barbeque lit). Dry the beef well with kitchen paper, then smear the oil over the beef. Char-grill it until medium rare (still soft when you press it with your finger, but dark and crusty on the outside). Set it aside until it has cooled.

Meanwhile, slice the onions finely and soak them in several changes of cold water to make them milder.

A few minutes before serving, halve the cucumber lengthways, and slice finely. Sprinkle with a little salt and set aside.

Slice the beef very finely. Mix it with all other ingredients except the cucumber and salad leaves. Taste. It should be a refreshing balance of hot, sour and salty. Add extra chilli, lime juice or fish sauce as you feel necessary.

Make a mound of salad leaves and cucumber, and pile the spicy beef strips on top of that. Serve soon, before the dressing 'cooks' the rare beef.

ANNE'S SALAD: SEARED BEEF RIBBONS AND PARSLEY

You don't need exotic herbs for exciting char-grilled salads . . .

SERVES 6–8 AS A STARTER OR PART OF A BUFFET, 4 AS A MORE SUBSTANTIAL MEAL

about 800 g thick sirloin or striploin steaks

1 clove garlic

a little olive oil

3–4 tbsp very fresh parsley, very finely chopped

Classic French Vinaigrette (see p. 70)

4–6 small courgettes (optional)

Leave a thin strip of fat on the steaks for better flavour as you fry (you'll trim it later). Crush the garlic and smear it over the meat; leave it to permeate for half an hour or so.

Rub a little olive oil over the meat and char-grill on a preheated searingly hot pan until rare or medium-rare. Set it aside to cool, on a rack, so it doesn't go soggy.

Shortly before serving, trim off the fat and any gristle, then slice the meat finely and turn it gently in the parsley and enough vinaigrette to coat it. Taste for seasonings.

Serve just as it is, or with salad leaves, or with **Seared Courgettes:** Slice the courgettes into long slices at an angle, then toss in a tsp olive oil to coat them, and char-grill them on a hot pan on both sides until striped and tender.

FISH ON THE CHAR-GRILL

Most fish don't take very well to the char-grill pan: the heat's simply too fierce and the fish tends to stick, then disintegrate. But there are a few exceptions. **Salmon** is a little borderline, but can work if you buy skin-on fillets and cook them by the no-turn method for frying a fish, described on pp. 32–3.

Tuna is fantastic. Its flesh is sturdy enough to cope, and its oily flavours are excellent combined with a few char-grilled stripes. Fry a tuna steak just like a piece of meat. It's a doddle to cook, since you can see the flesh turning opaque towards the centre as it gets done. No guesswork involved. One warning: tuna tastes best when still slightly rare in the centre. If well done, it dries out.

Squid is excellent on the char-grill — the seared flavours magnify its shellfishy sweetness. It's best to grill it when it's cut open and lying flat, but you can grill the tentacles too, so do your best to get hold of them as they look so exciting on the plate.

For instructions on cleaning squid, see p. 39. Cut the squid bodies open to lay them flat, and after cleaning, dry them well and oil them with a little olive oil.

Heat the char-grill pan, dry, on a medium heat until it's very hot — hold your hand just above it to test. Then lay the oiled squid on for half a minute, turn, and cook on the other side until opaque. If the squid is any good at all it'll be delightfully tender now. Serve right away.

Here are some ideas:

— Just drizzle with olive oil, and scatter with sea salt and finely chopped parsley.
— Add a scattering of finely chopped fresh red chilli if you like, or, as they do at London's River Cafe, rocket and red chilli, lemon and olive oil. Or serve on a bed of lightly dressed salad leaves, or with roasted red pepper strips, or some Puy lentils freshly cooked and dressed with garlicky vinaigrette while still warm.
— Or serve with a salsa or relish, see pp. 33 and 92–4.

salads

Once upon a time there was just shy flopsy butterhead, sadly squashed by a thick glob of salad cream and the spreading stain of pickled beetroot. Next, iceberg rushed in — but she was cold comfort, with her bulky, tasteless crunch. And then suddenly, it happened. There are now lettuces, herbs, even flowers galore; most look frilly, vivacious and fun — and are very tasty indeed.

A good green salad has never been easier. Yet we're still inclined to underestimate the magnificent glory which a bowl of spry, vital greens can bring to the table: a lush course by themselves, not just a thought on the side.

The leaves
They should be good enough to eat without a dressing. This is a counsel of perfection, though.

Every now and again I come across some, and wonder at the miracle of modern food production. Three-day-old lettuce from Spain, looking fresh and tasting of nothing? No problem. Flavourful lettuce picked three hours ago from a drill just around the corner? Well-nigh impossible.

In season, abandon the supermarket. Seek out markets and enlightened shopkeepers for one of the greatest pleasures summer can bring: just-picked leaves. (And if you ever find yourself in Sligo, go into Tir na nÓg and pick up some of Eden Plants' extraordinary organic leaves and herbs, grown by Rod Alston. The best I've ever tasted, anywhere.)

The best flavour of all comes from leaves which have never seen a fridge, and are still alive with the warm scent of soil and greenery. Don't scorn a beautiful butterhead if you see one, resonant with soft, earthy, minerally flavours. It can, if well grown, be delicious.

Look for all sorts of other greenery too. Baby spears of **spinach** are tender; **rocket** and **cress** are deliciously peppery. Herbs add life to the bowl: a handful of chopped **parsley** or **chives**, **dill** or **basil leaves**, or all of them together. Beware **curly endive** and **radicchio**. These bitter leaves may look smart, but a whole mouthful of them just doesn't taste good.

Unfortunately, supermarket bags of mixed salad leaves are still very unimaginative — and pretty tasteless — here in Ireland.

Washing — and drying
Wash briskly under cold running water, or in at least 2 changes of water, to be sure of freeing all the grit. Don't soak the flavour out of your leaves by abandoning them in a basin of water.

It's important to dry lettuce carefully, or the salad will taste soggy, the dressing diluted. A salad spinner is one of the most effective, underrated kitchen appliances of all (and it's cheap). Spin each batch of leaves twice.

Storing
This is best not done at all, but of course we all do. The best way to keep greens lively is to wash and dry them, then put them in a Ziploc vegetable bag (they have perforations), which allows them to breathe. Herbs? Don't wash in advance — it greatly reduces their flavour.

Tearing
Lettuce pieces must be mouth-sized if you don't want to end up with dressing all over your face. With soft lettuces, raggedy, torn edges look much more natural than the clean ribbons produced by the swathe of a knife. But rip gently, and never twist the leaves. You're not trying to wring their necks, and if you do violence to the delicate tissues now, you'll have sodden salad as soon as the dressing soaks into those bruised cells.

Firmer leaves need to be cut with a knife. Be sure it's sharp or they'll bruise.

The dressing
Apparently, an area of great mystique. Thousands of ready-made dressings sell in the supermarkets, almost all of them vastly inferior to anything you could rustle up at home in 3 minutes.

BASIC DRESSING
1. The jam jar
The simplest way to make up a dressing. Just shake it all up in a wide-necked jam jar. Remember to screw the lid on tightly first!

2. Don't move
I used to get into a complete tizz about dressings until it occurred to me that I kept every single ingredient in a different part of the kitchen. Store them all together, within arm's reach of the counter, including the garlic, salt and pepper grinder. (But always keep mustard, especially smooth Dijon, in the fridge, so it doesn't go off.)

3. The ingredients
Look for a fruity-flavoured extra virgin olive oil, a not-too-sharp wine vinegar, a zippy Dijon mustard. Sea salt and a pepper mill for black pepper are essential. These will cover the basics. (If you find extra virgin olive oil too strong, or too expensive, I wouldn't recommend inferior 'pure' olive oils. Stick to the extra virgin, and dilute with sunflower oil. The flavour's better.)

Then the fun begins. Splash out one day on a single-estate extra virgin olive oil for the purest, simplest dressings (see pp. 70–71). Add balsamic vinegar to the shelf, and perhaps some Mileeven cider vinegar with honey. Soon there'll be no stopping you . . .

4. The dressing
Put **4 parts olive oil** to **1 part wine vinegar** (red or white) to half-fill your jam jar. Add **a tsp Dijon mustard, a little salt and pepper**, close the jar and shake.

Taste. Remember the effect will be diluted by the leaves. Now adjust the ingredients to arrive at a flavour you like. Temper acidity by adding more mustard or salt before you add more oil. Add more vinegar if the dressing tastes flat. And that's it!

salads

Tossing the salad

Don't. Better to turn the leaves rather than toss them. To be honest, salad is best turned with your hands — they do the job more sensitively than any fancy fork and spoon. If you do this, however, I suggest you keep yourself out of view of your guests . . .

Use as little dressing as possible. The leaves should barely glisten. If there's a puddle at the bottom of the bowl, you used too much.

SIMPLE GREEN SALAD WITH CHIVES

SERVES 4–6

1 head of lettuce — butterhead or another
or 4 big handfuls mixed leaves, herbs and flowers
Classic French Vinaigrette (see below)
3 tbsp chopped chives

DRESSING TIPS

- The 'classic' proportions of 3 parts oil to 1 part vinegar are still often recommended. This is almost invariably far too acidic. 4:1 is usually good. 5:1 may even be right if the vinegar is sharp.
- Recipes for dressings can never be exact, since the strengths of oils and vinegars vary so greatly. Always, always taste . . .
- Dressing is best made fresh, but many will keep for several days in the fridge. Just remember that garlic goes rancid in a dressing after a few hours. If you want to make dressing in advance, or make a large quantity to keep in the fridge and use over several days, make it without the garlic, and add garlic in shortly before serving.

Toss the washed and dried lettuce (torn if necessary) with just enough vinaigrette to coat the leaves lightly, then scatter the chopped chives over it.

CLASSIC FRENCH VINAIGRETTE

If you want to jizz it up, add some chopped chives or another fresh herb.

MAKES ENOUGH FOR 1 MEDIUM GREEN SALAD, TO SERVE 4–6

4 tbsp extra virgin olive oil
1 tbsp wine vinegar
½ tsp Dijon mustard
1 small clove garlic, crushed
a generous pinch salt
freshly ground black pepper

Shake everything in a jam jar. Taste and adjust seasonings as necessary.

Some variations on the theme:

- Try **Balsamic Dressing**, **Purest Dressing**, **Buttermilk Dressing**, **Asian Dressing** or **Walnut and Balsamic Dressing** instead (see below).
- Add **1–2 tsp dry-toasted sesame seeds** to the salad. This works well with the Classic French Vinaigrette, Balsamic or Asian dressings. To dry-toast sesame seeds, heat them in a dry frying pan until they start to pop and jump around.
- Or add **3 tbsp crumbled or squished blue cheese nuggets**. Ripe Cashel Blue is a favourite, but you can use any blue. Dress with Classic French Vinaigrette.
- Or add some **Parmesan**, **Gabriel**, **Desmond** or **Mizen**, shaved with a vegetable parer into thin curls. Balance them on top of the greens. Dress with Classic French Vinaigrette or Balsamic Dressing.

- Use different **herbs**. A few small whole fresh basil leaves are lovely, or some chervil; try dill as well.
- **Asian green salad** — it's utterly untraditional, and it's very good. Any salad leaves work well, but if you can find some Asian ones too, so much the better. Baby pak choi or mizuna are two favourites. Other peppery leaves like rocket taste very good too. Finish with Asian Dressing, some toasted sesame seeds and, if you have it, a little fresh coriander.

BALSAMIC DRESSING

Balsamic vinegar is much less acidic than wine vinegars, so use about 3 parts oil to 1 part vinegar.

MAKES ENOUGH FOR 1 MEDIUM GREEN SALAD, TO SERVE 4–6

4 tbsp extra virgin olive oil
1½ tbsp balsamic vinegar
1 small clove garlic, crushed
salt

Shake it all up in a jam jar and taste. Add **1 tsp wine vinegar** if the flavour's a little flat.

PUREST DRESSING

When you have indulged in a single-estate, extra virgin olive oil, the kind that can cost £10 or £20 a bottle, don't muddy it up with any other ingredients. Don't even shake it.

Just coat the leaves with the best wine or balsamic vinegar you have, then the oil, using 1 part vinegar to 3 parts oil (if using balsamic) or 4 parts oil (if using wine vinegar). Add salt, preferably Maldon sea salt flakes (and maybe a little pepper). Toss.

The best vinegar? It's odd that, with so much fuss made about extra virgin olive oils, it's rare to find a superb vinegar to match them. My favourites (I prefer them to most balsamics) are the Spanish **Forum** vinegars, made on the small Puig Roca vineyard on the coast just south of Barcelona. With stunning slightly sweet/sour flavours, they're the very best partner for a beautiful oil and wonderful leaves. The red is made from **Cabernet Sauvignon**, the white from **Chardonnay** and they're crying out to be discovered more widely.

BUTTERMILK DRESSING

Low-fat salad dressings are usually just horrid, based on water and stabilisers and thickeners and God knows what else. This, on the other hand, is really rather good. Use a punchily flavoured oil. The dressing keeps well in the fridge for a few days.

MAKES ABOUT 150 ML, ENOUGH FOR A GREEN SALAD FOR 6–8

80 ml buttermilk
1 tbsp lemon juice
1 tbsp balsamic vinegar
1–2 tbsp extra virgin olive oil
1 tbsp Greek yoghurt
½ tsp smooth Dijon mustard
1 tsp sugar
generous pinch salt

Put them all in a jam jar, screw the lid on tightly and shake well. Taste and adjust seasonings as necessary.

ASIAN DRESSING

MAKES ABOUT 130 ML, ENOUGH FOR A GREEN SALAD FOR 6–8

4 tbsp sunflower oil
2 tbsp sesame oil
1½ tbsp wine vinegar
1 tbsp Thai fish sauce (nam pla)
½ tsp soy sauce
1 clove garlic, crushed
chopped fresh chilli to taste

Shake everything in a jam jar. Taste and adjust seasonings as necessary.

Note: If you can't find Thai fish sauce (nam pla), use 1 tsp soy sauce instead.

COS SALAD WITH BLACK OLIVES

SERVES ABOUT 4

1 cos lettuce
a handful tasty black olives
Parmesan (or another very hard, piquant cheese) for shaving in curls
Rich Savoury Dressing (see below)

Wash the lettuce; leave the long cos leaves whole or tear them, whichever you prefer. Scatter with the olives and curls of cheese shaved off with a vegetable parer. Pour over dressing in a thin stream in zigzag lines, and serve extra dressing on the side.

RICH SAVOURY DRESSING

Since this dressing contains raw egg, be careful to whom you serve it (see p. 5). This makes a lot of dressing, but you'll quickly find many uses for it. Keep it in the fridge and eat within 3 days.

1 large very fresh free-range egg
5 (or more) anchovy fillets
1 generous bunch fresh parsley
2 tbsp wine vinegar
2 tbsp freshly grated Parmesan
1 clove garlic, crushed
1 tsp Worcestershire sauce
1 tsp Dijon mustard
200 ml sunflower or peanut oil
100 ml extra virgin olive oil

Whizz everything except the oils in a food processor or blender. With the motor running, pour in the oils in a steady stream until the sauce is thick. Taste and adjust the seasoning if necessary.

Other things to do with this dressing:

● **Avocado and rocket salad.** For 4, halve and slice 2 avocados and rinse quickly under the cold tap (this stops the avocado from browning); pat dry with kitchen paper and arrange with 2 handfuls of rocket. Serve with the dressing.

● **Avocado and spiced beef salad.** Top slices of spiced beef with slices of avocado, then spoon some dressing over. Serve with crusty bread or steamed potatoes.

● **Young waxy potatoes** are delicious scattered with a generous handful of chopped parsley and served with the dressing on the side, while they're still warm.

SURPRISING GREEN SALAD

My uncle Hasse, who cooks with verve and feeling, is renowned far and wide for this salad. Excellent as a side salad with grilled meats, as part of a mixed salad plate, or as a simple supper with small, steamed, thin-skinned potatoes.

SERVES ABOUT 6–8

1 medium head of crispy lettuce (preferably cos or a flavoursome crisp)
1 small fragrant green-fleshed melon
½ large cucumber
Yoghurt, Garlic and Caper Dressing (see below)

Tear the washed, dried lettuce into bite-sized pieces. Cut the melon flesh into bite-sized cubes. Peel the cucumber leaving thin stripes of skin and cut into chunks. Toss with enough of the following dressing to coat more generously than you would with a vinaigrette.

salads

YOGHURT, GARLIC AND CAPER DRESSING

50 ml olive oil
50 ml sunflower oil
2 tbsp wine vinegar
1 tbsp capers (or more to taste)
1 heaped tbsp smooth Dijon or sweet German mustard
3–4 heaped tbsp plain yoghurt
3–4 fat cloves garlic, crushed
⅓ tsp curry powder
½ tsp sugar
salt and pepper

Shake everything very vigorously in a jam jar to emulsify.

Other things to do with this dressing:
● Serve it with the salad above, using halved seedless grapes (green or black) instead of the melon.
● Or steam courgettes, slice them lengthways, allow to cool, cover with the dressing and finish with lots of chopped parsley.
● Use it as a dressing for potato salad.

LITTLE GEMS IN A PUDDLE

The dress code for most salads requires them to be scantily clad. This one is different. Halved tiny lettuces are perched in a puddle of the lightest blue cheese dressing you've ever tasted. The salad is finished with tiny squares of sheep's cheese and a scattering of chives.

It's best of all made with Little Gem (sometimes called Baby Cos) — sweet and crunchy baby lettuce hearts which need only be halved to serve them. If you can't get them, ask for them — it's time we created demand for this excellent lettuce. You can use a cos lettuce instead, keeping the leaves whole as for a Caesar salad. Cratloe Hills is a lovely Irish mild, sweet, hard

sheep's cheese, available from good cheese shops, delis and some supermarkets.

SERVES ABOUT 3–4
125 ml whole milk
100 ml cream
30 g not-too-blue Cabrales, Roquefort or ripe Cashel Blue
about 200 g (trimmed weight) Little Gems or cos lettuce
40 g Cratloe Hills sheep's cheese (or another hard sheep's cheese)
1 tbsp chopped chives (and some chive flowers if possible)

Heat the milk, cream and blue cheese in a pan, whisking to mix in the cheese. Simmer gently until it has reduced a little and the salty, blue flavour has intensified. (It should now measure about 175 ml.) It should still be very runny. If it has darkened or thickened too much, stir in a little extra milk. Set aside and chill it.

Rinse the Little Gems whole. Dry them and cut them in half lengthways (or quarters if they're large). Lay them on a large, not-quite-flat plate onto which you have poured most of the cold dressing; then pour the last of it over the greens. Slice the Cratloe Hills very thinly and cut the slices into tiny squares; scatter them all over, along with the chives. Purple chive flowers make a lovely edible garnish if you can get some.

2 MAIN COURSE GREEN SALADS

WARM SALAD OF DUCK, GRAPES AND WALNUTS WITH A WALNUT AND BALSAMIC DRESSING

This is rich enough for a meal on its own, especially if you then finish with a piece of ripe cheese. Great crusty bread essential.

SERVES 4
4 small (or 2 very large) duck breasts
250 g tasty black grapes
about 24 walnut halves
4 portions of mixed salad leaves, including some spicy or bitter ones (e.g. endive, radicchio or rocket)

Walnut and Balsamic Dressing
4 tbsp olive oil
4 tbsp sunflower oil
2 tbsp walnut oil
2–4 tsp wine vinegar
4 tsp balsamic vinegar
1 clove garlic, well crushed
1 tsp Dijon mustard
salt and pepper

With a sharp knife, slash several lines through the skin on the duck breasts, without cutting into the meat. Season the duck with salt and plenty of coarsely ground black pepper. Heat a heavy frying pan, then lie the breasts skin-side down on it. As they fry, a lot of fat will be released — spoon this off regularly. (Don't throw it away! It makes the best fried potatoes.)

After about 10 minutes, when the skin is deep mahogany, turn the duck breasts and fry the other side until they're done to your liking (about another 5–15 minutes, depending on their size).

Working for Christ

To do the work of Christ is really quite simple.
It means to be faithful in little things,
for to be faithful in little things is a big thing.
It means to do one's task, no matter how humble,
not only thoroughly but joyfully.
It means to make oneself available,
yet never to seek the limelight.
It means to make oneself useful,
without seeking to push oneself.
It means to carry one's own burden, without,
as far as possible, becoming a burden on others.
In a word, it means to be at one's post,
helpful and faithful, loyal and constant.
Lord, make me an instrument
for the building of your kingdom.

Mass Intentions for the week.

Monday 17 July:
12 noon ..... Margaret Lyons and decd. membs. of the Lyons and Henry Families. Anniv.

Tuesday 18 July:
12 noon ..... O'Brien Family, R.I.P. Eden.

Wednesday 19 July:
12 noon ..... Hunt Family, Cloonfaughna.
3.00 p.m...... Decd. membs. of the Lavin Family, Shanvaghera.
5.00 p.m...... James and Margaret Mulkeen, Coogue North. Anniv.

Thursday 20 July:
7.30 p.m...... Margaret Ryan, Meeltrane. 1st Anniv.

Friday 21 July:
12 noon ..... James and Nellie Johnston and decd. membs. of the Johnston Family, Cloonternane.
3.00 p.m...... Holy Souls.

Saturday 22 July:
12 noon ..... Tommy and Mai Carney, Coogue. Anniv.
5.00 p.m...... Family Life.

Shanvaghera:

Sunday 23 July:
Teddy Campbell, Shanvaghera. 1st Anniv.

Meanwhile, halve the grapes lengthways and flick out their seeds. Shake all the dressing ingredients in a jam jar and taste for balance.

When the duck breasts are done, put them on a plate in a barely warm oven to rest for 5 minutes, but don't wash the frying pan — leave just 1 tsp duck fat in it. Then slice the duck breasts at an angle. Add all the juices they have released to the dressing, and put the meat back in the oven.

Toss the lettuce and grape halves with the dressing and pile them high on 4 plates. Heat the frying pan quickly, and stir-fry the walnuts until they colour. Arrange the duck and walnuts on the salad, trying not to squash the leaves.

Eat immediately.

TOASTED GOATS' CHEESE SALAD

This is fancy cheese on toast. Now a bistro classic, it's particularly tasty if the cheese is superb.

SERVES 4

150–200 g goats' cheese log (e.g. mature St Tola or Míne Gabhar)

1 slender baguette

a little olive oil

1 clove garlic, cut in half

really good salad leaves for 4 people

Classic French Vinaigrette or Balsamic Dressing (p. 70)

½ tsp fresh thyme or marjoram leaves

Turn on the grill. Cut the cheese into thick slices to divide it between 4; slice enough bread to fit neatly under the cheese. (How many pieces you end up with depends on the width of the cheese rounds.) Have all ingredients and serving plates ready.

Toast the bread on both sides; as soon as it's done, sprinkle a few drops of olive oil onto one side and rub with the cut clove of garlic. Toss the salad leaves in the dressing and divide between 4 plates. Place the cheese on the toast and put it back under the grill; keep an eye on it. It is done quickly; don't wait for it to melt, because goats' cheese doesn't.

Balance the toast on the leaves, sprinkle the herbs on each toast, and serve at once.

roasting vegetables

There's such pleasure in roasting vegetables. A few handfuls will do the trick: perhaps some carrots, an onion, a few potatoes. Chop the potatoes into long wedges, the onions into quarters, the carrots into chunks and tumble them all into a good-looking oven dish. Next comes a little splosh of olive oil, and the veg are turned in it till they glisten. To finish them, a scatter of sea salt and a few sprigs from the rosemary bush or a twig of thyme, and into the oven they go. Forty minutes later, they're fragrant, crusty-edged, dense, sweet and caramelised.

Roasting in winter
Roasting brings out the sweetness in winter's bland vegetables; best of all are carrots, parsnips, onions and pumpkins.

- Cut **carrots** and **parsnips** into quarters if they're small, and into chunky wedges if they're large.
- Peel **onions**, but leave the root on. Cut them into quarters through the root, so it holds them together. Allow 30–40 minutes' roasting time for root vegetables.
- **Tasty pumpkins**: Avoid gigantic Hallowe'en pumpkins; they're pumped-up and watery. Look for dense, orange-fleshed pumpkins (their skins may be orange or pewter). Roast in pieces, with the tough skin on, with olive oil or butter and herbs. Amazingly, the skin becomes thin and tender during the roasting; and the flesh will be exquisitely melting.
- **Potatoes**: Don't forget about roasting potatoes. See Rosemary and Olive Oil Roast Potato Wedges, p. 23, or roast them along with the rest of the vegetables, as in this next recipe. There's no need to peel if the skins are thin. Simply cut the potatoes into quarters or eighths, lengthways.

How to roast
Turn the oven on to 220C/425F/ Gas 7. Cut the vegetables to similar sizes (cut carrots a bit smaller than the rest since they

take longer to cook). Spread them in a jumbled single layer in a gratin dish or a roasting tin; don't overcrowd them too much. Turn them in a few tbsp of olive oil. Add some sea salt, preferably tender flakes of Maldon salt, and herbs if you have them. Roast until they're done; turn them once or twice while they're roasting. Allow 45 minutes– 1 hour.

ROAST VEGETABLES WITH OLIVE OIL AND THYME

Excellent with, or without, your Sunday roast.

SERVES 4
4 large potatoes
3 large carrots
2 parsnips
2 onions
2–3 tbsp olive oil
salt (Maldon if possible)
2 tsp thyme leaves

Cut the vegetables into wedges and chunks as described above. Put them in a single layer in a large roasting tin or gratin dish; turn them in just enough olive oil to coat them lightly. Scatter with salt and thyme. Roast at 220C/425F/Gas 7 for about 50 minutes, depending on the size of the chunks you have cut.

Variations:
Roast vegetables with parsley: Roast with a good handful of chopped parsley, which will go dark and crispy in the oven, and top with another few tbsp chopped parsley just before serving.
Tip: There's often debate about the merits of organic veg and whether it has any culinary advantage. Here's one case where there's no doubt. Organic vegetables roast much better. They

have more texture. Chemical-boosted vegetables tend to wilt rather pathetically — their inferior structures, it seems, just can't stand the heat.

Serve with . . .
Roast vegetables are great with roast meat; doing several different vegetables together makes for such an easy meal. Roast the vegetables at the top of the oven and the meat at the bottom.

But they certainly don't need to be relegated to a support act; roast veg are good enough to eat on their own, and are one of my favourite light suppers. See the salsas (pp. 92–4) for lots of accompaniments, or simply serve with some soft goats' cheese, or with a good plain yoghurt such as Glenisk Probiotic, stirred with plenty of finely chopped chives or scallion greens, and a little salt.

ROAST COURGETTES, AUBERGINES AND YOUNG ONIONS

SERVES 4 AS AN ACCOMPANIMENT OR 2 AS A MAIN DISH
2 medium or 4 small courgettes
2 smallish aubergines
2 small new season, juicy onions (red, white or yellow)
2–3 tbsp olive oil
salt
fresh thyme or marjoram leaves

Turn the oven to 220C/425F/Gas 7. Cut the courgettes and aubergines into quarters lengthways, then halve these long wedges. Quarter the onions through the root, so it holds the quarters together. Put them all in a single layer in a roasting dish, turn them in oil and salt, and add herbs if you're using them.

These softer vegetables will be done in 20–30 minutes. They taste good warm or at room temperature.

ROAST PEPPERS

If you've never done this before, start now. There are so many things you can do with a home-roast pepper.

Try using them instead of some of the tomatoes in the No-cook Fresh Tomato and Fresh Herb Sauce (p. 13), or make Roasted Red Relish (p. 33) or a Red and Yellow Salsa (p. 93). Or just serve as they are, on slices of crusty, toasted bread rubbed with olive oil and garlic.

- Roast red and yellow peppers. Green ones are unripe, not as sweet, and look dirty when roasted.
- Peppers are best roasted whole, so their precious juices are not lost. Just lay them on a baking sheet at 200C/400F/Gas 6 (no oil needed) and roast until blackened and blistering; they'll need a few turns. It should take about 20 minutes.
- Once blackened on all sides, take them out of the oven and put in a bowl; cover with cling film and leave them to steam and cool down. This makes the skin easier to remove.
- When they're cool enough to handle, lift them onto a large plate. Gently tear them open, remove stem and seeds, and peel them. Don't lose the juices! Store the peeled pepper pieces in the juice; they will keep in the fridge for the best part of a week.

steaming vegetables

This is one of life's great pleasures. In the kitchen, just back from a Saturday morning market visit. There is a jumbled still life of vibrant vegetables on the counter; I have bought too much, again. I want to make them the focal point for a weekend lunch, and I certainly don't want to lose their extra-fresh, just-picked flavours. What will I do?

It depends on my mood. Perhaps I'll just pour a little extra virgin olive oil and a few drops of balsamic vinegar on some green beans; perhaps I'll whisk up a Golden Lemon Dressing for some purple sprouting broccoli; maybe I'll dip pale cauliflower florets into a Roasted Red Relish. Or there might be a spicy Peanut Sambal in the centre of a whole glorious mixed platter of vegetables and other things, including sticky-yolked hard-boiled egg quarters.
But one thing is clear. I will steam the vegetables.

I know that steamed vegetables have the dastardly air of diets and deprivation about them, but it's time to cast all that aside. A light steaming will actually maximise their flavours, and will preserve their fresh squeak. It will keep them looking glorious — translucent and vivid, and they will make a stunning, simple meal. Whatever the sauce, the real basic is to start with the firmest, freshest veg — and not to be turned off by the idea of steaming them.

Sauces for steamed vegetables:
— Extra virgin olive oil, and lemon wedges
— Golden Lemon Dressing (see below)
— Roasted Red Relish (p. 33)
— Milder Salsa Verde (p. 94)
— Mayonnaise, Very Slightly Lighter Mayonnaise or Aioli (pp. 99–100)
— Peanut Sambal (see below)

The steaming itself is simple:
- Steam sturdy greens (and potatoes). They must be extra-fresh. Best bets? Asparagus, broccoli, cauliflower, French beans, small courgettes and green cabbage. (Yes, cabbage. A very fresh, small Savoy cabbage or a spring or York cabbage works best.)
- With a swivel veggie peeler, trim thick skin from stalks of asparagus, broccoli florets and cauliflower florets. Steam beans and courgettes whole. Cut cabbage into wedges.
- A folding petal-like metal steamer, set into a pot, is cheapest and most flexible.
- When steaming, start with those which take the longest to cook. This partly depends on size, of course. As a rough guide, allow 6–8 minutes for broccoli and cauliflower florets, 5–8 minutes for whole courgettes, 4–7 minutes for French beans, 5 minutes for cabbage wedges, 3–5 minutes for asparagus.
- Stay alert: sniff for cooked-vegetable smells, look for colour changes, and pierce with the tip of a sharp knife to check. Quickly lift out those which are done.

- Spread them out in a single layer to cool so they don't continue to cook. Slice courgettes right away.
- Eat them while they still have a trace of living warmth in them.

STEAMED GREENS WITH OLIVE OIL AND BALSAMIC VINEGAR

2–4 courgettes, or 2 large handfuls French beans, or 1 small bunch asparagus
2 tbsp extra virgin olive oil
1 tbsp balsamic vinegar
salt, preferably Maldon flakes
1–2 tbsp finely chopped chives

Prepare and steam the vegetables as described above, then allow to cool a little. Slice courgettes as described; leave beans or asparagus whole.

Stir together the oil and balsamic vinegar and pour them over the vegetables. Scatter with salt and chives. Serve while they still have a trace of warmth in them.

GOLDEN LEMON DRESSING

This very lemony dressing goes beautifully with all the vegetables described above, warm or cooled, singly or mixed. I'm particularly fond of it with broccoli and wedges of cabbage.

It's also excellent with tomatoes, eggs, pan-fried, grilled or barbequed fish and with cheeses like feta, so it works well for large, mixed, summery platters. One of those really useful recipes you'll find yourself returning to time and time again.

4 tbsp lemon juice (about 1 medium lemon)

4 tbsp fruity extra virgin olive oil

very finely diced red chilli, to taste

2–3 pinches salt

Whisk all the ingredients together or shake them up in a jam jar. Be generous with the salt, to balance the lemon juice. Pour over the steamed vegetables which you have arranged beautifully in a single layer on large plates, and serve any extra in little bowls on the side.

PEANUT SAMBAL

A spicy relish, it makes a wonderful meal of a large platter of steamed and raw vegetables. If you have some toasted peanuts this sauce/dip is done in moments; otherwise allow 15 minutes to make it.

Serve with a combination of:
Steamed courgettes, cabbage, broccoli, cauliflower, cabbage wedges, French beans, asparagus, potato quarters.
Raw tomato wedges, lettuce shreds.
Boiled eggs with dark yellow sticky yolks, quartered lengthways.

100 g raw (unsalted) shelled peanuts, toasted (see below)

4–6 long green chillies

6–8 cloves garlic

4 tbsp light soy sauce

1½ tbsp light muscovado sugar

6 tbsp lime juice (2–3 limes)

First dry-toast the peanuts (see p. 79). It's worth toasting plenty extra — they keep for ages.

To make the sauce: Deseed the chillies; smash the garlic flat to spread its fibres, then peel it. Whizz the peeled toasted peanuts with everything else in a blender or food processor. Taste to check the seasoning and serve in little bowls with platters of steamed veg.

HOW TO PEEL GARLIC

Oh, to think of all the wasted hours of my life laboriously spent prising the tight papery skin off garlic cloves before I discovered how to do this!

Cut the root end off the clove of garlic. Lie the garlic clove flat on the chopping board and lie the blade of a large knife flat on it. Lean heavily on the flat knife blade with the heel of your hand. The garlic clove cracks, and is released from its papery skin.

You can vary the effect by varying the strength of your lean. If you lean gently, the garlic will have a single small crack, good enough for when you want a whole clove. If you want crushed garlic, just lean much harder and the clove underneath will be reduced to mashed, splayed fibres. Then you can simply chop those, and you won't even have to bother with a garlic press.

stir-frying vegetables

When stir-frying vegetables, of course all the basic principles of stir-frying apply. The wok, hot as dragon's breath. The food spluttering in it, picking up smoky 'wok fragrance'. The speed. Have a look at the stir-frying section for how to do it (pp. 62–4).

Steam-frying

Still, there's one important extra. First, as with meat, the vegetables sizzle in the wok's smoking heat to absorb that delicious seared wok flavour. But they then need a little steam or they'll stay raw inside. So you now add a few tbsp water or stock to make a whoosh of bubbles and steam. Put on the lid, and simmer. This is steam-frying.

It applies to all vegetables. Leafy greens like spinach or pak choi need only a couple of tbsp liquid which will produce one big whoosh. More sturdy greens — like French beans — need a touch more, and a few moments' bubbling. The really chunky ones — carrots, broccoli, cauliflower — need a little more again.

And if the vegetables aren't quite done, just add some more water, and steam once again.

STIR-FRIED GREEN BEANS

SERVES 2–4

400 g green beans (French beans or Chinese long beans)
2 cloves garlic
1 tsp finely grated root ginger
1 tbsp sunflower or peanut oil
100 ml light stock
pinch of salt

Top and tail the beans and cut if they're very long. Smash the garlic with the flat of a large knife or cleaver, remove the peel and chop it. Heat the wok until it's smoking, add the oil and swirl it. Add the garlic and ginger, turn once, then add the beans. Sear them, tossing as necessary. When they have picked up flavour, add the stock and salt, let it whoosh up, turn the beans and cover the wok. Simmer briefly until they're tender but firm.

Serve right away.

With sesame: Dry-toast **1 tsp sesame seeds** in the wok first, then tip them out and fry the beans. When the beans are on the serving plate, scatter with the fragrant sesame seeds and shake **a few drops of sesame oil** over them.

STIR-FRIED RED PEPPERS WITH OLIVE OIL

Stir-frying doesn't need to be all Chinese. These are quick, and great both hot and cold.

SERVES 2–4

1 onion
2 large red peppers
2 tbsp olive oil
3 tbsp vegetable stock
2 sun-dried tomatoes in oil, very finely chopped
2 tsp balsamic vinegar
salt

Peel and halve the onion, then cut it lengthways into slivers.

Peel the peppers with a swivel vegetable peeler; halve, de-stalk and deseed, and cut into slivers.

Heat a large frying pan or wok until very hot, then add 1 tbsp olive oil, swirl it round, and add the onion. It should sizzle and crackle. Stir-fry over very high heat until it's blackening, then tip it out onto the serving plate.

Add 1 tbsp olive oil, heat the wok again, and add the peppers. Again, fry fiercely until they're charring a little. Add the onion and stock. Bubble briefly. Tip it all out onto the serving plate.

Add the sun-dried tomatoes to the wok, fry briefly till they're crisping and darkening, then add to the peppers. Finish the dish with the balsamic vinegar and a sprinkle of salt.

Serve now, later or tomorrow.

ROLL-CUTTING

Here's a good way to cut firm, long, round vegetables like carrots and courgettes for stir-frying. Cut a chunk off the top of the carrot or courgette at a fairly steep angle. Roll the veg a quarter-turn, then cut again. Roll once more, and cut again. As you continue, you should get bite-sized chunks with 3 cut, angled sides and 1 outside rounded one. They're easier to fry and nicer to eat.

STIR-FRIED VEGETABLES WITH SPICES, COCONUT MILK AND TOASTED PEANUTS

This is such a lovely way to make dinner. Stir-fry the vegetables, adding them one by one to the pan or wok, then simmer for a moment with coconut milk and spices. Top with the chopped toasted peanuts, and it's done. Serve with rice.

SERVES 3–4

4 tbsp raw unsalted peanuts
1 fresh red chilli
4 cloves garlic
1 heaped tbsp grated root ginger
2 onions
200 g carrots
200 g cauliflower or broccoli
200 g courgettes
200 g cabbage (trimmed weight)
2 tbsp sunflower or peanut oil
200 ml coconut milk
2 tbsp Thai fish sauce (nam pla)
1 large lemon or 1–2 limes
salt
fresh coriander (optional)

First dry-toast the peanuts (see the panel).

Chop the chilli into large pieces and crush the garlic; set aside with the ginger.

Peel and halve the onions and slice finely lengthways.

Peel the carrots and roll-cut them (see the panel on p. 78).

Snap tiny florets off the cauliflower or broccoli, then peel the remaining stalk with a vegetable peeler and roll-cut it.

Top and tail the courgettes, then roll-cut them.
Cut the core out of the cabbage and shred it finely.

Heat the wok, add the oil, swirl it around, then add the chilli, ginger and garlic. Stir quickly; when they're aromatic, add the onion, carrots and broccoli/cauli stalks. Stir-fry for flavour, then add 50 ml water, cover, and simmer for a couple of minutes, until the water's gone.

Add the florets and courgettes to the wok, stir-fry, then add in another splash of water. When it has evaporated, add the cabbage. Stir-fry, then add the coconut milk, another 100 ml water, the fish sauce and lime/lemon juice to taste. Simmer briefly. Salt to taste, then top with the chopped peanuts and coriander if you have it.

TO DRY-TOAST AND PEEL PEANUTS

Leave them in their papery red skins and put them in a dry frying pan or wok. Toast slowly, stirring frequently, for about 10 minutes over a low-medium heat. You'll get black patches on the skins, but don't char the nuts too badly.

Leave the nuts to cool, then put them in a colander and set it over the bin or the sink. With your hands, rub and roll the nuts around. The skins will fall through the holes. (A few bits remaining don't matter.)

ANCHOVIES AND FISH SAUCE

Smelly fish – why does it crop up regularly in my recipes? You'll find anchovies, those pungent little powerhouses of flavour, in several sauces and relishes. Smelly fish sauce, the liquid produced from fermenting tiny Asian fish, and an essential ingredient in Thai and Vietnamese cooking, also makes many appearances. (It's called nam pla in Thailand and nuoc mam in Vietnam, and is as essential to them as soy sauce is to the Chinese.)

The curious thing about these fishy flavours is that while they are undeniably whiffy on their own, they meet their match in other strong flavours. Suddenly the fishy element is tamed; it turns into a rich, salty, savoury background that gives the food structure and depth. Go on, be brave — try it and see!

brassicas

Broccoli, cauliflower, cabbages and sprouts are imposters on the veg counter. They're actually flowers and flower buds, and some are even beautiful enough to stick in a vase. Even the taken-for-granted cabbages can be pretty. Consider the dusty bloom on a heartless spring cabbage, or the wet inky tips of a bundle just-steamed purple sprouting broccoli; imagine those stern, crinkled viridian leaves of a football-sized Savoy cabbage, the tiny frizzle of a pile of shredded sprouts, the ivory mini-florets of cauliflower.

And think of the smell!

Yes, they're notorious. Raw brassicas contain mustard oils. These can give tremendous hot fresh, sparky flavours — if you don't boil them away. In cooking, they break down to hydrogen sulphide — the smell of rotten eggs — and other odiferous compounds. In the 5th–7th minute of cooking, the hydrogen sulphide content of many cabbages doubles.

There are two rules in my kitchen for brassicas.
1. **Don't boil them.** The waterlogged squelch of boiled sprouts or broccoli florets is just unpleasant; so is the wet flab of boiled cabbage. And it does them no favours anyway, leaching away the taste. Stir-fry them, steam them, spice them instead, and they'll come to life.
2. **Stop cooking before the smell sets in.** That doesn't, incidentally, always mean you should leave them nearly raw — some cabbages and kales are quite tough and need to be well softened before they're nice to eat. Keep smelling, and keep tasting.

STIR-FRIED CABBAGE SHREDS IN OLIVE OIL

Include as many outer green leaves as possible with the cabbage, but be sure they're not too coarse.

SERVES 4
3 tbsp olive oil
1 tsp (or plenty more) red chilli, very finely chopped (optional)
5 large handfuls very finely shredded York, spring or Savoy cabbage
salt and pepper

Put a wok or very large frying pan onto the highest possible heat. Pour the oil in the wok and swirl it around. Add the chilli, then the cabbage, and stir-fry until the cabbage is cooked. A little blackening makes it extra tasty. If the cabbage is still a little tough, add a few tbsp of water to create steam, then cover with a lid to cook it through. Season to taste. Serve immediately.

STIR-FRIED CABBAGE WITH RED CHILLI AND BALSAMIC VINEGAR

Finish with 1–2 tbsp balsamic vinegar in the pan before seasoning the cabbage.

STIR-FRIED CABBAGE WITH RED CHILLI AND GINGER

Add 1–2 tsp grated root ginger to the chilli when frying.

And more . . .
— Add 2 cloves garlic, finely chopped
— Or 2 anchovy fillets, finely chopped
— or both

— Asian-style, stir-fry the cabbage with peanut or vegetable oil instead, with any of the above flavourings.

STIR-FRIED CABBAGE WITH RASHERS
SERVES 4

Chop 2–3 streaky rashers finely and fry in 1–2 tbsp butter until they release their fat. Add 5 handfuls shredded cabbage and stir-fry until tender, adding a little water if necessary. Finish with a few tbsp cream (optional), salt and plenty of pepper.

STIR-FRIED SPROUTS

The best way to eat them. Unlike whole sprouts, shredded sprouts don't go squelchy when cooked. Instead they are tender and delicate and crinkly: surprisingly pretty.

SERVES 4–5

Use 600 g sprouts (untrimmed weight) instead of the cabbage, for any of the above recipes. Trim them, cutting more of the base off than you would if leaving them whole, and shred on the thick slicing disc of a food processor, or slice finely by hand.

JADE BROCCOLI

Peel broccoli stalks and slice them fairly thickly. Steam them until they're translucent like jade. Then add a squirt of lemon and toss them in butter with a few tsp chopped fresh herbs mashed in, or serve with a Ripe Tomato Salsa or a Zesty Green Coriander and Lime Salsa (p. 92). Everyone will want to know what this lovely, sweet, green, mysterious new vegetable is.

INDIAN GINGERED CAULIFLOWER WITH SPICES

This is my favourite way of cooking cauliflower: vivid and bright, it's a revelation. It can also be prepared in advance, something that's not too advisable with brassicas otherwise. I've adapted it from Julie Sahni's *Classic Indian Cooking.*

SERVES 4–6

1 large head cauliflower
3 tbsp sunflower oil
2 tsp coriander seeds
2 tbsp grated root ginger
1–2 fresh green chillies, seeded and chopped
$\frac{1}{2}$ tsp turmeric
$\frac{1}{2}$ tsp salt
juice of $\frac{1}{2}$ lemon
2 tbsp fresh coriander leaves, or finely shredded green scallion tops

Separate the cauliflower into mini-florets. Use the stalk, ribs and any clean inside leaves too, cut to floret-size. Have ready the coriander seeds, ginger, chilli, turmeric, salt and 50 ml water, all next to the cooker.

Heat a large frying pan and add the oil. When it's very hot, add the coriander seeds; fry for a few seconds. Add the ginger and chillies; stir until fragrant. Immediately add the turmeric and salt, stir, then tip in all the cauliflower and stir quickly and thoroughly to coat the cauli in the turmeric. Add the 50 ml water, reduce the heat and cover the pan. Simmer very gently until the cauliflower is not quite done (15–20 minutes). At this stage the cauliflower can be set

aside, uncovered (for up to a few hours), if this suits you.

Finish the cauliflower by cooking it, uncovered, over a medium heat to evaporate any remaining moisture. Add 2 tsp lemon juice; taste and adjust for salt, lemon juice and chilli if necessary. Add the coriander leaves or scallion tops and serve immediately.

PURPLE SPROUTING BROCCOLI

The thunderous Calabrese variety with its tree-trunk stalks has become so ubiquitous that we all call it broccoli now, but Purple Sprouting is the one which I'd choose every time. Its stalks are slender, and the flowery tips have a purple bloom on them. It has the delicate sweet flavour common to other tender spring shoots. It's seasonal — late spring is its time, and its appearance marks the first emergence from the barren winter months. Look out for it — it's a gem.

KNIVES

A good knife is a joy to use, and there are three things that make a knife good. Of course, there is sharpness. A sharp knife saves energy and time, allowing you to glide through your food, rather than hack at it; and contrary to popular assumption, sharp knives are actually safer. They are less likely to slip, and stab your finger instead of the onion.

To keep a knife sharp, you need a sharpening steel or gadget. The steel — if you don't mind using it — produces a better edge; the little gadgets can be pretty rough on an edge, but they're better than nothing. Stroke a knife on your sharpener a few times before every use and it'll always be sharp.

A good knife should also have weight and balance; it should feel solid and fairly heavy. A little veggie paring knife is the only exception to this. Cheaper knives, which may well be sharp, tend to fall down on this test. Weight and balance can only be judged in your hand, so don't buy a knife that you haven't held yourself to check.

Taste in knives is very personal, and the right knife for you is the knife that feels comfortable in your hand. I don't recommend knife sets. Buy knives one at a time. My personal all-round, all-time favourite? A 16-cm Wusthof Classic. It has good balance, it isn't too heavy, and it's manoeuvrable enough in the hand to peel an onion, yet big and heavy enough to chop it too.

roots

The sweet underground vegetables of the dark, those roots which see us through the winter, are full of mysterious sweetnesses, and there are wonderful things we can do with them.

Above all, roast them. It transforms them, caramelising and concentrating their natural sugars. After you've roasted carrots and parsnips, you'll never accuse them of being dull again. See pp. 74–5 for the details.

There are other options. A slow-simmered carrot can be magnificent, a gently spiced parsnip can be splendid. And bash them all about, and add plenty of butter, or cream, or maybe both, and they'll turn into soothing winter purées and mash, for which we should perhaps be most grateful of all.

HOW TO COOK A CARROT

If you just boil and boil a carrot in lots of water, it will drown. Its amazing rooty sweet flavour will be gone, and you'll be left with something that does look like a carrot — but it won't taste much like a carrot.

But if you boil the water off until it all evaporates, and moisten the carrot with a touch of butter, it will glisten and glow. And be delicious.

SERVES 4

600 g carrots

1 high heaped tsp butter

1 tsp sugar

pinch salt

Put on the kettle. Peel and trim the carrots, then cut them into thickish diagonal slices. Put the butter in a saucepan, not too large, and melt it on a medium heat. Add the carrots, and turn them in the butter for a minute.

Pour in water from the hot kettle to come halfway up the carrots; add sugar and salt, and cover with a lid. Simmer them gently until they're nearly done. Check after 15 minutes, but it does depend on the carrots (they can vary a lot) and on how thickly you've sliced them. They may take 25 or 30 minutes. When they're just about done, take off the lid and allow the remaining water to evaporate. The carrots will get a lovely sheen; stand over them, turning them as the water disappears, or they may burn.

Serve as they are, or

With herbs: with 1–2 tsp **finely chopped dill**, or **parsley**, or **chives**, or **chervil**

Or:

— add a **scant tsp finely grated ginger** with the butter

— simmer the carrots in **freshly squeezed orange juice** instead of water

— simmer the carrots in **light stock** instead of water

— use **2 tsp olive oil** instead of the butter, then dress the carrots with the **Golden Lemon Dressing** (p. 76–7). Serve warm or at room temperature.

SPICED CARROTS WITH SULTANAS AND PINE NUTS

A Middle Eastern variation on the theme.

SERVES 4–5

2–3 tbsp pine nuts
1 large onion, sliced
2 tbsp olive oil
600 g carrots, washed, trimmed and cut in thick diagonal slices
1 tsp ground cinnamon
1 tsp sugar
salt and pepper
3 tbsp juicy sultanas

Heat a large frying pan gently, then toast the pine nuts carefully in it until they're very lightly browned. Tip them out of the pan to cool. Fry the onion in the olive oil until golden; add the carrots, cinnamon, sugar, salt and pepper and fry for a few minutes. Add the sultanas along with 100 ml water and cook, covered, for 30–40 minutes, until the carrots are soft, the sultanas plump and the water has evaporated. Serve sprinkled with the toasted pine nuts.

HOW TO COOK A PARSNIP

There's no point in relying on fine words or healthy eating theories to butter your parsnips. Only butter will do the job. Peel and trim the parsnips, then cut them in quarters lengthways. Cut out the core if the parsnips are large. Put them into plenty of boiling salted water and simmer till done. They always cook more quickly than you think they will, so be sure to catch them before they become waterlogged. (Although they look so similar, parsnips cook much more quickly than carrots, so don't risk boiling the two veg in one pot together.)

When they're done, drain, return to the pot and add a knob of butter. At this stage I'd also add some grated fresh ginger and perhaps some cayenne too, then turn the parsnips in the buttery spice over a medium heat for a few moments. Parsnips have a strong flavour which is best balanced with other strong flavours. It makes all the difference.

GOLDEN MASH WITH GINGER

The hot breath of fresh ginger juice lifts not just parsnips but turnips out of the ordinary. This rough golden mash is fantastic with roasts, especially with porky things, and excellent with slices of fried black and white pudding.

SERVES 4–6

3 medium parsnips
1 medium swede turnip
large knob root ginger
30 ml cream
salt

Peel and trim the swede and parsnip. You should have around 900 g swede and 450 g parsnip. Slice them both, then simmer the swede in plenty of salted water until nearly done, then add the parsnip. When both vegetables are soft, drain and return to the saucepan.

Meanwhile, while the swedes cook, peel and grate the root ginger until you have about 3 tbsp. Squeeze it through a garlic crusher to get ginger juice and some fine purée; you will need about 3 tsp in total.

Mash the vegetables roughly with a potato masher. Add the cream and some salt. Stir in the ginger juice, starting with 2 tsp and adding the rest if you want a stronger flavour.

TURNIP AND CARROT PURÉE

Two kinds of rooty sweetness combine for wintry pleasure.

SERVES 4–6

1 medium-sized swede turnip
250 g carrots
salt
about 100 g crème fraîche
black pepper

Put two pans of well-salted water on to boil. Top and tail and peel the swede and carrots. Cut into even-sized chunks. Simmer in separate pans until just soft. Drain, then purée in a food processor or put through a mouli-légumes. Stir in crème fraîche to taste, plenty of freshly ground black pepper and a little extra salt if necessary.

soup

Soup. It's one of the most basic things of all. It can keep body and soul together. It is simple, soothing and satisfying. There are five soupy S's to remember:

Sweat

Not yours! The only thing which may need to sweat when making soup is the onion. Many soups start with a gently cooked base of onion (and often other flavourings — perhaps garlic, or leeks, or some root vegetables). They're stewed slowly in a little butter or olive oil. This is a very important bit which mustn't be rushed. For the onions to develop maximum sweetness, they need to seethe slowly and moistly (that's the 'sweating'), not to sizzle and fry. They shouldn't colour at all. To get this effect, keep the heat as low as you possibly can, lay a sheet of greaseproof paper (or the butter wrapper) on the onions, and keep the lid on. Check once or twice to be sure they don't burn.

Some soups look for brighter flavours, and the onion is quicker-fried. See the Black Bean Soup on p. 86.

Stock

Some soups can work with water. Others simply need a really good home-made stock if they're to

8 4

taste nice. With some highly flavoured soups, you can get away with using stock-cube stock. But the stock-cube flavour will more than likely shout through all the other ingredients at you, so be very careful how you use it, and always make it weaker than the pack recommends, at least to start with.

Simmer

A gentle simmer is best for your ingredients.

Stir

Stir from time to time, to be sure the solids aren't sticking to the bottom of the pot.

Soft

If your soup is to be blended or puréed, be sure all the ingredients are fully softened before you start to whizz. A blender can't deliver smooth purée from still-firm vegetables. Press a piece of vegetable or bean against the side of the pot with the wooden spoon. It should squash easily.

Once they're soft, there are several ways you can get a purée:

1. **A hand-held stick blender which you immerse into the pot.** These are great — there's no pouring hot soup from one thing to another, and less washing up. Keep it submerged while it's switched on or you'll splatter the kitchen.
2. **A blender.** Hold the lid on tight as you switch it on, or you may get soup on the ceiling.
3. **A food processor.** It works (sort of), but many of them

leak, so you may get soup on the kitchen counter. Do the soup in small batches.

4. **A mouli-légumes.** This low-tech French strainer has a handle which you turn to make sieving easy. It retains bits and gives a very fine purée. Excellent for tomato soups — it will hold back seeds and skins. Not so good for chunkier soups.
5. **A sieve.** See no. 4 above, but much harder work!

VELVET ROOT SOUP

They don't come much simpler, or cheaper, than this. We don't make nearly enough potato-based soup here, a mystery since we have the perfect ingredients for it: fabulous floury spuds which turn soups to thick velvet without any other thickener.

SERVES 6–8

3 onions
3 cloves garlic
½ fresh red chilli, deseeded
50 g butter
500 g carrots and/or parsnips
1 kg floury potatoes
1.5 litres light stock — chicken or vegetable
1 tsp salt
2 bay leaves

Chop the onions, garlic and chilli quite finely and sweat them in the butter until soft, sweet and glassy. Meanwhile peel and trim the carrots and/or parsnips and cut into chunks; add to the onions and continue to sweat the vegetables slowly while you prepare the potatoes.

Peel the potatoes and cut into chunks. Add to the pot with the stock, salt and bay leaves. Simmer until the vegetables are soft (the carrots will take longest),

then fish out the bay leaves and whizz the soup (with a hand-held stick blender, or in a blender or food processor) or put it through a mouli. Check the seasoning and serve.

POTATO, COURGETTE AND PIQUANT CHEESE SOUP

This great soup doesn't even need puréeing. You can also use overgrown marrows instead of the courgettes. For the cheese, choose **fresh-grated** Parmesan, Grana Padano, Pecorino or Regato, Manchego or Gabriel, Desmond or Mizen. No Parmesan in tubs — you'll ruin the soup!

SERVES 6–8

2 onions
1 big knob butter
1 kg floury potatoes
2 tsp salt
1 litre light stock
1 kg courgette or marrow
100 g freshly grated piquant hard cheese (see above)
optional: crème fraîche and/or chives to serve

Dice the onions very finely and, in a large pot, sweat them on a very low heat with the butter. Meanwhile, peel the potatoes and chop into medium chunks. When the onions are sweet and soft, add the potatoes, salt and stock. Cover and simmer.

Meanwhile, trim the courgette or marrow. If the marrow is a real prizewinning knockout size, halve it lengthways and scoop out its large seeds. Grate the courgette/marrow, skin and all, on the large holes of a grater. Add it to the simmering soup and put on the lid again. Stir from time to time.

After about 15 minutes, check the soup. The potato should have

soup

disintegrated and the courgette should be tender, but it should all have a little texture. Check carefully for seasoning as the ingredients are pretty bland. Just before serving, stir in the cheese. I like this soup served with a dollop of crème fraîche and a scattering of chopped chives, but it's good and satisfying without them too.

BLACK BEAN SOUP

This Mexican-style recipe makes a filling all-in-one soup. Serve with a good crusty bread or sourdough for a truly satisfying experience. Beer is perfect with it.

SERVES 4–6

500 g cooked black beans (from 2 tins or 225 g dried — see note below)

2 tsp cumin seeds

1 tsp coriander seeds

1 bunch scallions

5 cloves garlic

2–3 long green chillies, deseeded

4 soft oil-preserved sun-dried tomatoes (or 2 tsp tomato purée)

2 tbsp olive oil

1 litre chicken or vegetable stock

1 heaped tbsp dark muscovado sugar

1 small bunch fresh coriander

salt and pepper

about 4 tbsp Greek-style yoghurt

Prepare the beans (see below). If using tinned, rinse very well. Dry-fry the cumin and coriander seeds until they are fragrant; grind them in a pestle and mortar or coffee grinder.

Finely chop the scallions, garlic, chillies and tomatoes. As you are doing this, set aside 1 heaped tsp chilli and 1 heaped tbsp scallions for garnishing the soup.

Heat the olive oil in a large, heavy-based saucepan. Add the scallions and

fry for a few seconds until they're bright and fragrant. Add the garlic, chillies, sun-dried tomatoes (or purée) and ground cumin and coriander. Stir until they have released their fragrance, then add the beans, stock and sugar. Season with salt and plenty of black pepper and simmer briskly, part-covered, for about 20 minutes.

Meanwhile, pick off a few coriander leaves for garnishing; chop the rest of the bunch roughly. Add this to the soup, then blend it (but not too smoothly) with an immersion stick-blender. Alternatively, with a slotted spoon, scoop most of the solids out of the soup into a food processor or liquidiser. Purée them with the fresh coriander and a little of the liquid, then return to the pot. Check the seasoning and bring back to a simmer.

To serve: Ladle the soup into bowls. Sprinkle with the chopped scallions and the coriander leaves; you can use the chilli or not depending on how hot the soup tastes. Finally, dollop about 1 tbsp Greek yoghurt into each plate as elegantly as possible.

The beans: You can use dried or tinned black beans. Little ones, sometimes called turtle beans, are ideal, but black kidney beans will do too. **225 g dried beans, or 2 x 425 g or 450 g tins will yield about 500 g ready-to-cook weight.**

If you are using **dried beans** you need to start well in advance. It's worth it, though — the flavour's better, and they're cheaper. **First soak the beans:** either in cold water overnight, or cover them with water in a saucepan, boil for 2 minutes and leave to stand for an hour. **Then cook them:** drain and cover with fresh water; simmer until soft, 1½–2 hours depending on the quality, age and size of the beans. You

can do this in advance and keep them in the fridge or freeze them if that suits. Save the cooking water to use in place of some of the stock.

If you are using **tinned beans**, drain them and rinse very well in a sieve to rid them of that yucky tinny-tasting goo.

THAI-STYLE HOT AND SOUR SOUP

Hot, spicy and sour, this Thai-style broth soup is pure and light — but needs a good stock to taste right.

THIS POT OF SOUP WILL FILL 4 STANDARD BOWLS OR 8 OF THOSE DAINTY ASIAN ONES

1.3 litres light but well-flavoured chicken, fish or vegetable stock (see pp. 88–91)

3 stalks lemon grass

2 shallots

1 lime

4 kaffir lime leaves, if available

4 slices root ginger

200 g sliced mushrooms (preferably oyster)

or boneless fish or squid slivers

3 tbsp Thai fish sauce (nam pla)

pinch sugar

1 red chilli

1 green chilli

½ handful fresh coriander

Begin by checking the stock is not fatty — scoop or scrape any off the top. Trim the lemon grass: cut off the top half, the base, and peel off the outside leaves. Peel the shallots. Lay lemon grass and shallots on a chopping board and whack them vigorously with the base of a heavy pan. They should splay out, their fibres broken, but still hold together. (This will help them to release their flavours when simmered with the broth.) Peel the lime rind in wide strips with a vegetable parer if you have no kaffir lime leaves.

In a large saucepan, simmer the stock with the lemon grass, shallots, lime rind or lime leaves and ginger for 10 minutes. Then lift out these aromatics with a slotted spoon and discard them.

Add the mushrooms (or fish/squid), fish sauce and sugar to the pan. Decide how much chilli you want to use. Last time I made this, 4 slender slices each of red and green chilli (no seeds) was plenty. Simmer for 5 minutes.

Squeeze the juice of about $\frac{2}{3}$ of the lime and add it to the pan. Taste and check for seasoning. Does it need more sour (lime), salt (fish sauce), or heat (chilli), or does it need to be tempered with another small pinch of sugar?

Ladle into bowls, add the coriander leaves and serve.

YELLOW PEA AND MARJORAM SOUP

A rich, savoury, satisfying flavour for zero effort; you don't even need any stock, nor is there any blending. This is a Swedish classic.

SERVES 4–6
500 g dried split yellow peas
a meaty ham bone, or a 200 g piece of smoked bacon (see note below)
1½ tsp dried marjoram

Put the peas and ham bone or bacon in a large heavy pot. Pour in cold water until the water above the peas is knuckle-deep on your thumb.

Simmer, part-covered, for about an hour, until the peas are soft and the soup is quite thick. It will need the occasional stir and may need extra water.

Turn off the heat, then fish out the bacon or the ham bone. Allow the soup to stand for a couple of minutes, then skim any fat off the surface. Add the marjoram and check the soup for salt. Simmer for a further 5 minutes and slice the meat if you intend to serve it too.

Note: The traditional flavouring for this is a meaty smoked ham bone. These are in short supply in most households these days, except after Christmas and perhaps at Eastertime, though if you have a good local butcher or deli who bake their own ham it would be well worth filching theirs. Alternatively, a piece of smoked bacon is delicious too. Cut off the fat before putting it in the pan, but use the rind. Remove the rind before serving and slice the bacon to serve with the soup. If you want to make a meatier meal, use a larger piece of smoked bacon, but be sure it's not too salty.

CALDO VERDE

It sounds like a bad joke of old Irish cooking: a soup of potatoes and kale, boiled in water. Nothing else, except perhaps the odd clove of garlic. But no, this dish is a pillar of Portuguese cuisine. I'd venture to suggest that Ireland may have the upper hand here: we have excellent floury potatoes which collapse perfectly for soup-making. A tiny puddle of extra virgin olive oil finishes the soup, its fruity aromas carried to your nostrils by the hot steam.

If you have tasty potatoes and good fresh flavoursome kale, there is a delightful purity to this soup made on water. However, some prefer it made with stock — chicken or vegetable. Just bear in mind that there's nowhere for stock cube flavour to hide here, so if you want to use stock, use real stock.

SERVES 4–6
1.3 kg best floury potatoes, such as Golden Wonders or Records
2 cloves garlic
2 litres water or stock
about 500 g kale
extra virgin olive oil
salt and freshly ground black pepper

Peel and trim the potatoes — you want a total of about 900 g. Cut them into quarters. Crush the garlic cloves under the flat blade of a large knife, then chop roughly.

Put the potatoes and garlic in a large pot and cover with 2 litres cold water. Simmer, part-covered, until they have broken down.

Meanwhile, prepare the kale. Cut out the thick stalks until you have 200 g leaves. You now need to slice them sliver-thin, or you'll have ugly lumpy bits in the soup; it's a bit like slicing great big clumpy parsley. Scrunch leafy clusters into tight balls. Hold them firmly in place with the fingers of one hand while you slice as finely as you possibly can.

When the potatoes have collapsed, add the kale and 1 tsp salt. Simmer until the kale is tender — this may take just a minute, or significantly longer, depending on the variety. Check the seasoning.

Ladle the soup into bowls and trickle 1 tsp of olive oil into the centre of each.

Variation: This soup can be garnished with chorizo. You'll need soft cooking chorizo, not the more dried salami-style stuff. Slice and fry gently in a pan (no fat needed) until it releases its fat and crisps up a little. Allow 150 g, which is usually 2 short little sausages, for the quantity above.

stock

It's time to take the plunge: into the stockpot.

Most of us make excuses to put off this job. Me too. I'm not squeamish — wrestling with a raw chicken is fine by me — but I find stock-making distasteful. Perhaps it's the smell of boiling bones. Perhaps it's the thought of washing up that big sticky pot which doesn't quite fit in the sink; perhaps it's pouring the hot splashy liquid. The colander leaks, a giblet escapes, stock spatters on your shoes.

Even the language seems to belong to another era. 'Scum'. 'Strain'. 'Degrease'. Unappealing words, which evoke thoughts of sweatshop kitchens, like those Orwell described so graphically in *Down and Out in Paris and London*.

But yes, I do still make stock. And whenever I get around to it, I wish I did it much more often, for a world of cooking opens up before me once again; delicate broths with a few aromatics poached in them, well-flavoured soups, just-right gravy. Stock really is the foundation of flavour.

Above all, stock in the freezer means freedom from shop-bought stock cubes. Cook's little helper they may be, but one sliver too much and they can wreck a dish with their overbearing taste (see p. 91 for reasonably good ones).

Be a scavenger

The pleasure of stock? Creating something wonderful from scraps destined for the bin or the cat. The freezer is your greatest ally. Save chicken carcasses, raw or cooked; bones and giblets too. Freeze them all, ready to be plonked in a pot when the stock-making mood strikes.

The stockpot is not a compost heap

They do have similarities: both create gold from scraps. The difference is that the stockpot needs its contents alive. If vegetables are tired-looking, don't leave them to go slimy or sprout a new set of hairs. Trim them as appropriate and bag in the freezer along with the bones.

Onion, carrot and celery

Bones aside, these are the perfect trio of stock flavour. They provide pungency, sweetness and crisp astringency. If you have nothing else, you can make a stock with these three alone, though they do perform better when supported by parsley stalks and a bay leaf.

Do you need a stockpot?

No. It is an immensely useful item: once you're committed to hours of simmering you may as well simmer a lot. But you can make stock in an ordinary large pot.

Stock-making equipment: A **large pot.** If you're thinking of buying a stock/pasta pot, remember this is one pot which can be cheap and light — since it's always full of lots of liquid, there's none of the usual worry about food burning if the pot's base isn't good and thick. A **large slotted spoon** or (better again) **a long-handled wire mesh strainer** (usually cheaper in Chinese supply stores). A **colander,** a **sieve, large bowls.** Plus . . . **extra ice cube trays, freezer bags** and an **indelible marker.**

10-STEP CHICKEN STOCK

The most useful, all-round stock. It can be used for fish and vegetable soups and sauces too. This quantity is for a large stockpot — halve for a saucepan.

2 kg chicken bits — see below
4 onions
4 carrots
4 sticks celery
2 bay leaves
stalks from 2 bunches parsley
2 sprigs fresh thyme
2 tsp whole peppercorns

The chicken bits: Remove any saved goodies from the freezer. Add some raw pieces for extra flavour if your saved scraps are mostly cooked. Giblets (minus liver) are good, if you can get them. If you need more meat, add a tray of chicken wings (chop them crossways with a cleaver). Avoid using too much skin: it's very fatty.

1. The chicken: Put all the chicken bits in a large pot (you can use them frozen), leaving room for the veg later. Cover with cold water. Bring slowly to a very, very, very gentle simmer.

2. The scum: Once the water simmers, take a large serving spoon and scoop off the scum and fat which rise to the surface. Do this from time to time as you're passing, for the next half-hour or so. You'll fill a soup bowl with the stuff.

3. The aromatics: Meanwhile, prepare the vegetables. Peel and quarter the onions. Peel, top and tail and slice the carrots thickly. Wash and roughly chop the celery (use its leaves too); wash the parsley stalks and thyme.

4. The simmering: Add the vegetables, herbs and peppercorns to the pot. Simmer for another hour or two, or as convenient. Continue to skim the scum when you can.

5. The colander: Set a colander into a large bowl. With a long-handled strainer or large slotted spoon, lift most of the solids out of the stock into the colander. (This makes the hot stock much easier to pour.) Finally pour the stock through.

   You can pour the stock, bits and all, straight into the colander — but watch out for spills and hot splashes, and keep an eye on the liquid level in the bowl, lest it spill over. It usually does.

6. The sieve: Have a clean large saucepan ready, or wash the stockpot. Set a fine sieve over the clean pot. Pour the stock through it.

7. The degreasing: Leave the stock to settle for 5 minutes or so. With a large spoon, scoop off any fat floating on the surface.

8. The kitchen paper: You may wish to remove the last scraps of fat. Lay a square of kitchen paper on

stock

the surface of the stock, then quickly lift it off, drips and all, and discard. Repeat this as necessary.

9. **The reduction:** Now for the finale. Simmer briskly until the stock has reduced. Be sure it doesn't burn on the side of the pot as you do this. The result should be a dark, syrupy liquid, rich-flavoured but not bitter.

10. **The stock cubes!** Pour it into ice cube trays and freeze. Now you have your very own, utterly delicious stock cubes, ready to be added to gravy, soups, sauces and more.

SOME STOCKS ARE SPEEDY

You don't need an entire afternoon of your life for stock. Only meat stocks need hours to extract their flavour. First to the one which no one makes, and which everyone ought to, for it's a brief, 20-minute job.

FISH STOCK

Fish stock is unusual, because although it does involve bones, it's done quickly. Fish surrenders its flavour easily. Indeed if you simmer too long, the stock turns bitter.

The bones

However, there is one problem, and that's finding the bones. It's most frustrating. 'Ask your fishmonger,' cookbooks counsel breezily, but those books were clearly written in the days before most fishmongers folded and most supermarkets decided to fillet their fish centrally. Blank stares and bored glances in the direction of the bin are all you get when you ask for fish bones at many supermarket fish counters now.

— Don't just give up and head for the stock cube section. Get talking. Ask for white fish bones in advance. If you strike lucky, take all the bones they can give you and bundle them into the freezer until you have half an hour for the stock. Remember: if nobody ever asks for bones, the supermarkets will assume nobody wants them.

— What kind of bones? Bones from oily fish such as mackerel or herring are too coarse. White fish are best, and if you can snaffle turbot and sole bones, you've got the prize specimens.
— And if you've no luck at all, take a few fillets of whiting or another cheap white fish to do the job instead.

Other flavours

— Don't scorn shells and heads. Lobster, prawns, shrimp, crab . . . they all yield exquisite depth of flavour. Never throw them away. Keep them in the freezer until it's time for stock.

— Fishy flavours need balance in a stock, so the more astringent aromatic come to the fore here. Leave out the carrot — it's too sweet — and concentrate on onion and celery instead. If you can spare a glass or two of dry white wine, the stock will be all the better for it.

500 g fish bones and/or shellfish shells and/or cheap white fish — see above	
1 onion, sliced	
2 sticks celery, sliced	
½ bay leaf	
stalks of a bunch of parsley	
1 tsp peppercorns	
1 or 2 glasses of dry white wine — optional	

If you're using fresh fish bones, rinse them in cold water before starting; check for any traces of blood and guts which would taint the stock and give it a bitter flavour. Put everything in a saucepan, cover generously with water and simmer uncovered for 20 minutes (no longer). Strain through a fine sieve to remove as much debris as possible. Clean the saucepan, then simmer the stock again to reduce it to your desired strength, and use right away or freeze in small batches.

VEGETABLE STOCK

Finally, we get to the bone-free stocks. Vegetable stocks are underrated. Their flavours aren't as deep as meaty stocks, but they're quick and straightforward, and the ingredients are always to hand. Here's a simple one:

3 onions
3 sticks celery
3 leeks
3 carrots
1 handful parsley
1 small sprig fresh thyme
30 g butter or 2 tbsp olive oil

Wash, peel, trim and roughly chop all the vegetables. When doing the leeks, slice them in half lengthways first, then rinse the halves under running water; check all the layers to be sure you've freed any trapped mud.

In a large pan, turn the chopped vegetables in the butter or oil over a low heat until they release fragrance and soften, about 5 minutes. Don't let them darken. Cover with cold water, bring to a simmer and simmer for about 45 minutes. Strain. Reduce and freeze.

Note: Many other vegetables can be added to the stock. Tomatoes, mushrooms, aubergines, courgettes, lettuce leaves, halved cloves of garlic and peppers all work well. Avoid the brassica (cabbage/broccoli/cauliflower) family, which is too smelly. Finally, if you're in search of greater depth of flavour, add a few dried mushrooms to the pot.

KOMBU VEGETABLE STOCK

This is the simplest, purest of them all. But what's kombu?

Kombu is a seaweed and is one of the 2 ingredients of the basic Japanese stock known as *dashi*. (The other ingredient is flakes of dried bonito fish.) Kombu is also known as kelp, or laminaria, and grows on our shores as well as in Japan. You'll find it, dried, in Asian stores — or in health food shops as one of the wonderful Carraig Fhada seaweed range. It gives a quite surprising backbone to the flavour of a vegetable stock, a steely bedrock which I wouldn't do without. This is my favourite vegetable stock.

1 small or ½ large head of celery
1 large onion
1 medium carrot
3 strips kombu (see note above)

Trim, peel and slice the vegetables; include the celery leaves. Put them and the kombu in a medium saucepan, cover with water and simmer very gently, uncovered, for half an hour. Remove the kombu (easier said than done — by now it's like real strips of weed again and is very slippery!) and continue to simmer the veg for about 20 minutes, until they are spent (they'll look pale and wan). Strain.

Of course we all use bought stocks, whether cubes or fresh.

— Freshly made frozen stocks taste best. You're most likely to find these in local delis and caterers', and if you feel like moaning about the price they charge, just think of the fresh ingredients — and all the simmering! Some supermarkets have McNean Cuisine stocks, which are excellent.

— Tinned stocks usually just taste tinny, but I've found John Lusty fish stock OK (though I didn't like its meat ones).

— Of the meaty cubes, Kallo's Just Bouillon Chicken is OK. As an all-purpose cube I'd stick to the vegetable ones, which have fewer funny flavours. Marigold Swiss Vegetable Bouillon Powder and Kallo Just Bouillon are my favourites.

salsas and relishes

The way we cook has changed, and so has the way we eat. Until recently, a sauce was most likely hot and smooth and one colour only. But then we encountered zippy relishes, herb-laced, freshly chopped sauces, things based on fresh herbs, citrus fruits or olive oil, sauces which could be stirred together in moments, and we haven't looked back. Whether they're Mexican, Spanish, Italian or mixem-gatherem, salsas are in the ascendant.

The burning question is: what *is* a salsa? The answer these days is: just about anything. The word exists in both Spanish and Italian, and it can be, depending on where you go, cooked or raw; hot or cold; fiery or mild; fruity or veggie or herby; oily or not . . . But in general, in English, the word has now come to mean a fresh sauce, a cold one, based on herbs, vegetables or fruit — and plenty of seasonings. Salsa should taste like an all-singing, all-dancing kind of sauce, something that will pep up your steak, chop, beans, sandwich or roasted aubergine wedges — just about anything you fancy. Make one, and you're guaranteed to find new uses for it.

SALSA TIPS

- Most salsas don't keep well. Chop them fresh and use them quickly. Tomatoes especially will go woolly; and onions will go smelly. Think of them as salads; you wouldn't serve yesterday's tossed lettuce, would you?
- Only the best will do. Ripe tomatoes. Firm, fresh onions and garlic. Vibrant herbs.

With these sauces, there's nowhere for sad ingredients to hide.

RIPE TOMATO SALSA

This classic all-rounder is probably the most useful salsa of all. You'll have fun varying it, depending on your mood, what you're serving and which herbs are available. You'll find it's good with almost anything. Try it with:

- any grilled or roast meat, or vegetables
- spicy sausages
- grilled aubergine and courgette slices
- new potatoes, rice or bulgar
- hot, fresh-cooked pulses which have just had a few tbsp gutsy olive oil stirred into them
- piled into pittas along with just about anything you fancy . . .

SERVES ABOUT 4–6
300 g tomatoes, which must be sweet, red and ripe
1 large shallot
enough fresh chilli to make your tongue tingle (see below)
2 tbsp (or more) chopped fresh coriander leaves
salt
juice of about ½ lemon or 1 juicy lime

Chop the tomatoes into fairly small pieces, saving all the juice as you do. Slice the shallot finely and chop the chilli into tiny dice. Add the rest of the ingredients, mix everything together and taste. The salsa should be crunchy with the shallot and fairly chunky; if it isn't, add more shallot. Add chilli until the salsa makes your eyes smart a little, remembering that its effect will be diluted by the rest of the food on the plate. This salsa is best fresh and really only keeps for a couple of hours.

Options:
— Use mint instead of coriander, or try marjoram or basil instead.
— Add some garlic.
— Add 3 tbsp gutsy olive oil.

ZESTY GREEN CORIANDER AND LIME SALSA

Although the ingredients are nearly identical, this couldn't be more different. It's really more of a herb relish, fairly concentrated and with the zesty punch of chilli and lime peel. This is one salsa which keeps quite well.

It's good in small spoonfuls with just about anything, especially fish (any kind), grilled meats, rice and yoghurt.

SERVES 4–8
1 large handful fresh coriander leaves and slender stalks
4 fat scallions
2 very ripe tomatoes
fresh chilli, to taste
1–2 limes
generous pinch salt

Chop coriander, scallions, tomatoes and chilli very finely. On a fine grater or with a zester, scrape the zest of 1 lime, then squeeze its juice. Stir everything together and taste: it should pack quite a punch. Use juice from the second lime if you need it. Add salt to taste.

Option: Stir in some olive oil.

RED AND YELLOW SALSA

Made with red and yellow peppers and some sweetcorn, this has great textural contrasts between silken and crunch. Allow about 45 minutes to roast and steam the peppers if you haven't any ready-roasted.

SERVES ABOUT 4

1 red pepper and 1 yellow pepper

(Roast them whole in a hot oven for 20–30 minutes, turning them to blacken each side. When each side has a few blisters and black spots, put them in a bowl and cover with cling film until cooler. Peel them and remove the seeds, saving any juices. Chop the flesh into little slippery, glowing squares.)

1 shallot
2 tsp red wine vinegar
1 tsp sugar
3 tbsp tinned or defrosted corn kernels
juice of ½ lemon
2 tbsp pepper juices (see recipe above)
enough fresh chilli to tickle your tongue
1 tsp finely chopped fresh marjoram (optional)

While the peppers are cooking and cooling, macerate the sliced shallot in the vinegar and sugar. Then combine all ingredients and taste to get a good flavour balance. You may wish to add more pepper juices, or more sugar. This salsa keeps well for several hours.

Options: Vary the herbs, or add olive oil. Or do both.

QUICKEST CORN SALSA

Very simple, very easy, very nice.

SERVES 4–6

2 x 198 g tins Green Giant Extra Crisp Corn
juice of 1 lemon
chopped fresh red chilli to taste
salt

Mix all ingredients. A relish-cum-salsa. Pure, clean and very tasty — but it really should be that particular corn, which is significantly tastier than any other.

Serve with grilled meats or vegetables, or as a side relish with quesadillas, filled pittas or on a mixed salad plate.

PINEAPPLE AND LIME SALSA

This is delicious with a well-seasoned, fiery grilled pork chop, and also tasty with ham and robust spicy sausages as well as various fowl.

SERVES 4–6

1 medium pineapple, about 1 kg weight
1 lime
2 fat scallions, finely sliced
fresh red or green chilli, very finely chopped
1 tsp sugar
½ tsp salt

Peel the pineapple and trim it till there are no 'eyes' left. Cut it in quarters lengthways and cut out the core. Cut the flesh into small pieces. Grate the zest from the lime with a fine grater or zester. Roll it on the work surface, pressing down hard to release the juice; then squeeze it. Mix all the ingredients together and taste for a good sweet/savoury/hot balance, adding chilli to a proportion which pleases you. This salsa keeps very well for several hours.

THAI DIPPING RELISH WITH LIME, GARLIC AND CHILLI

This is a runny, light dip — good with grilled or barbequed fish, with chicken or pork, or even just stirred into plain steamed rice along with some stir-fried vegetables.

SERVES 4–6

2 cloves garlic
2 red chillies
2 tbsp fresh coriander stalks
½ tsp salt
2 tbsp lime juice
1 tbsp Thai fish sauce (nam pla)
2 tsp sugar

Chop garlic, chillies and coriander very finely. Mash them with the salt, in a pestle and mortar, or on the chopping board, using the flat side of a large knife blade. When the mix softens, and starts to squelch and glisten, stir in the rest of the ingredients until the sugar has dissolved. Taste to check the balance. Serve in small quantities!

THAI TOMATO DRESSING

This can be quite like a dressing, or chunkier like a salad, depending on how much juice your tomatoes contain and how finely you chop them.

SERVES 2–6

2 ripe tomatoes
2 cloves garlic, mashed
1 green chilli (or more), deseeded and finely chopped
2 tbsp Thai fish sauce (nam pla)
1 tbsp light muscovado sugar
grated zest of 1–2 limes
juice of 1–2 limes

Skin the tomatoes by putting them in a bowl of just-boiled water for 10 seconds. Then cut a nick in the skin and it should slither off. Chop roughly, saving all juices and seeds, then combine with all the other ingredients.

salsas and relishes

Start with zest and juice of 1 lime and add more if it needs it.

SALSA VERDE

And now for something *completely* different . . . Here's an Italian-style salsa verde. It looks rather like a pesto: a concentrated, pounded mix of green herbs and other flavourings, but it's smoother and punchier-flavoured. Salsa verde is perfect with meat — grilled, poached and roast — and salads. It's great with steak or a big rib roast, excellent with a pork chop, tasty with chicken; the minty version is particularly good with lamb, the coriander one is wonderful dotted onto boiled eggs and it is generally a paragon of all-round virtue. It even keeps well for several days in the fridge. Be warned, this sauce is addictive.

SERVES ABOUT 8

40–50 g fresh parsley (weight of leaves and slender stalks)
a handful of fresh basil, mint or coriander
4–6 anchovy fillets
1 heaped tbsp well-rinsed capers
1 tbsp red wine vinegar
2 rounded tsp smooth Dijon mustard
2 cloves garlic
salt and pepper
150 ml olive oil

Chop the herbs roughly and put them in a food processor with all other ingredients except the oil. Mix to a paste, then add the oil in a steady stream with the blade turning to form a sauce. Taste it and see. Does it need more pepper, more anchovy, another dollop of mustard? Keep tasting until you've got the balance right.

Option: Coriander salsa verde is great: use all coriander instead of the other herbs, about 60 g of leaves and slender stalks.

MILDER SALSA VERDE

Here's one for people who just can't abide anchovies, no matter how well disguised.

SERVES ABOUT 8

1 large bunch fresh parsley
a small handful fresh basil or mint leaves
1 tbsp tender white scallion parts
2 tbsp well-rinsed capers
1 tbsp smooth Dijon mustard
2 tbsp wine vinegar
125–50 ml extra virgin olive oil
salt and pepper

Chop the herbs and scallions roughly and put them in a food processor with all the other ingredients except the oil. Chop to a paste, then add the oil in a steady stream with the motor running. Taste and season.

SPICY YOGHURT RELISH WITH MINT AND CORIANDER

Is it a sauce? Is it a dip? Is it a relish? It's all of them, and you could eat it all summer long. You probably will. This herby 2-minute sauce is hot with the bite of green chillies, smooth with the pure balm of yoghurt, fresh with the zip of mint.

Use as

● a sauce for crisp-skinned grilled or barbequed chicken
● sweet grilled or roast lamb
● a wonderful dip for anything — tortilla chips, crudités, roast or barbequed veg
● a perfect (naturally low-fat) dressing for a tomato salad
● a superb light potato salad dressing
● it's great with just about anything deep-fried (naturally, not so low-fat any more). It's so clean-tasting, it even makes chips feel healthy.

This makes a small bowl of dip; enough dressing for a large tomato salad or a small potato one; or enough sauce for 4–6 generous servings.

½ medium onion
½–1 large green chilli, deseeded
small piece root ginger
½ handful fresh mint leaves
1½ handfuls fresh coriander leaves
about 300 g plain yoghurt
½ tsp salt

Chop the onion finely and the chilli roughly. Peel a little skin off a tip of the ginger root and grate it very finely until you have about ½ tsp ginger. Roughly chop the mint and coriander leaves. Put all ingredients in the food processor and whizz to a pale green, herb-flecked, slightly frothy sauce. Taste for the balance of flavourings. You can, for example, start with less chilli and add more as your tastebuds deem necessary.

Chill . . . and serve with everything.

More sauces?
Peanut Sambal, p. 77
Mayonnaises, pp. 99–100
Bon Bon Chicken, p. 56
Golden Lemon Dressing, pp. 76–7
Roasted Red Relish, p. 33

white sauce

Parsley Sauce

Flour-based sauces have fallen out of favour. You can see why. In theory, they should be a delicate veil of velvet cream, but so often the result is sticky goo instead. Madame de Bovet, a French visitor to Ireland in the 19th century, described being served chicken 'dishonoured', she said, 'by a white paste with parsley in it, the national sauce'.

In the 1970s, nouvelle cuisine banished flour-thickened sauces; they were considered heavy and had too often been used to mask inferior ingredients. They were replaced with intense reductions, buttery things, the *jus* and the coulis. And lately oils, vinegars and salsas have taken over on our plates.

And yet . . . white sauce is essential, for all sorts of cooking. You need it for lasagne (though it'll most likely be referred to as béchamel or balsamella). Try a soufflé, and you'll need one too. Cook up those wonderful winter comforters, cauliflower or macaroni cheese, and a smooth, delicate white sauce is where you start.

And of course, there's parsley sauce. It's time we rescued its reputation. The version over the page might do the trick. Parsley sauce *can* be delicate, fresh, green and *elegant*. (Honest!) It's just perfect for moistening a burst floury spud or three, or as a silky friend for a slice of bacon, or a soft coat to envelop sweet carrots. You just want to make sure that it's velvety light, and that it doesn't taste of raw flour, but (what an extraordinary thought) actually tastes of parsley instead.

white sauce

The roux

Flour-based sauces — béchamel, white sauce, parsley sauce, cheese sauce, mornay, soubise, call them what you will, are all based on roux. This is a cooked mixture of butter and flour, and it's right here that you do one of the most important things: banish the taste of raw flour. Melt the butter in a pot over a very low flame, then stir in the flour. Keep stirring. (This will take about 3 minutes.) The sticky lump becomes a grainy mass. Keep stirring. Suddenly you can smell cooked pastry, and soon after it will turn into a slick, glossy liquid. Keep the heat as low as possible so that these two sensitive ingredients don't burn; they should hardly change colour at all.

Your roux is cooked.

You can proceed to make the sauce right away. But it's also very handy to know that roux hardens when cold and keeps for weeks in the fridge. If it's to hand, you can add a little into a gravy to thicken it, or make a quicker white sauce by crumbling the roux directly into hot milk.

The liquid

It can be all milk. Or you can substitute half the milk with stock, depending on what you're cooking. A cheese sauce for fish is excellent with some fish stock in it; if you're making cauliflower cheese, the cauliflower cooking water is a very tasty enrichment.

The infusion

Especially if you're using milk alone, it pays to infuse it with flavourings such as spices and onion. See the recipe below. There's no extra work, it just

means starting a little earlier. If you're really pushed for time, you can skip this step, but it does make the difference between a rather bland, one-dimensional sauce and one with richer flavours.

The sauce

It induces fear, because lumps can be a problem. The solution? Add the milk carefully. When the hot roux is done in the pan, take it off the heat and get a whisk. Add just a few tbsp liquid and stir. It will suddenly form a very thick sticky mass. Keep adding just a few tbsp milk at a time, and whisk each lot in until it's incorporated. When you have a smooth wet sauce, you can add the rest of the liquid. The sauce will now be very runny. Return it to the cooker and pick up your wooden spoon again. Heat the sauce until it simmers, when it will thicken. Stir it all the time so it doesn't stick to the bottom of the pot.

(If, despite your best efforts, you have lumpy sauce, whisk it vigorously, or sieve it.)

Sticky goo?

These flour-based sauces thicken as they cook, but they also thicken rapidly as they cool. They even thicken in those few degrees from the pan to the table, and that's one of their problems. Parsley sauce which seemed perfect in the pot will be sticky by the time it hits someone's plate. Stop cooking a flour-based sauce when it's a little more runny than you think it should be.

Or . . . use the whizz method for parsley sauce which I describe below. I don't know why, but it

thins a sauce to a delicious, light cream.

BASIC WHITE SAUCE

| 500 ml milk |
| 1 onion, roughly chopped |
| 2 whole cloves |
| 2 bay leaves |
| 1 tsp peppercorns |
| 1 rounded tbsp softish butter (25 g) |
| 2 rounded tbsp plain flour (25 g) |

First flavour the milk. Pour it into a small pan and add the onion, cloves, bay leaves and peppercorns. Heat until the milk simmers, cover the pan, turn off the heat and leave to infuse for as long as suits — about 15–30 minutes should do.

Meanwhile, make the roux. In a heavy-bottomed saucepan large enough to take the milk, melt the butter. Add the flour and stir to cook, for about 3 minutes, as described above.

Finally, make the sauce. Through a sieve, pour the hot infused milk back into the measuring jug. Whisk it in to the roux, a little at a time, as described above. Heat the sauce until it simmers, stirring all the while, then simmer very gently until it reaches its required consistency.

GREEN PARSLEY SAUCE

SERVES ABOUT 4–6

to the **Basic White Sauce (above)**
add

| 2 bunches fresh parsley and the greens of 2 scallions, all chopped |

When the white sauce is cooked, add the parsley and scallions. Then whizz the sauce with one of those stick-like blenders which you insert into a pot of soup. (You can also do it in a blender or food processor, but it means more washing up.) Magic! Dubious white stodge is gone; the sauce turns green, light and slightly frothy. This is even good enough to convert parsley sauce haters.

CAULIFLOWER CHEESE

Cauliflower in a silky cheesy sauce is an old favourite — with good reason. This sauce is great with carrots and broccoli as well. Just be sure to use very piquant hard cheese (Mizen, Gabriel, Parmesan, Gruyère, very mature Cheddar) or you'll have a tasteless Cauliflower White Sauce instead.

SERVES 4–6

to the **Basic White Sauce (using just 300 ml milk)**

add

1 large cauliflower

100 g tasty hard cheese (see note above)

2 tsp Dijon mustard

(optional: 2 tbsp grated cheese and 1 handful fresh white breadcrumbs)

Use 300 ml milk to infuse as described for the white sauce above.

While the milk infuses, cook the cauliflower. Trim only the battered leaves. Put it whole in a pot in which it fits snugly, with just 2 cm water in it. Cook with the lid on for about 15 minutes, until the cauliflower isn't quite done. (It'll go on cooking as you finish the sauce.) Remove, keep the cooking water, and cut up into florets.

When making the sauce, add 200 ml cauliflower cooking water to it, then the cheese and mustard. Coat the cauliflower with the sauce. Serve as it is, or put in an ovenproof dish, scatter with cheese and crumbs, and bake in a preheated medium oven until hot and bubbling.

MACARONI CHEESE

If you get macaroni cheese right everyone will love you for it.

There are two schools of thought on this subject. Some prefer it just-made, when the cheese sauce is still a little runny, like a creamy pasta sauce. Others (me included) prefer it more like a gratin, when the pasta and sauce have been given time to meld together and are then reheated in the oven, and the pasta is very tender and conceals pockets of hot, smooth cheesy sauce. If you're planning on serving it immediately, I'd recommend you simmer the white sauce gently for 3–5 minutes, stirring all the while, before you add the cheese, to be sure the raw flour taste is all gone.

Finally, use a tubular pasta of some kind; other twists and twirls aren't quite as good.

SERVES 4–6

1.1 litres whole milk

2 onions

1 tsp peppercorns

4 cloves

a chip of a nutmeg

2 bay leaves

parsley stalks

250 g tubular pasta, preferably pipe rigate (big elbows), or penne or macaroni

60 g butter

60 g flour

2 tsp smooth Dijon mustard

175 g grated or crumbled cheese (see note below)

salt and pepper

2 tbsp finely chopped fresh chives or parsley (optional)

a handful of breadcrumbs (optional)

Pour the milk into a saucepan and add the onions, peppercorns, cloves, nutmeg, bay leaves and parsley stalks. Bring to a simmer, take off the heat

and cover with a lid. Leave to infuse for 15–30 minutes, then strain the milk and discard the aromatics.

Boil up a pot of salted water and put the pasta on to cook.

In a big heavy-based saucepan, make a white sauce (as described above) by cooking the butter and flour, then whisking in the hot milk. Stir in the mustard and cheese, reserving a handful of cheese for the topping. Add salt and pepper to taste, and the chives or parsley if you're using them.

When the pasta is just done (don't overcook it — very important), drain it well to be sure there's no water trapped in the shapes, then stir it into the cheese sauce. Pour it all into a large ovenproof serving dish (of about 1½–2 litres capacity). Top it with the reserved cheese, mixed with breadcrumbs if you're using them.

To serve the dish right away: Put the dish under a hot grill until the topping is crusty, then serve.

To serve later (I prefer it this way): Allow to cool. Reheat later, or the next day, in a preheated 200C/400F/Gas 6 oven, until it's hot all the way through. Depending on the shape of your dish and how cold it was when it went into the oven, this will take about 30–40 minutes.

The cheese: Tasty cheese makes a big difference to the dish. Cheddar is traditional, but unless you can find a really exceptional, well-matured one, the flavour is disappointing. I'd use two cheeses: half or more of a very hard, tangy cheese such as Gruyère, Gabriel or Desmond; the rest of a softer, flavoursome cheese such as a well-matured Ardrahan, Durrus or Lavistown. Or you could experiment with your favourite goats', sheep's or blue cheeses. Have fun!

mayonnaise

Mayonnaise. Making it seems to suit the slow air of warm days. The job can't be hurried. It has its own rhythm. It's best done sitting on a kitchen chair at the sunny back door, the bowl jammed tight between your knees. The olive oil drip-drips. The whisk beats. Frothy egg yolks are transformed to sticky, shiny gold: stiff yet wobbly like a belly dancer's tummy.

Mayonnaise-making is a skill often overlooked nowadays; after all, isn't there plenty in the supermarket? Forget it. They don't come close. Your own

mayonnaise will make a feast of the simplest ingredients. It will be opulent and fruity with olive oil. It will enhance even a boiled potato — and it will make a platter of vegetables a sensuous experience, as you dip into the sauce again, and again, and when the vegetables run out a finger will do the dipping just as well.

There is mystery surrounding mayonnaise. Some even consider it divine. 'It was patently absurd', Alice Thomas Ellis's Aunt Irene said, 'to suppose that mayonnaise had come about through random chance . . . An angel must have

divulged that recipe, and then explained what to do with the leftover egg whites.' Who indeed could have foretold that an egg yolk could hold a million miniscule droplets of oil in quivering suspense?

And the mystery is not quite solved. Scientist Harold McGee devotes twelve pages of *On Food and Cooking* to the subject, and they're brimful of lecithins, livetins, colloids and surface tension. Still he concludes that 'we really have no idea . . .' of why these sauces work.

Never mind — ignorance can be bliss. We may not know exactly *why* it works — but do we know *how* to make a bowl of glorious mayonnaise? We certainly do. Here goes.

— **Use wonderful ingredients**. It is very easy to make boring mayo: just use dull oil and battery eggs. You'll wonder why you bothered, though.

— **The egg yolks**. They must be from the freshest, free-range eggs. There are several reasons. There's flavour, of course. But there are sound technical reasons, too. First, ageing eggs don't emulsify so well. Second, free-range eggs tend to have a higher lipid content than battery eggs, so they make a better emulsion. An egg that's both super-fresh *and* free-range will make the stiffest mayonnaise of all.

Also, if you're going to eat something raw, it's only common sense that it should be as fresh as could be. (The fresher an egg, the less chance it will have had to multiply any salmonella it might possibly contain. Salmonella is not a huge problem in eggs from the Republic, but remember it is still safer not to serve raw egg foods to people who are very young, old, unwell or pregnant.)

— **The oil**. It must be good. Mayonnaise has a funny habit of magnifying an oil's characteristics. A strong, dark, green olive oil will make nasty, bitter mayo. The best recipe is to use about half olive oil, half sunflower. And the olive oil should be a mellow, rounded, fruity extra virgin. If you find the olive flavour strong, use less olive oil and more sunflower instead.

— **The temperature**. Ingredients emulsify better if they are at the same temperature, so after you have cracked them into the bowl let the egg yolks warm up a little to room temperature.

— **Patience** is the final ingredient. Not a lot of it, just 5 minutes' worth. That's all it takes to make a hand-whisked, lustrous, ravishing mayonnaise. Here's how.

MAYONNAISE

MAKES ABOUT 300 ML

2 large very fresh free-range egg yolks

1 tsp Dijon mustard

½ tsp salt

lemon juice to taste

250 ml oil (about half olive, half sunflower)

Take a large bowl, sit down and hold it tight with your legs. (You can stand it on a work surface, steadied on a damp tea towel if you prefer.) Whisk the egg yolks with mustard, salt and 1 tsp lemon juice until they thicken a little. Drip the oil in, drop by drop, whisking continuously. Do this until you have a sticky paste. Now add the oil in a thin trickle, still whisking all the time, until all the oil is incorporated. Taste. You'll need more lemon juice, perhaps a little salt. Add enough warm water until it has the consistency you require.

— **Don't panic** if the mayonnaise doesn't thicken. This means it has 'curdled' — a rather confusing term, since it often doesn't look like curdled milk or cake mixture, it just stays runny for a while and then separates. All you need to do is to start the process all over again. Put another egg yolk into a bowl. Whisk the curdled mixture into it — more slowly this time!

— You can make this mayo in the food processor if your blade sits very close to the base of the bowl, or if you use 3 yolks (and half as much again of all the other ingredients).

---

3 KITCHEN STARS

Here are three really useful — and very cheap — items of kitchen gear with which I wish I'd made my acquaintance much earlier. Every kitchen should have these.

1. **The Salad Spinner**. It produces dry salad leaves, so the dressing isn't diluted. Spin each batch of leaves twice.

2. **The Petal Steamer**. It fits into any sized saucepan and folds down very small for easy storage. Essential for potatoes. Good for the rest of the veg too.

3. **The Spatter-guard**. It looks like a flat, very fine-meshed sieve. Lie it on a frying pan and it stops most oil from spattering around, but still allows hot air to escape so there's no condensation in the pan.

mayonnaise

VERY SLIGHTLY LIGHTER MAYONNAISE

A food processor mayo for when you want something with less oomph, or when you're in a terrible hurry. You use the whole egg, not just the yolk. It's very, very tasty, but just not as sensuous as the yolk-only version.

MAKES ABOUT 275 ML

1 large very fresh free-range egg
1 tsp Dijon mustard
½ tsp salt
lemon juice
200–250 ml oil (half olive and half sunflower, as above)

Place everything except the oil (using 1 tsp lemon juice) in the food processor bowl; mix. With the motor running, drip in the oil as described above. When the sauce is thicker, you can add the oil more quickly. Finish as for the handmade version.

AIOLI

To either of the above versions, add 1–10 well-mashed cloves of garlic when you start whisking the egg yolks.

CHEAT'S AIOLI

There are always times when you want just a little garlicky, olive-oily mayo to flavour a dish or a dressing, or even just to dunk a salty, late-night chip into. In which case, take **1 heaped tbsp of Hellman's** and stir in **3 tbsp extra virgin olive oil**, then add **2 large cloves of garlic, thoroughly mashed**. It's really rather good . . .

HERB MAYONNAISE FOR SHELLFISH (OR CHICKEN OR VEGETABLES)

This mayo is lightened, so it's not too intrusive for the delicate flavour of shellfish. It's perfect for mixing with crabmeat, piled high with avocado or simply on fresh crusty brown bread.

MAKES ABOUT 275 ML

1 free-range very fresh egg
1 tsp Dijon mustard
½ tsp salt
1 tbsp lemon juice
50 ml olive oil
150 ml sunflower oil
about 2 tbsp (or more) plain yoghurt
chopped fresh chives

Make as for food processor mayonnaise, starting with the egg, mustard, salt and lemon juice. Add the oils drop by drop as the blade turns round, then in a trickle. Stir in yoghurt and chives at the end, and taste to check the seasoning.

PRAWN COCKTAIL

Every rule has an exception, as parents and teachers always said when they wanted to be inconsistent. You can use your own delicious mayo for this, and it will be lovely. And you can do as I always do, and use Hellman's, and then it'll taste just perfect.

This, incidentally, is a good use for frozen cooked prawns which are a bit lacking in the flavour department.

SERVES 4

250 g cooked prawns (shelled weight)
1 ripe avocado
Salad leaves, preferably including something peppery such as rocket or watercress, or a little radicchio

Sauce

4 heaped tbsp Hellman's (or your own) mayo
1 level tbsp Heinz ketchup
2 tsp brandy
¼ tsp curry powder
Tabasco and salt

If the prawns were cooked and frozen defrost them slowly (ideally overnight in the fridge). If fresh, steam them in the shell for a few minutes until the flesh is opaque, then shell them. Drain them well and dry on kitchen paper. Halve the avocado and get the stone out by spearing it with a sharp knife. Scoop out the flesh and cut it into prawn-sized bits. Tear the salad leaves into manageable sizes if necessary.

In a large bowl, stir all the sauce ingredients together, adding Tabasco and salt to taste. Turn the prawns and avocado in it. Taste again for seasoning. Pile the mix high on salad leaves, and serve.

Eating the mayonnaise . . .

This, you will discover, can easily be accomplished straight from the fridge. More orthodox uses:

In the centre of a platter of mixed foods. This is the Provençal principle for aioli, their staggeringly garlicky mayonnaise. 'Aioli intoxicates gently, fills the body with warmth, and the soul with enthusiasm,' said Mistral, the Provençal poet. It would, with the amount of garlic that goes in: 14 cloves per batch of mayonnaise. It accompanies everything from boiled snails (Christmas Eve) to dried cod (Ash Wednesday) to simply cooked meats and boiled and raw veg (summer festivals).

Garlic quantities are variable, of course. Try aioli with:

- boiled new potatoes, mealy and comforting
- quick-steamed French beans, bright green and still squeaky
- ripest red tomatoes, cradling slurpy jellied seeds
- little courgettes, nutty and crisp, steamed briefly, then cut open and cooled (see p. 75)
- poached chicken (see pp. 54–6), or steamed salmon, cooked until its white curds have just set (see pp. 34–5), or mussels, cockles, squid, oysters . . .

Anything is possible, and everything is made more special, you'll discover, when there's a pot of the magic stuff to dip into.

- Mayonnaise goes well with any robust salad ingredients. Just don't glop it onto salad leaves, which it will floor with a single punch.
- Thin it out with warm water to use as a dressing for potato salads or poached chicken.
- Use it neat to make the best BLT you'll ever eat.
- Try it in a chorizo and rocket sandwich, preferably made with ciabatta; or with tomatoes and fresh herbs; or with cold roast lamb.
- Or squished into any other sandwich that takes your fancy.

COOKING WITH THE SEASONS

No, I'm not fanatical about this. I'm just as partial to a fragrant Thai curry in deepest midwinter as anyone else, its creamy coconut sauce pepped up with the irreplaceable citrus whiff of flown-in kaffir lime leaves and imported ginger root. And I don't want to eat parsnips and turnips and sprouts all winter long.

But there's no doubt that shopping and cooking with the seasons is one of the most important Basics of all. Why? Because when food is freshest, it tastes best. And when it is grown as naturally as possible (with natural light, heat, soil and fertilisers), it tends to taste much better too.

It can be pretty hard to know what the seasons are these days. If you shop only in supermarkets, you'll see much the same fruit and veg all year round, and most of it has very little flavour at all. But why bother with a tasteless strawberry in January, when if you wait till June you'll savour intense berry heaven? Why settle for dull old chunky supermarket Calabrese broccoli in spring, when if you go to a market, you'll find slender stalks of dusky-bloomed, sweetly tender purple sprouting broccoli instead? Why bother with a pale watery Dutch hothouse tomato in November, when September brings ripe, red tomatoes from the south?

Keep an eye out for seasonal foods, and for those grown close by. You'll be amazed at the difference it'll make to your cooking.

pancakes

My mum, who can still do cartwheels to delight her grandchildren, always tossed her pancakes high into the air. Round and round they flipped, narrowly missing the ceiling, and down they came, and they always landed back in the pan. Every time. We gazed, enthralled. (These are the moments when the childhood myth of parental invincibility is formed.) The dog gazed and drooled and waited, in vain.

I can't toss pancakes, but I do still love to make them. The simple pleasure's enough, the pleasure of a hot thin pancake fresh from the pan, tender, eggy and buttery, crisp at the edges. It's ready to be rolled around a zesty squirt of lemon juice, plus a scattering of sharp little crystals of granulated sugar which will stick to the corner of your mouth, and have to be found and licked off with the tip of your tongue.

Pancakes are perfect instant food (and no, you don't need a packet of pancake mix). They're for quick suppers, and slow breakfasts. And for desserts, and for emergency hunger in the middle of the day. And the beauty of it is that once you know you can whisk up a quick 'n' easy batter, you can make plenty of other things too. A hot and steamy Plum Clafoutis, perhaps. See the next pages for some of them.

But first, the pancake batter basics.

Lumps in the batter?
Going slowly when adding the milk is the key to avoiding lumps in the batter.

Put the flour in a large bowl, and hollow out a dip in it. Crack the eggs into the dip. Poke them with a whisk to break the yolks. Stir the eggs gently with the whisk, incorporating just a little of the flour, until you have sticky opaque goo.

Add a little milk, just enough to soften the goo, and keep stirring gently to incorporate a little more flour at a time. Keep going like this until all the flour is absorbed. At this stage there will probably be a few lumps left.

Add just a little milk and whisk vigorously until the lumps are gone; then whisk in the rest of the milk. That's all there is to it.

The pan
Worried the pancakes might stick? A non-stick pan is the answer. Don't worry if the first pancake looks like a dog's dinner. It always does! (Give it to the drooling dog.) The process of frying it will have seasoned the pan and the rest will be just fine.

Tossing and turning
Tossing the pancakes is strictly optional; a spatula or fish slice does the job of turning them just as well.

The frying
Heat a non-stick pan to medium and add a big lump of butter to it (about 50 g). Swirl the butter round to melt it, then pour it all into a small bowl. Turn the heat up. Ladle in just enough pancake batter to cover the base of the hot pan thinly. Pour it into the centre of the pan, then tip the pan to swirl the batter round to the edges. (If you've poured too much batter into the pan, just pour the extra back out again into the bowl of batter, or the pancake will be thick and stodgy.)

After a minute or so, lift the corner to look underneath: if the base is speckled buttery and brown, slide the slice under it and turn it over to cook the other side.

After every pancake, add a few more drops of the melted butter.

Serving pancakes
There's no question that pancakes taste best for about 5 seconds after they have left the pan, and that's how they should be eaten: straight from the kitchen, one by one. However, they can be made in advance for serving when the hot buttery crispness doesn't matter, such as in the orange sauce on the next page.

PANCAKE BATTER
MAKES ABOUT 12 LARGE PANCAKES

175 g plain flour
pinch of salt
2 large eggs
475 ml milk
butter, to fry

Sift the flour and salt into a large bowl, make a dip in the middle and crack the eggs into it. Break the yolks up with the whisk, then beat gently and start to incorporate the flour surrounding them. Add a little milk to help the whisking, but keep it thick until all the flour is gone. Then slowly add the rest of the milk, whisking energetically to disperse the lumps.

You can leave this batter aside for a while, or keep it in the fridge overnight, or use it right away. (Recipes usually advise you to let it stand for half an hour before using but I can't say I've ever noticed a great difference.)

Remember: the first pancake will almost certainly be a mess. But the rest will be fine!

To serve with pancakes:
Fresh-squeezed lemon and granulated sugar. Or maple syrup. Maybe an easy chocolate sauce (see p. 125). Apple slices, or banana, gently fried in a little butter . . .

pancakes

PANCAKE FANS WITH INDULGENT ORANGE SAUCE

The effect is similar to Crêpes Suzette, but minus the singed eyebrows.

SERVES 6

1 recipe pancakes (see p. 103)

Make the pancakes, as described, in a pan 23/24 cm across the base; you should have 12. They must be thin. If you want to go for a more dainty effect but a bit more work, make the pancakes in a smaller pan, and you'll then have more than 2 per person. Pile the pancakes in a layer on a plate. They can be made up to a day ahead.

Sauce

4 oranges

150 g unsalted butter

150 g icing sugar

50 ml Cointreau or Grand Marnier

Grate the zest from 2 of the oranges and squeeze the juice of 4. Put zest and juice in the pancake pan. Add the butter and icing sugar. Heat and whisk until the sauce is homogeneous. Off the heat, add the booze.

To serve:

Return the pan to a gentle heat: One by one, lay a pancake into hot sauce. Fold it in half, then fold over again (to make a fan-shape, a quarter of the circle). Lay on a warm serving dish and keep warm. Keep going with the rest of the pancakes until all are covered in the rich orangey sauce. They will happily keep warm for a little while now.

BUTTERMILK PANCAKES

These are quite different from thin, sweet-milk pancakes: thick yet light and slightly risen, they have a lovely fresh flavour from the buttermilk. They're particularly good for breakfast,

with jam, or maple syrup, or savoury things like a crisp streaky rasher that shatters as you bite into it. (But they don't work with lemon juice — too acidic all round.)

SERVES 4–5. MAKES ABOUT 16 SMALL PANCAKES

230 g plain flour

1 scant level tsp bread soda

1 tsp salt

1 tsp caster sugar

1 egg

400 ml buttermilk

Sieve flour, soda, salt and sugar into a large bowl. Make a dip in the centre and crack the egg into it. Poke the egg yolk with a whisk to break it up, then add a little buttermilk. Keep whisking this thick gooey paste, drawing in the flour bit by bit. Add a little buttermilk as the paste gets too stiff, but keep it thick until all the flour is incorporated. At this stage there will still be some lumps. Whisk vigorously as you gradually add the rest of the buttermilk. The lumps will go.

Use the batter within minutes or it won't rise so well. Fry the pancakes on a griddle or non-stick frying pan. Small pancakes about the width of your hand are the right size for this batter. Heat the pan, then melt a big knob of butter. Pour the butter into a bowl, then pour in the batter from a ladle. You should fit 3 in a large pan. Leave it untouched until it has airy bubbles all over and is nearly set on top, then turn it. Cook on the other side. It's important to cook pancakes like these until they're done — raw batter in the centre is not at all pleasant.

Eat immediately.

PLUM CLAFOUTIS

If you can make pancake batter, you can make this hot baked pudding. The result? Hot, syrupy plummy juices mingle with the custardy, risen batter.

SERVES 4–6

6–7 very large under-ripe plums, about 550 g

50 g butter

3 eggs

2 heaped tbsp plain flour

2 heaped tbsp caster sugar

1 tsp vanilla extract or ½ tsp essence

250 ml milk

1 tbsp light muscovado sugar

Turn on the oven to 200C/400F/ Gas 6. Quarter the plums and discard the stones. Find a shallow ovenproof dish with about 2 litres capacity; put the butter in it and put the dish in the heating oven to melt the butter.

In a large bowl, whisk the eggs. Whisk in the flour, sugar and vanilla and keep going until the lumps are gone. Gradually whisk in the milk.

When the butter has melted, swirl it around to coat the inside of the dish, then pour the rest into the bowl of batter. Arrange the plums cut side up in the dish. Scatter with the brown sugar and put the dish in the oven for 10 minutes, until the plums are starting to brown at the tips. Then pour the batter into the dish — slowly, so the hot plums don't rise up and float all over the place. Return it to the oven for a further 15–25 minutes, until it's well risen, just set in the centre, but still tender. Serve while still hot, with cold cream, or vanilla ice cream.

'DIMPAS' BAKED APPLE SLICES WITH BUTTER CINNAMON CRUNCH

This is an old family favourite, a lovely simple supper dessert. The thing that makes it special is its final flourish: the hot risen apple batter is dotted with butter, scattered with cinnamon sugar and given a lift with a squeeze of lemon juice. It's just the thing for a winter's evening with a big steaming bowl of milky coffee.

SERVES 4

butter for the dish
3 eggs
1 tbsp sugar
2 heaped tbsp plain flour
½ tsp salt
50 ml milk
2–4 tart apples (depending on size), such as Granny Smith or Braeburn

To serve

1–2 tbsp butter
2 tbsp sugar
½ tsp cinnamon
2 tsp lemon juice

Turn the oven on to 190C/375F/ Gas 5. Generously butter a 1.2-litre capacity ovenproof soufflé or gratin dish. In a large bowl, whisk the eggs with the sugar until they're light, then whisk in the flour and salt alternately with the milk.

Peel, quarter, core and slice the apples fairly thinly. Turn them in the batter. Scrape the mix into the prepared dish and bake it for 20 minutes, then cover it and bake for another 15 minutes. The apples should be soft and the batter risen (though it will fall as you serve it).

Dot the top with 1–2 tbsp butter. Mix the sugar and cinnamon and strew this over, then add the lemon juice. Serve hot, while the butter's just melting.

egg whites...

Whisking egg whites? It's a kitchen miracle. You begin with a glob of slithery mucus at the bottom of a bowl. Next thing it's frothing like sea spume. Beat a bit longer and it's creamily firm. Keep going and you've a bowlful of snow, so full of trapped air bubbles it'll defy gravity if you turn it upside down. This brinkmanship was my favourite cooking task when I was a child. I can still never resist upending the bowl, just to see if the foam really will stay there, or whether it might slither out and land on my head.

And once the whites are whisked, the miracle continues, as they transfer all those air bubbles to bring an incredible lightness to mousses and soufflés, omelettes and cakes. Or you can simply bake them with sugar, and make meringues: soft, marshmallow meringues, parchment-coloured, frail and tender.

There's a bit of detail in the tips below, but don't get the idea that this is a difficult job. Perfectionists might insist on copper bowls, balloon whisks, lemon halves and sprinklings of salt. But Karen Blixen (who wrote *Out of Africa*) had a Kikuyu chef called Kamante. He scorned the egg beater she offered him, opting instead for an old knife which she used for weeding. The result? 'His whites of eggs towered up like light clouds.'

The eggs
Important: This is one time you don't want your eggs ultra-fresh. Eggs just 1 or 2 days old are too moist. They will never whip up properly. They must be at least 3–4 days old.

Squeaky clean . . .
Egg whites are amazing, expanding to 8 times their volume if you get it right. But their greatest enemy is fat. So the only kind of grease allowed in their vicinity is elbow grease (and if you don't have an electrical beater you'll need plenty of that). Bowls and beaters must be, literally, squeaky clean.

The bowl
The *best* egg white foam is made in a copper bowl. This is no affectation, it's chemistry (the copper provides ions to the metal-binding protein conalbumin, if you must know). But don't rush out to buy one — other metals do fine. Plastic bowls are not fine — they're chemically too similar to oil, so they don't get squeaky clean enough.

Separating . . .
Be careful when separating the eggs. It's important to keep the yolk out of whites which are destined for whisking: yolks contain fat too, and can reduce volume by as much as $\frac{2}{3}$. (If some yolk slips in, slip it out again with a piece of eggshell.)

So, unless you like living dangerously, use three bowls. One to crack each egg over; one for the whites; and one for the yolks. Tap the egg on the side of the bowl smartly to crack it, then break it open into two clean halves. Slide the whole yolk back and forth between the shells until all the white has slithered out into the bowl below. And always have an extra egg or two, in case a yolk breaks.

The temperature
This is not crucial, but egg whites do whip best at room temperature.

The sugar
This *is* crucial: only use caster or sieved icing sugar. Granulated is too coarse to dissolve properly. Golden icing sugar is the tastiest of all — look out for it.

Whisking
— Keep moving the beaters around; don't leave slithery unbeaten white at the edges.
— For sweet mixes, most recipes suggest whisking the whites first, then gradually adding sugar — I just whisk them together and it works fine.

Cookbooks say they're done when 'stiff but not dry'. What does that mean?

- The whites should look opaque and creamy. They should have the dense look of shaving foam, rather than the foamy appearance of shampoo lather. There should be sharp little peaks. Are they a bit lumpy and granular? You have not beaten long enough. Don't overbeat, or they'll go lumpy again and start to collapse.
- If you've whisked in sugar, they should be stiff and glossy, like satin, with sharp little peaks. Either way, you will be able to turn the bowl upside down without getting egg on your face.
- If you are worried about overbeating, you can add a pinch of cream of tartar or a dribble of vinegar to the whites, though this is less

and meringues

necessary when using sugar (it stabilises the foam too).

- If you have overwhisked a little, whisk another white separately, then carefully beat the overwhisked whites into it.
- If you're using plain whites (e.g. for a soufflé), use them as soon as they're whisked, as the foam will break down rapidly. Sugary ones will hold for some time.

Do your whites need folding?

Folding egg whites is one of those standard kitchen moves. If you're wondering how to perform this incongruous-sounding manoeuvre see p. 108.

A few tips for meringues

- Bake on non-stick parchment paper (Bakewell).
- Leave some room between them — they may rise or expand.
- Check them during cooking time, and if necessary turn the tray for even cooking.
- The harder they are, the longer they'll keep.

TENDER MERINGUES

The flimsiest crisp crust coats these enormous marshmallowy puffs, which are delightfully insubstantial inside. They crack a little as they cool. Serve with soft summer fruits, or poached fruits, and whipped cream mixed with crème fraîche or Greek yoghurt.

SERVES 4
4 egg whites
115 g caster sugar
15 g dark muscovado sugar
1 tsp real vanilla extract (or a few drops essence)
1 tsp white wine vinegar

Turn the oven on to 130C/250F/ Gas ½. Put everything in a bowl, having squished the brown sugar through your fingers to ease out any hard lumps.

Whisk with electric beaters until it is stiff and glossy. This will take nearly 10 minutes. Lay non-stick baking parchment on a baking tray. Pile the meringue to form 4 high mounds (with space between them). Bake for about an hour. They should be firm to the touch on the outside but perceptibly softer within. Leave to cool a little before peeling the parchment away carefully. These meringues are at their best for a few hours. They still taste good the next day, but do sag a little.

ALMOND MERINGUE

The scent of toasted nuts rises from the oven when these are done. You can make lots of little round blobs, or two large flat discs for a cake-like effect. Either way, fill with whipped cream and fruit, or whipped cream flavoured with a few tbsp of brandy or whiskey.

75 g whole unpeeled almonds
3 large egg whites
150 g caster sugar

(You can use nibbed almonds if you're in a rush, but freshly peeled and chopped almonds retain much more of their aromatic oils.)

Turn on the oven to 140C/275F/ Gas 1. Simmer the almonds in water for a minute, then drain. When cooler, squeeze the wet skins and the nuts will shoot out. Dry well, then chop to the texture of nibbed (coarse-ground) almonds.

Whisk the egg whites and sugar until glossy and stiff. Gently stir in the almonds. Lay baking parchment on two baking trays. Spoon the meringue on to the parchment and flatten it out into 2 circles about 23 cm/9" wide. They don't need to be particularly even but it helps if the edges aren't too thin.

Bake for 45 minutes–1 hour, until the aroma of toasted nuts drifts out of the oven. You may need to switch the trays around during baking to cook them evenly.

Cool a little, then store in a dry or airtight place.

soufflés

Soufflés are mysterious things. Not so much because they rise up to teeter splendidly in mid-air. Not even because of their fabled detumescent tendencies (which really need concern only those of you who have several miles of cold corridor between oven and table). No, the mystery of the soufflé lies in the fact that everyone is so terrified of making them.

In fact, baking a soufflé is pretty easy. It's certainly one of the simplest ways I know to gain oohs of appreciation, except popping the cork on a bottle of champagne. (There's a bit more hassle in the washing up, but we'll gloss over that one. Making a soufflé always seems to use up too many bowls.) Soufflés are great store cupboard suppers — look at the simple ingredients for the cheese soufflé below. And they're such fun. Light, trembling and insubstantial, every mouthful surrenders soft little breaths of hot air as you eat.

All soufflés work the same basic way — and if you've ever made chocolate mousse, you'll know all the moves. First, you make a thick, sticky sauce. Then you beat egg yolks into it. Some whisked egg white is stirred into this sticky mix, to loosen it, and then the rest of the egg white is folded in — as gently and as lightly as possible, in order to hold in the air which is trapped in it.

And that's it. You don't even have to bake it straight away. A soufflé, once it comes out of the oven, does need to be eaten pronto. But a prepared soufflé will happily wait in the fridge for 1 or 2 hours before being baked, and will rise just the same.

For soufflé success:
— Use a straight-sided dish, and butter it generously. Always use the size of dish specified in the recipe.

— With savoury soufflé mixes, overseason the thick sauce, to compensate for the bland egg whites which will be added.

— For the low-down on egg whites and how to beat them best, see p. 106. This is important!

— How do you fold an egg white? With a spatula. Pile the whisked whites on top of the thicker mix. Slice the spatula through the centre, to the bottom of the bowl, and with a turn of your wrist bring the spatula up and over. Keep doing this, cutting into the fluffy egg white with the edge of the spatula and then scooping the heavier mix up from the bottom. Gradually, the egg white foam will be incorporated. The trick is to get it done with as few scoops as possible, and to scoop from the base of the bowl, so no unmixed stuff lurks down there.

— Is it done? Knowing when a soufflé is done does take a little practice. It should be golden and crusty on the outside, with a soft (but not gooey) heart. It should still have a little wobble to it. If you're not sure, carefully slide in a skewer to test. Just don't fiddle around with the thing too much. And don't open the oven door to look at it, no matter how tempted you are, until nearly the end of its baking time.

CHEESE SOUFFLÉ

Such effect for such ordinary ingredients! I like savoury soufflés to be slightly more substantial and stronger-flavoured than their sweet relations, so I use fewer egg whites than many recipes.

Most important of all: use a really hard, tangy cheese, or you'll just end up with a kind of pointless eggy squidge. My favourites? Desmond, Gabriel or Mizen, Pecorino or Parmesan (freshly grated *only*), or a really mature Cheddar — a hard, flaky farmhouse one, not a sticky factory

version. A little Gruyère can add life to the mix as well.

SERVES 4 AS A MAIN COURSE, 6–8 AS A STARTER

50 g butter, plus extra for the dish

40 g plain flour

300 ml milk

4 large free-range eggs, separated

150 g grated hard cheese (see note above)

1–2 tsp Dijon mustard

salt, pepper and cayenne pepper

Butter a 2-litre capacity soufflé dish (or six to eight 250 ml ramekins) and turn the oven on to 200C/400F/Gas 6 with a baking tray in it. Melt the butter in a large heavy saucepan and add the flour; cook gently, stirring, for 2 minutes. Whisk in the milk to make a (very thick paste-like) white sauce (see pp. 95–7 for more about these). Beat in the egg yolks, cheese and mustard. Take the pan off the heat, taste and season it with salt, pepper and cayenne, remembering to overseason.

Whisk the egg whites until firm but not grainy. Stir a quarter of the foam into the sauce to lighten it. Fold the rest of the egg whites in. Pour the mix into the prepared dish(es). Put it in the oven on the baking tray immediately — or leave it in the fridge for up to 3 hours.

A large soufflé will take 25–30 minutes, small ones about 10 minutes. Allow a few minutes extra if baking from the fridge.

CHOCOLATE SOUFFLÉ

SERVES 6–8

butter for the dish

150 g dark chocolate, preferably 70% cocoa solids

125 ml cream

3 egg yolks

1 tbsp brandy

5 egg whites

60 g caster sugar

pouring cream, to serve

Turn the oven to 220C/425F/Gas 7. Thickly butter a 2-litre soufflé dish. Put the chocolate and cream in a heavy pan, stirring carefully over a very low heat to form a smooth sauce. Take it off the heat and beat in the egg yolks and the brandy. Set it aside to cool.

Whisk the egg whites and sugar until stiff and glassy. Stir a quarter of the egg whites into the cooled chocolate mixture to loosen it; fold the rest in lightly. Spoon the mix into the prepared dish. Bake it right away for about 18 minutes, or first keep it in the fridge for a few hours (allowing a few minutes' extra baking time if you do). It should be soft, nearly runny in the centre. Serve with the cream.

quick breads

Quick 'n' easy soda breads, if they hadn't already been invented, would be a 21st-century advertiser's dream. Speed is their essence: they're stirred in seconds, baked in minutes, and ought to be eaten within hours. It's a shame they're weighed down with the air of tradition. It can be the only reason we have abandoned baking them. Ironically, for a food thought of as so utterly, quintessentially traditional, soda breads are one of Ireland's most recent acquisitions. Bicarbonate of soda arrived here only early in the 19th century. Within a few short decades it had swept across the country to transform bread-making. It's no wonder, when you think of the options at the time: coarse, flat oaten and barley breads, breads leavened with fermented oat juice, or soured potato juice.

In Ireland, bicarbonate of soda met its destiny: wonderful tangy Irish buttermilk. The chemistry was right. Alkaline bicarbonate of soda combined with acidic buttermilk and together they created enough gas to rise a loaf of bread. We took bicarbonate of soda to our hearts, rechristened it bread soda, and the rest is culinary history.

The abysmal quality of most commercially baked soda breads is a good reason to be able to turn out a quick loaf of your own. The fact that soda breads really taste good only for a few hours after baking is another. But even if you had a wonderful bakery just around the corner I'd reckon that being able to bake a batch of scones or a loaf of soda bread was one of the most basic skills of all. When unexpected guests show up and there's nothing in the house but a hunk of cheese, or when you get up on a Sunday morning and realise there's not a crust in the bread bin: those are the moments when a batch of quick 'n' easy scones will be a blessing.

The basics

All these breads need quick mixing. Unlike yeast breads, which need time and a great deal of bashing about, quick breads call for a rapid, featherlight touch. (Your hands will do the job better than any machine could.) Think of stroking a cat.

Preheat the oven fully before allowing wet and dry to meet

Whether your recipe uses bread soda with buttermilk, bread soda plus cream of tartar, or just baking powder, it works because acid and alkali react with each other to create carbon dioxide. This reaction gets going as soon as the wet ingredients meet the dry ones. So switch on the oven before you even get the flour out, and before you add the wet ingredient, check the oven is ready.

Sieve the bread soda

It's inclined to be lumpy, which not only will give you an uneven rise, but may give your bread green spots when baked.

Add almost all the liquid at once

Adding the liquid a trickle at a time slows you down and means the dough will be handled too much.

Always stir gently but quickly

You want to avoid dissipating the gas and toughening the dough.

Aim for a dough which is soft but not sticky or sloppy

This is something you will learn only with hands-on experience. Flour varies. Relative humidity varies. The amount of liquid you add to a pound of flour can vary by up to 80 ml (3 fl oz).

Get to know your own kitchen

The wisest words on bread-making come from Ken Buggy, master soda bread maker, of Buggy's Glencairn Inn near Lismore in Co. Waterford. 'No two ovens are the same. No two teaspoons are the same.' Expect some trial and error . . .

To check the bread is done

Tapping the base and listening for hollow sounds is usually recommended. With soda scones or loaves you can also (carefully!) break them open a little where they have a natural crack: at the cross of a loaf, or in the centre of a risen scone. If the dough looks wet, it isn't done. Put it back in the oven.

Eat the bread quickly!

Or freeze it on the day you baked it. If you won't eat it for a few hours, sprinkle the loaf with a little water and wrap in a clean tea towel to prevent the crust becoming too hard.

BASIC SODA BREAD OR SCONES

This is my basic recipe. I'm most likely to make scones: ready in 15 minutes. You can turn it into one large loaf, or enjoy any of the variations listed below. For urgent moments when the cupboard is bare of buttermilk, it works just as well to sour ordinary milk with lemon juice (see the recipe for proportions).

This is one of the only recipes for which I still use imperial measurements: take a look at how easy they are to remember!

MAKES ABOUT 10 SCONES OR 1 LOAF

1 lb (450 g) flour (see below)

1 tsp salt

1 level tsp bread soda (baking/bicarbonate of soda), sieved

1 tsp caster sugar

1 oz (30 g) butter

10 fl. oz (300 ml) approx. buttermilk (or milk, plus 1½ tbsp lemon juice)

— For a light, brown mix use about three-quarters plain or cream flour and one-quarter coarse stoneground wholemeal.
— For a delicious, slightly sweeter flavour use half granary malted flour and half plain or cream flour.
— For a sterner brown mix use half wholemeal and half plain or cream flour.

Preheat the oven to 220C/425F/Gas 7. (If using milk, mix it with lemon juice now.)

In a large bowl, mix all dry ingredients well. Rub in the butter with your fingertips until it's dispersed through the flour in tiny pieces. Make a well in the centre. Check the oven is fully heated. Pour all the buttermilk or sour milk in. With a spoon, gently and quickly stir the liquid into the flour. It should be soft, but not sticky. You may need an extra few drops — or even 25–50 ml — of buttermilk. Flour the work surface. Turn the mix out onto it and pat into a 2–3 cm high round. To make scones, cut into 10 large triangles with a knife. Lightly flour a baking tray and place the scones on it. Bake immediately for about 15 minutes. Cool on a wire rack. Eat within hours, or freeze.

Variations:

To bake a loaf: Shape the dough into a round. Place on the floured baking tray. Cut a deep cross with a sharp knife. Bake in the preheated oven for 20 minutes, then reduce the heat to 200C/400F/Gas 6 and continue to bake. It should take about 40 minutes in total. See p. 110 to check if it's done.

Different flavours:

Scallion: Add ½ bunch very finely chopped scallions to the mix before adding the buttermilk.
Herb: Add 3 tbsp chopped herbs to the mix before adding the buttermilk.
Richer: Place 1 beaten egg, or about 50 ml cream, in the measuring jug; add buttermilk to bring it up to 300 ml.
Nutty: Add 1–2 tbsp very finely chopped nuts, or toasted sesame seeds, or pinhead oatmeal to the mix before adding the buttermilk.

SOUR-SKONS

This crisp oaty scone from Orkney is just delicious: tangy and full-flavoured from the combination of buttermilk and bread soda, nutty from the oatflakes, crunchy on the outside, very tender within. Perfect with cheese as well as with morning marmalade.

MAKES 6 SCONES

175 g plain flour, plus extra for dusting

1 level tsp bread baking soda

1 level tsp (baking) powder

pinch salt

60 g small oatflakes

140 ml buttermilk (approx.)

Preheat the oven to 220C/425F/Gas 7. Sift flour, bread soda, baking powder and salt into a large bowl. Stir in the oatflakes and mix evenly. Stir while you pour in the buttermilk and mix to a soft but not sticky dough. Place on a well-floured baking tray. Pat quickly into a round, about 1 cm thick. With a knife, score it quite deeply into 6 wedges, like a shortbread round. Bake in the oven for about 20 minutes, or until golden brown. Place on a wire rack to cool for about 15 minutes. Best served warm.

quick breads

CORN BREAD

This is a wonderful brunch bread, an American classic which uses corn (maize) meal. It's soft and cake-like, with a warm savoury flavour and bright yellow colour, plus a lively little crunch from the cornmeal.

It's excellent with a good jam, but is also good with savoury things — in America it's traditionally eaten with chilli and other spicy stews.

MAKES 1 LOAF

25 g butter, plus extra for the tin
150 g plain flour
150 g cornmeal (maizemeal)
2 tbsp sugar
2½ tsp baking powder
½ tsp salt
2 eggs
225 ml milk

Turn the oven on to 200C/400F/Gas 6 and butter the inside of a large loaf tin (about 900 g–1 kg).

Melt the butter. In a large bowl, stir together the flour and cornmeal, sugar, baking powder and salt. Beat the eggs, then stir the milk and cooled butter into them. Make a dip in the middle of the dry ingredients, then pour in the wet ones. Mix as briefly as possible to a sloppy, almost pourable dough. Scrape it into the tin and bake it for about 35 minutes, until a toothpick slid into the centre of the loaf comes out clean. Serve very fresh.

Note: You can use coarse or fine cornmeal, maizemeal or polenta for this, but not maize *flour*, which is too finely ground, nor cornflour/cornstarch, which is something quite different.

Variations: Add one (or more) of the following:
2 tsp (or more) very finely chopped fresh red chilli
a few tbsp chopped fresh coriander
chopped scallions
3 tbsp tiny cubes firm, tasty cheese

ORANGE AND POPPY SEED MUFFINS

MAKES 16–24

50 g butter
sunflower oil for greasing the tins
375 g plain flour
2 tsp baking powder
1 tsp bread (baking) soda
½ tsp salt
150 g caster sugar
1 heaped tbsp poppy seeds
3 oranges
2 eggs
50–100 ml milk

Turn the oven on to 200C/400F/Gas 6. Melt the butter and set it aside to cool. Using kitchen paper, lightly grease two 12-muffin trays. Depending on their depth, the mix will make 16–24.
Sieve the flour, baking powder, bread (baking) soda and salt into a large bowl. Lightly stir in the sugar and poppy seeds. Grate the rind of the oranges, and squeeze the juice of 2 of them.
In a bowl, beat the eggs. Stir in the cooled melted butter, orange juice and rind and 50 ml milk. Make a dip in the flour, pour in the wet mix and stir quickly. Depending on how juicy the oranges were, you may need to add extra milk to make a soft but not floppy batter.

Spoon this into the muffin trays, filling them just ⅔ full. Bake for 20–25 minutes. Serve soon.

ORANGES AND LEMONS (AND LIMES)

Plenty of recipes in this book use the grated rind of citrus fruits. These fruits are sprayed with many, many chemicals during growing and before storage, to make them look perfect and to last forever in storage and in your fruit bowl. Choose organic fruits wherever possible when you're planning on cooking with the skins, and keep them in the fridge or use them quickly; you'll find they go mouldy otherwise.

yeast bread

Yeast? It has a bit of a reputation. It's allegedly delicate, moody, time-consuming, hard work and fearful of draughts.

It does sound awful, but I think it all rather misses the point. Yeast is one of the world's great survivors. You can compress it, dry it, chill it and freeze it. You can bash it about and give it a very hard time indeed. And yet all it needs is a hint of cosseting, and this incredible single-celled fungus bounds into action. It begins a frenzy of feeding (it gobbles carbohydrates), burping (it expels carbon dioxide which rises the bread or, indeed, puts the bubbles in champagne), and reproduction (when warm and well-fed it reproduces rampantly). A teaspoon of yeast contains billions of cells, all of them frantically getting up to all that stuff in your bread dough. Wears you out just thinking about it.

So yes, making things with yeast is very, very hard work indeed — but you're not the one working. Your input is 10 minutes' kneading (or 3 with a machine), when you turn a wet sticky mess of a dough into a silken springy ball.

The yeast does the rest.

BAKING BREAD

The flour

To bake yeast bread, you must use *strong* flour for a good rise. Strong flour has a high protein content. When kneaded with water, it forms a stretchy substance called gluten, which is what gives yeast dough its springy, chewy bounce, as opposed to the tender, cake-like crumb of a bread made with a 'soft' flour and lifted with baking powder or bread soda.

— White flour rises better. The bran in brown interferes with gluten's bounce.

— My favourite bread-baking flour is Dove's Farm organic strong white flour (available in many health food shops). Many bakers cite Odlums strong white as a good flour.

The yeast

Yeast comes three ways nowadays.

— **Fresh** is hard to find, but is preferred by most bakers for flavour. Beg some from your local bakery; it freezes well. Older recipes may refer to fresh yeast as 'compressed'. To use fresh yeast, you must dissolve (or 'cream') it in a little warm water to get it going. A pinch of sugar helps.

There are two kinds of **dried yeast:**

— **Plain dried yeast** (usually in little tins) must also be dissolved in warm water to get it going. Wait till it's slightly bubbly to check it's active, and then use it just as fresh yeast.

— **Fast-action yeasts** (usually in sachets) have almost completely taken over on shop shelves. They include 'improvers' to speed up the action of the yeast, so you can add the yeast directly to the dry ingredients, and even make bread with just one rising. This does make for slightly faster bread, which is trumpeted as a great advantage, but the texture and flavour of one-rising breads are usually inferior.

However, contrary to what many books say, you *can* use fast-action yeasts in ordinary yeast bread recipes where the dough is risen twice, and even in more complex recipes which involve an initial 'sponge' dough, or yeast-based 'starters'. Just follow the recipe, omitting the first dissolving of yeast in water.

— *If substituting in a recipe, use half the weight of either of the dried yeasts to fresh yeast.*
— *Watch the 'best before' dates; dried yeasts last a long time, but not forever.*

The temperature

Yeast does grow quickest at around 34 °C. But it doesn't have to be somewhere hot to rise; it rises perfectly well at the temperature of a cool room, and in fact I much prefer the flavour and texture of breads when the dough hasn't risen too quickly. A yeast dough will even rise overnight in the fridge. In fact, the biggest danger with yeast is killing it by letting it get too hot.

I think this may be where many of us got into trouble with our first yeasty endeavours. Having been told that yeast needs warmth, we thought that warmer would be better, and killed the yeast with too-hot water, or too hot a rising place. Which is why...

The water

When adding water, make sure it's not too hot. Always stick your finger in it first to check it's on the cool side of lukewarm — you

yeast bread

should barely feel it. One part just-boiled water from the kettle to two parts from the cold tap usually gets it right.

The mixing

Roll up your sleeves, and take off your watch and rings before starting. When mixing in water to make the dough, err a little on the sticky side. It's much, much easier to knead extra flour into a wet, sticky dough than it is to try squelching water into a tough, dry dough.

The kneading

This is your 10-minute upper-body-workout. If you don't feel slightly out of breath, you didn't knead hard enough!

Lightly flour the kitchen table. (A work surface is usually too high.) Plonk the slightly sticky dough on it. Rub off the bits stuck on your fingers, but only add them to the dough if they're very soft — no crusty bits! Pick up the far end of the ball of dough and fold it back towards you with both hands, then press down hard with the heels of both hands, pushing the dough away from you and stretching it along the table. Turn it a quarter turn, then repeat the action. You will build up speed and a satisfying rhythm. Lean into the dough with the full weight of your body from your hips.

—10 minutes is usually right for hand-kneading. Keep an eye on the clock; it's always longer than you think.

— You can knead with the dough hook of a mixer or even the blade of a food processor. When using machines, be careful not to over-knead: 2–5 minutes is enough.

— If you are taken away from kneading the dough, cover it with cling film or a tea towel so it doesn't form a crust.

When is it kneaded enough?

After a while, the dough suddenly feels different — slightly bouncy and silky, memorably described by that great Californian chef Alice Waters as feeling like your 'relaxed inner thigh'. And it should be just as silken as an inner thigh to stroke! Keep going for another couple of minutes after that stage.

Rather more orthodox tests usually advise poking the dough with your finger. It should spring back and start to fill in the hole quite smartly (though the dent won't disappear completely).

The rising (or 'proving')

To rise bread dough, rub the inside of a very large bowl with 1 tsp oil, then turn the dough ball in this, then cover the bowl with clingfilm.

Where to put it? Just about anywhere. It would probably rise on your back doorstep with a stiff breeze blowing, as long as it was well covered. You can rise dough overnight in the fridge if you want fresh bread from the oven for brunch in the morning.

I usually leave the bowl on the kitchen table. This produces a gentle, even rise.

— Rising times are guides only. Allow dough to rise until it's about 1½ times or twice its original size. If it goes over twice its size it's in danger of over-rising.

— If you suddenly remember you've got to go out while the bread is rising, put it in the fridge. This slows it down for several hours.

'Knocking back'

This means punching the spongy, light, risen dough down. It is then kneaded very briefly, and shaped to rise a second time until it's ready for the oven.

The oven

Must be hot, so preheat it properly.

And is it done?

Unfortunately the heavenly, homely, torturing smell of bread is no guide. Tap the base of the loaf and it should sound hollow. Honest. An underdone loaf, with stodgy dough inside, sounds dead; when the loaf is airy inside, the sound resonates a little.

MORE IS NOT BETTER.

Being accurate with baking recipes is important. More yeast will just give your bread an excessively yeasty flavour. More heat will, as we've seen, kill the yeast. And more of a rise doesn't result in lighter bread, it just courts the danger of a collapsed loaf.

focaccia, pizza

FOCACCIA, PIZZA AND A LOAF OF BREAD

So now to the baking.

You'd think I might suggest you start off with a basic loaf of bread. Nope. In my experience, simple, basic loaves of bread are not the easiest for beginners to master, especially if you can't get hold of fresh yeast for the best flavour. Getting a really good result, with great texture and a good rise, does take a little practice, and if you're going to all that trouble, you do want to end up with something which tastes significantly better than a reasonable shop-bought loaf. So I reckon flat yeast breads are the place to start, and I have chosen two: focaccia and pizza.

However, you can also use this dough to bake a tasty loaf of bread if you'd like to give it a go.

The basic dough

This dough makes enough for 2 focacce, or about 8 individual pizzas, or 2 loaves of bread. It uses a little bit of rye for texture, but you can use all white flour if you prefer. Extra dough can, of course, be frozen for another day.

600 g strong white flour, plus extra for dusting
50 g rye flour (or use all strong white)
1 tsp caster sugar
1 x 7 g sachet fast-action yeast
2 tsp salt
400–450 ml lukewarm water
2 tbsp olive oil, plus a little extra

Take off your rings and roll up your sleeves. Mix all the dry ingredients in a very large bowl with your hands. Pour in the water and oil, and stir it to a moist, tender, slightly sticky dough. If you're not too sure, err on the side of

wetness. It's easy to knead in extra flour, and it's very difficult to incorporate water.

On a lightly floured table or worktop, knead energetically for 10 minutes, until the dough ball is silky and elastic, adding only as much extra flour as is absolutely necessary to work it — the moister the dough, the lighter and crisper the pizza or focaccia will be.

Clean out the bowl. Rub the ball of dough in a little extra olive oil and put it in the bowl. Cover the bowl with clingfilm and leave the dough to rise to 1½ times or twice its bulk. It will take 1 hour in a warm place, about 2 at room temperature, overnight in the fridge.

FOCACCIA

Focaccia is one yeast bread that's really worth going to the trouble to bake yourself, even if you're lucky enough to be able to buy good yeast breads. This salty, crusty, herby, olive-oil-fragrant Italian flat bread is easy to bake, hard to come by, and ridiculously expensive when you do find it. And it tastes so much better when extra-fresh (although it responds well to toasting too).
— The dough above makes enough for 2 focacce, and each provides enough bread for 4–8 people, so I generally use half the dough to bake one focaccia. I freeze the other half of the dough for another day, or divide it into four portions for pizzas and freeze those.

focaccia, pizza

FOR ONE LARGE FOCACCIA

1–2 tsp chopped fresh rosemary or sage

half–1 tsp Maldon salt or not-too-coarse sea salt

1–2 tbsp olive oil

When the basic dough (p. 115) has risen, peel it out of the bowl and knead it briefly to redistribute the air pockets. Divide it in two. Leave it to rest, covered with a tea towel, for 10 minutes. Then roll one half of the dough out to a large circle, about 26–8 cm across (or the size of your baking tray), and put it on a lightly oiled baking tray. Cover with a tea towel and leave for half an hour to rise just a little. Preheat the oven to 200C/400F/Gas 6.

(Freeze the other half, or prepare it for baking as well, or keep it tightly-wrapped in the fridge for a day or two.)

Finally, push deep dimples all over the risen dough with your fingers. Scatter with the rosemary or sage, salt and olive oil. Put it in the fully heated oven until crusty and golden, about half an hour.

Focaccia: variations

● After punching down the risen basic dough, divide it in two. Knead in 2 tsp chopped rosemary, sage or thyme to each half, then rest, covered with a tea towel for 10 minutes, roll out and proceed as described above.

● Or knead in a small handful of roughly-chopped green or black olives to each half of the dough.

PIZZA

As for pizza — it certainly is worth making it at home, no matter how many zillions are available in supermarket freezer cabinets, because your own pizza will taste much better.

Your dough will explode into life as it hits the hot baking tray, and make a bubbly, crispy, chewy, base, full of life and flavour. You'll have the wonderful aroma of fresh-baked bread in the kitchen. And everyone will have such fun creating their own toppings — with fresh ingredients, and no modified starch in the sauce giving your dinner that weird gloopy texture and processed-food flavour.

Make and rise the basic dough above on p. 115.

The oven

It must be fully heated to its maximum, as close to 250C/500F/Gas 9 as you can get it. If it goes higher, so much the better. You will need flat baking trays — no rims, so you can slide the pizza straight onto the hot tray. *The trays (very important) must preheat with the oven.*

Pizza baking stones or unglazed quarry tiles can do a good job of baking pizza. Heat them with the oven.

If you have a Stanley or an Aga, lucky you: you can bake the pizza directly on the oven floor, just like in a wood-burning oven.

The toppings

Just remember this: real pizzas are light on toppings, so as not to drown out that tasty base. The bread's the thing! Keep the toppings simple, or they'll overwhelm the thin bread and squash it wet and flat.

Tomatoes: No need to cook them, nor even to peel, de-seed or chop. Use tinned chopped tomatoes; drain them well in a sieve set over a bowl, then tip them into another bowl, season them with salt and pepper and stir in a few tablespoons of olive oil for a shot of flavour.

A LOAF OF BREAD

You can also use this dough to bake 2 simple loaves of bread. Just divide the dough in two after punching down, shape into 2 fat sausages and tuck them into two 1 kg loaf tins (approx 21 x 11 x 6 cm) which have been lightly oiled. Cover loosely with cling film and rise for about an hour, or until the dough's a few centimetres above the tins. Put the bread in a preheated 230C/450F/Gas 8 oven, and immediately turn the heat down to 200C/400F/Gas 6. Bake for 45–50 minutes, or until done.

Of course you can also knead herbs or olives into this dough (try the proportions described above for the focaccia) and then bake the loaves.

— If you get the yeast bread baking bug, check the bibliography at the back of the book for those baking books which I have found really useful.

— If you're on the look-out for recipes, here's a tip: be suspicious of yeast bread recipes which promise quick results. Good flavour in most yeast breads comes with time. Yeast doughs are like fruits: they ripen. The slower the rising, and the longer the process, the better the flavour and texture of the finished bread.

If you want great flavours, search out recipes which use sponge doughs, starters and which keep back a portion of the dough for the next baking. Those methods take more time, yes. But they are the ones which will make it worth it, with results which are truly worth savouring.

Cheese: If you're using mozzarella, try a real mozzarella, the ones that come swimming in a little bag of water. Brick-like Irish or Danish 'mozzarella' is stretchy, but it's also pretty heavy, gummy and tasteless.

Mind you, there's no law that says that because it's pizza, it has to be mozzarella. Many other softer cheeses are superb — in fact, you'll get more flavour from them. See the Milleens pizza below for inspiration. I also like to use mature Ardrahan, Durrus and Gubbeen.

Other flavours: keep it simple. A little chopped rosemary or sage. A scattering of pungent olives. Thin slivers of red onion. A smear of pesto. A few slices of spicy sausage. And so on...

Remember: the bread's the thing.

Assembling and baking the pizza

The pizza will take only 5–10 minutes to cook. Have everything ready, and toppings at room temperature. Be sure the oven is fully preheated, with the tray (or stone, or tiles) fully heated too.

Flour your work surface.

Peel the risen dough out of the bowl and knead it very briefly. Divide the dough into 8 small, fist-sized balls (each should weigh about 140 g to serve one person). Cover 7 with a tea towel. Roll one until it's about 20 cm wide and very thin (less than ½ cm high). Flour the removable base of a large round tart tin (or another flat baking tray) generously. You'll assemble the pizza on this, then slide it into the oven from this, and some of the pizza's flavour will come from the flour which will stick to the base of the dough and char in the oven.

Put the dough circle on the floured tin base or tray. Quickly scatter toppings over the dough with a very light hand — you should still be able to see the dough through them. Add a little splash of olive oil and flick the pizza straight into the oven, onto the preheated baking tray. Bake for 5–10 minutes.

If you find your oven is slow (needing 15–20 minutes to cook the pizzas), then roll the dough a little less thinly, or the base will be too crispy.

To serve it...

If you have some super-duper extra virgin single estate olive oil, now's the time to flourish it: sprinkle it onto the finished pizza and smell that rising fragrance. A little fresh basil or some dried chilli flakes are also good.

Baking more than one pizza

Most of the time you'll be baking more than one pizza. To do this:
— have a baking tray heating up in the oven on every oven shelf — the intense heat from it is important in cooking the pizza's base
— move the pizzas round as you bake; each one needs a blast at the top of the oven for maximum heat. Best to start them at the top, then move down later
— work quickly so you don't lose too much heat from the oven when the door's open.

PIZZA IDEAS...
Mozzarella and chilli

Scatter a few squares of tomato, prepared as described above, on the base. Add 3–5 slices mozzarella and chopped fresh red chilli to taste.

Cured ham and rocket

Bake the pizza 'white', with just some olive oil (and perhaps a little garlic and/or mozzarella if you like). When it's done, top it with thinly sliced Parma or Serrano ham. The heat just warms them slightly. Finish with whole leaves of tender rocket and a flourish of olive oil.

Milleens and marjoram

This inspired idea comes from Ireland's (now sadly retired) pizza wonderwoman, Bernadette O'Shea. You'll find it and many more besides in her book, *Pizza Defined*.

PER PERSON
1 ball pizza dough (about 140 g, one-eighth the above dough)
85 g soft sun-dried tomatoes preserved in oil, cut into slivers
85 g cream cheese
85 g Milleens, very finely sliced (remove the rind if you prefer)
fresh marjoram leaves

Roll or stretch the dough to a 20-cm circle. Brush it with oil from the sun-dried tomatoes. Scatter the sun-dried tomato slivers over the base, then dot it with cream cheese. Arrange the Milleens slices over the pizza. Bake on a preheated baking tray in the preheated oven (see the method described above) for 10 minutes or until done, then scatter with the fresh herbs and a little extra oil from the tomatoes (or extra virgin olive oil).

LEFTOVER DOUGH?

— Wrap it tightly in cling film (so no crust can form) and put it in the fridge. It will keep for 2–3 days and provide instant pizzas.
— Or freeze it in pizza-sized dough portions.
— Or make a little ciabatta: shape the dough into that characteristic low-slung loaf, allow it to rise again, then bake in a moderate oven for 15–20 minutes.

shortcrust pastry...

Pastry. The very word is enough to bring otherwise confident cooks out in a panicky sweat. Which, of course, is the last thing you want. With pastry, coolness and deftness is everything. Hot sticky fingers just won't do.

I know all about this because I am no natural when it comes to pastry. For years, my pastry was tough and my tarts' bottoms were soggy. I was unsure, and I found recipes unhelpful: when did the mix look like 'breadcrumbs'? What's 'enough' water? What's baking 'blind'? Still, achieving crumbly, buttery, delectable pastry for pies and tarts is a doddle once you know a few tricks. Here are mine.

- **Use a food processor**. It's quicker and colder than your hands will ever be.
- **Use butter**. It tastes better.
- **Use as little liquid as possible**. The pastry should not even feel damp — just cool. If your cooked pastry's tough, you probably used too much liquid.
- **Don't touch!** Handle pastry as little as possible. With bread dough, you want to develop the stringy, stretchy, elastic gluten in the flour. Here, the opposite applies. In addition, you want to keep it cool.

and a few tarts

- **When baking filled tarts, use a metal tin with a removable base.** Metal, because it conducts heat best. Removable base, because if the pastry stays in a container as it cools, the steam will make it soggy. (Removable-base tins aren't expensive and can be found at specialist kitchen shops.)
- **Don't be tempted to skip the bit in the recipe about baking blind.** It stops pastry going soggy, so it's worth it.

MAKING THE PASTRY

This step-by-step method is for any pastry recipe on the following pages.

1. **Cut in the butter**
   Scoop the flour and any other dry ingredients into the processor; whizz to mix them. Cut the cold butter into small cubes, add them to the flour, and whizz again until the mix looks like large rough oatflakes, just 6–10 seconds.

   (*By hand:* Sift dry ingredients into a bowl. Add tiny cubes of cold butter. Rub in with your fingertips as quickly as possible.)

2. **Add the liquid**
   Remember . . . you always need less than you think. With the processor blade running, pour in the egg yolk. As soon as the sound changes from whirring to a rumble, stop. The mix now looks sticky but has not yet formed a ball.

   (*By hand:* Mix the egg yolk in with a fork to the same stage: sticky, but not stuck.)

3. **Finish the pastry**
   Tip all the bits from the food processor onto the counter and give them 2 quick kneads so they cohere. If they really don't form a ball at this stage, just flick some cold water on with your fingers. But generally the warmth of your hand softening the butter will make the pastry come together.

4. **Wrap and rest**
   Form the pastry into a thick flat disc. Make it an even circle — it'll be easier to roll evenly later. Wrap it in cling film and rest it in the coldest part of the fridge for at least half an hour, or as long as suits.

5. **While there's mess everywhere . . .**
   Make another batch of pastry and keep it in the freezer for next time.

6. **Roll it out**
   After emerging from the fridge, the pastry needs to warm up a little at room temperature to become pliable. But then work quickly, or it will go floppy and oily. Touch it as little as possible. If it's too hard, whack it with the rolling pin. And don't panic if it cracks as you roll: just press the bits together again.

7. **Get the pastry into the tin**
   Advice is usually to fold the pastry, or roll it round a rolling pin. However, if you've worked quickly, the pastry will still be stiff and will probably crack. I just pick it up and lay it in the centre of the tin. Press it into the bottom edge quickly and firmly. Let the pastry peek a few millimetres above the rim to allow for shrinkage. You can crimp it with your fingers, or just neaten the edge with a sharp knife. There's no need at all to grease the tin.
   Tip: Keep the ball of trimmings . . .

8. **Bake blind (pre-baking the pastry)**
   Preheat the oven to 190C/375F/Gas 5. You now want to pre-bake the tart shell 'blind' (without its filling) to crisp it. Here's how:
   — Preheat a *heavy baking tray* in the oven to sit the tin on: it helps to cook the base.
   — Prick the pastry all over with a fork.
   — Use a few squares of *kitchen paper*, overlapping, to cover all the pastry. (Yes! Just ordinary kitchen paper. It won't burn. Foil or greaseproof are usually recommended, but my experience is that they often stick to the pastry. Alternatively, use non-stick baking parchment.)
   — Pour in enough *dried beans*, any kind (black beans, chickpeas, lentils, anything), to fill the tin. Bake the tart shell for 20 minutes. The beans stop the pastry from rising.

9. **The anti-soggy-bottom barrier**
   This extra step is really worth doing. Take the pastry shell out of the oven. Spoon out the beans (save them for next time you're pre-baking, they'll keep for ever — you can't boil them now). Lift off the kitchen paper squares. Brush the hot pastry liberally with the egg white left over from making the pastry, then put the shell back in the oven for another 10 minutes. No beans this time. The egg white forms a hard barrier between pastry and filling.

10. **Bake the tart**

This is unorthodox, but before you add the filling, take a look at the pastry shell. If it has any cracks, the filling will trickle out and burn in the oven. So patch it up now, with the saved pastry trimmings . . .

Tip: Don't fill the shell to the very top. The aroma of escaped filling burning on the oven floor will not enhance the tart. Fill it nearly full, and spoon in any extra once the tart has started to set, about 10 minutes into baking time.

FRESH HERB AND GOATS' CHEESE TART WITH A PECORINO CRUST

A tender tart with two cheeses for light lunching or an elegant starter. Use another very well-flavoured, very well-aged cheese (such as Gabriel or Desmond) if you can't get Pecorino.

SERVES ABOUT 6

Prepare and bake blind a 26 cm pastry shell with:

200 g plain flour, plus extra for dusting

80 g cold butter, diced

30 g finely grated Pecorino

1 egg yolk (keep the white for baking blind)

2–3 tbsp cold water

Filling

3 tbsp chopped fresh parsley

2 tbsp chopped fresh chives

1 tsp chopped fresh marjoram

50 g crumbled soft goats' cheese

4 eggs

400 ml cream

salt and pepper

a scrape of nutmeg

Make the pastry the usual way, stirring the grated Pecorino into the flour once you have cut or rubbed in the butter. Bake it blind at 190C/375F/Gas 5, not forgetting the anti-soggy-bottom barrier.

Scatter the herbs and cheese over the base of the tart. Whisk the eggs, cream and seasonings together and pour them in too. Bake in the oven (at the same temperature) for about 25 minutes, or until just set but still wobbly in the centre. Delicious warm or at room temperature. Serve it with crisp salad and several glasses of dry white wine.

CLASSIC QUICHE

A real quiche is a delicate, subtle thing — so abused that perhaps we ought to hide it under another name and call it Alsace tart instead.

SERVES 6

Prepare and bake blind a 26 cm pastry shell with:

200 g plain flour, plus extra for dusting

pinch salt

100 g cold butter

1 egg yolk (save the white for baking blind)

1–2 tbsp cold water

Filling

6 streaky bacon rashers

5 eggs

450 ml cream

pepper

freshly grated nutmeg

Bake the pastry blind at 190C/375F/Gas 5, not forgetting the anti-soggy-bottom barrier, then leave the oven at that temperature. Fry the rashers to crisp them a little, then cut them into shreds. Lay them on the baked pastry shell. Whisk together the eggs, cream,

pepper and a generous grating of nutmeg. Pour this into the shell and bake for about half an hour until the custard is just set, but still very tender and wobbly in the centre. Eat while warm, with salad and lots of white wine.

APPLE TART WITH TREMBLING CUSTARD

This has a vanilla-scented, just-set, custardy filling cosseting the fruit.

SERVES 6–8

Pastry

200 g plain flour, plus extra for dusting

1 heaped tbsp icing sugar

pinch salt

100 g cold butter

1 egg yolk (save the white for baking blind)

1–2 tbsp cold water

Filling

500 g tart dessert apples, such as Granny Smith or Braeburn

2 tbsp lemon juice

3 large free-range eggs

1 tsp real vanilla extract (or a few drops essence, or indeed the scraped seeds of a pod if you're feeling extravagant)

100 g sugar

125 ml cream

Make the pastry as usual and put it in the fridge.

Put a baking tray on a rack in the centre of the oven and turn the heat on to 200C/400F/Gas 6. Peel the apples, quarter them and core them, then slice them quite thickly and toss in a bowl with the lemon juice.

Roll out the pastry, line a 26 cm removable-base tart tin with it and prick it all over with a fork. Brush with

and a few tarts

the egg white, then lay the apple slices on the pastry, in a few concentric circles. Bake for half an hour on the baking tray in the hot oven. In a large bowl, whisk the eggs until quite light, then whisk in the vanilla, sugar and cream. Open the oven door. Slide the tray with the tart on it out towards you. Pour the egg mixture into the tart case slowly, whisking the mix again to get all the sugar into the tart. Slowly slide the tart back into the oven. Cook for another 30 minutes or so — until the custard is set at the rim and wobbly in the centre (it will continue to cook after coming out). It's heavenly served warm and it doesn't need any more cream.

CHOCOLATE TART

This, as far as I'm concerned, is irresistible. Theoretically, it can serve 6–8, but that's very theoretical.

Prepare and bake blind a 26 cm tart shell with:

175 g plain flour, plus extra for dusting

1 heaped tbsp icing sugar, plus extra for dusting

pinch salt

130 g cold butter

1 egg yolk (save the white for baking blind)

Filling

200 g plain chocolate (preferably 70% cocoa solids)

125 g unsalted butter

2 whole eggs and 3 yolks

40 g sugar

Bake the pastry blind at 190C/375F/Gas 5, not forgetting the anti-soggy-bottom barrier, then turn the oven down to 180C/350F/Gas 4.

Melt the butter in a small, heavy-based pan over a low heat. As it's melting, add the chocolate in small pieces, stirring constantly. Do all this carefully so the chocolate doesn't seize. Set the mix aside to cool.

In a large bowl, whisk the eggs and the yolks with the sugar until they're thick and creamy (5 minutes with an electric whisk). Gently stir in the cooled chocolate mix. Pour it into the pastry case. Bake for 15 minutes, or until barely set.

Serve dusted with a little icing sugar, and with very strong coffee.

TARTE TATIN

A French classic, this upside-down apple tart is sticky with buttery juices.

You need a piece of special equipment: a frying pan with an ovenproof (or removable) handle, 21 cm at the base. If you're thinking of buying a pan, look out for one of these, since they're so useful for savoury sautés and other dishes finished in the oven.

Pastry

120 g plain flour, plus extra for dusting

2 tbsp caster sugar

65 g cold butter

1 egg yolk

about 1 tbsp cold water

Filling

about 7 largeish eating apples, quite green and sharp (Braeburn or Granny Smith are good)

juice of ½ lemon

90 g butter

90 g caster sugar

1 tbsp dark muscovado sugar

Make the pastry in the usual way, wrap and leave in the fridge to rest.

Turn the oven on to 220C/425 F/Gas 7. Prepare the filling: peel, quarter and core the apples, dropping them into a large bowl and turning them in the lemon juice.

On the hob, melt the butter in the frying pan, then take it off the heat. Mix the two sugars well and strew evenly over the butter. Pack the apple quarters into the pan, standing them on their sides. (They will be very tight but will ease as they soften.) Put the pan in the hot oven for 10 minutes. Take it out, tip it and baste the apples with the melted butter using a teaspoon; put it back in for 5 minutes. Take it out again. The apples will be glistening gold, the buttery caramel bubbling up high. Cool for 5–10 minutes. The apples will be swimming in buttery ooze. Mmm.

Roll out the pastry just a fraction larger than the apples. Drape it over them. Use a round-bladed knife to tuck it in all around them. It may well crack and break somewhere, in which case just patch it up again. Put the pan in the oven for 20–25 minutes, until the pastry looks golden and cooked.

Leave the tart to cool for about 10 minutes before turning it out. Lay a serving plate on the pan, then put on thick oven gloves. Grasp both pan and plate firmly with both hands and flip them over with one quick movement. Lift the pan off and admire the dark gold, even apple quarters, the biscuity pastry, the oozing caramel soaking into it. And if bits have stuck to the pan, not to worry: just take them out and patch the tart up again.

This tart is very good served with crème fraîche.

fruit salad

I still remember the prickle of shock I felt the first time I was served an orange for dessert. It was in Andalusia, and the menu had said 'naranja'. I assumed that this meant an artful, elegant Spanish orange creation. In a way I was right. What arrived was an orange. A big orange, but just an orange all the same, a whole orange, in its skin, rolling slowly around and around on the plate.

Disappointed, I took up the sharp little dessert knife and started to peel, looking enviously at the 'flan' (crème caramel) everyone else was tucking into. As my knife cut into the fruit, a shower of

bitter-sweet orange oil filled the air and landed on my fingers. I separated the orange segments, bit into their juicy cold sweetness, and felt refreshed. It was a wonderful way to end a meal.

You wouldn't get away with it here, mind you, no matter how large and fine the orange, or how elegant the knife. For a family dinner, sure; but an unpeeled orange in a restaurant, or even for guests at home? Unthinkable.

So many of our dealings with food, when we are serving it to others, involve unacknowledged but profound notions of respect.

(These are incredibly subtle and can be hard to decode. An unpeeled orange for dessert just won't do, but a simple bunch of grapes would be fine. How about an unpeeled banana? The very idea would make you giggle.) In general, respect in our culture means you need to peel the fruit for your guests.

Which brings me to the subject of fruit salad. Where fruit salad is concerned, less is very definitely more. This can be a little hard to adjust to, for those of us who grew up with fruit salad as a kind of fresh tinned fruit cocktail. The immutable trio — apple, orange and banana — all bobbed in a tasteless sugar syrup. For special occasions a few strawberries or — in later years — some kiwi might have been sliced in. By the time you got around to eating, the bananas were furry, and the hard little chunks of apple had probably gone slightly brown.

I think the very best fruit salads are those which approach the bold simplicity of that single Spanish orange, rolling around on the plate. They don't drown everything in a confusing babel of conflicting flavours and clashing colours. They're made with fruit that's ripe enough, sweet enough, juicy enough not to need lashings of sugar and water to make it palatable. The best fruit salads feel luxurious and taste exciting and refreshing. Here are some ways to go about that.

Buy ripe fruit
This may sound ridiculously basic, but if the dessert is going to be fruit, hunt for the best. Start with one glorious, ripe fruit. It might be a fragrant, succulent melon, a large punnet of aromatic strawberries, some meltingly soft peaches. It might even be a fantastic, juicy orange. In fact oranges are the best fall-back of all, especially in winter, when other fruit is unavailable or disappointing.

Think colour
A fruit salad must look beautiful. Colours which go well together are essential. For really elegant restraint, stick to just two colours. The pale lime tones of green melon flesh plus purple globes of grapes look fantastic yet subtle

together. Add another colour and the effect may be spoiled.

Think texture
Melting, juicy softness is what you're after. Apples, pears and bananas just don't work. If you want to use apples or pears, poach them first in one of the flavoured syrups below. I'd save the banana for my cornflakes.

Oranges (and lemons)
These are the most useful fruit. Not just because oranges make a stunning fruit salad dessert all on their own, but because they bring out the best in other fruits too. Orange, lemon and lime juice in various combinations makes the perfect fruit salad dressing, with just a little sprinkling of caster sugar — no syrup necessary. It's light and it's refreshing.

Taste it
Don't ever blindly follow a recipe for fruit salad. Every fruit has a different sugar level and is a different size. Before you make the salad, taste the fruit. Is the pineapple disappointingly sour? Are the peaches harder than you thought? Time to poach them gently.

Mind the chopping board!
Be sure it's exceptionally well scrubbed. The lingering aroma of onion or garlic is not really a desirable addition to a bowl of fresh fruit flavours.

Flavoured syrups
These are wonderful for poaching hard or underripe fruit, or for flavouring some fruit salads. For fruit salad for 4, **400 ml water** and **100 g sugar** is right. Then add

the **juice of half a lemon** plus **3 sweet geranium** (pelargonium) leaves, OR **2** bashed and bruised stalks of **lemon grass**. Simmer for 5 minutes. The resulting syrup is delightfully fragrant. Strain it, then use it to dress the prepared fruit, or to poach apple or pear slices, or that disappointing pineapple.

Some favourites
The real fun with fruit salads is dreaming up your own creations with whatever's seasonal.

Oranges
These are the year-round stars of the show. A simple plate of sliced or segmented oranges does make a delightful dessert, now that you've peeled them!

- **Moroccan orange salad:** Sieve a little icing sugar (golden, preferably) over orange slices or segments, allowing 1 large or 2 small oranges per person. Dust with a *tiny* puff of cinnamon and chill. Just before serving, add a few drops of rose water or orange flower water and a little grated orange zest.
- **Orange salad with strawberries:** Add a punnet of sliced strawberries to the fruit above.

TO SEGMENT ORANGES

Peel them, removing every trace of white pith, catching juices as you do. Cradle the peeled orange in your left hand. With a small knife, cut out each segment from the membrane on each side. With a little practice, this is a quick job: the knife slides down inside the membrane, then your wrist turns to flick the segment out.

ruit salad

- **Boozy orange salad:** Segment or slice oranges, and dress with extra orange juice and a little sugar. Add a few tbsp brandy, Cointreau or Grand Marnier to taste. Chill well before serving.

MELON

Melon is wonderful as a fruit salad all on its own. Dress it with freshly squeezed orange and lime juice, or orange and lemon. Cut bite-sized chunks, or treat yourself to a melon-baller.

Two-tone Melon
SERVES 4–6

1 ripe green-fleshed melon
1 ripe orange-fleshed melon
juice of 1–2 oranges
1–2 limes

Scoop the melon flesh with a melon-baller or cut it into cubes. Dress with the orange and lime juice to taste.

Melon and Grapes
SERVES 4

1 ripe green-fleshed melon
a bunch of black grapes (or mixed black and green grapes)
juice of 1–2 oranges

Scoop the melon flesh with a melon-baller or cut it into cubes. Halve the grapes, and flick out the seeds if they're not seedless. Dress with orange juice, and sugar if necessary.

Melon and Berries
SERVES 4–6

1 ripe green-fleshed melon with a punnet of blueberries
or
1 ripe orange-fleshed melon with a punnet of raspberries

Dress just with a little squirt of lemon juice and some sugar.

Melon and Cardamom Cream

The subtle scent of cardamom mingles with the melon's perfume.

SERVES 4

3 cardamom pods
100 ml cream
1 tbsp icing sugar
1 ripe green-fleshed melon

Crush the cardamom pods with pestle and mortar (or any heavy object!) to open them, then crush the black seeds to a powder. Stir them into the cream with the sugar and place in the fridge to infuse for several hours. Place the melon in the fridge to chill as well.

Just before serving, cut the melon into quarters, remove the seeds and cut the flesh from the skin. Slice each quarter of flesh into thin slices. Fan these out on plates. Pour the cream over them in a thin stream through a little sieve. Serve.

Melon, Lychee and Lime Salad

Here's one dish where tinned lychees are fine.

SERVES 4

1 ripe green-fleshed melon
1 tin lychees, drained
1–2 limes
mint sprigs to decorate (optional)

If you have a melon-baller, scoop the flesh from the melon; otherwise cut it out and chop it into small chunks. Halve the lychees and put them in a bowl with the melon. Add enough lime juice to freshen the flavour of the mix without making it too acidic; this depends on the melon and on your own taste buds. Chill before serving. Decorate with mint sprigs.

PINEAPPLE

Pineapple and Mango Salad with Lemon Grass Syrup

SERVES 4–6

1 small ripe pineapple
1–2 ripe mangoes
lemon grass syrup (see p. 123)

Cut the flesh from the fruit (don't forget to core the pineapple and cut out all the little 'eyes'). Cover with the syrup and chill well before serving.

Pineapple also goes well with **strawberries**: dress with orange juice and sugar.

MIXED CITRUS SALAD

Use segments of as many different citrus fruits as you can find: orange, ruby grapefruit, ugli fruit, pomelo and more. Dress with orange and lime juice and a scattering of mint.

DISAPPOINTING STRAWBERRIES MADE BETTER . . .

To improve disappointing strawberries, slice them into freshly squeezed orange juice with a little sugar and serve as a strawberry fruit salad.

PEACHES IN WINE

Slice a peeled peach, or an unpeeled nectarine (1 per person) into red wine or a fruity white (1 glass per person). The fruit must be meltingly soft. Stir in sugar to taste.

SUMMER BERRY SALAD

Take a mix of best summer berries and redcurrants. Dress simply with lemon juice and a scattering of sugar. Alternatively, try a few tbsp of maraschino. Chill and allow the flavours to develop.

chocolate

It takes a stern soul to resist the lure of chocolate. Perhaps you dream of the tickle on your tongue as you suck on the crisp, malty-combed core of a Malteser. Maybe your downfall is those little caramel wisps which float out after each sweet-layered bite of a Mars bar. Perhaps you're more of a purist, and you long for the bitter shock of something austere and very dark, late at night. Whatever yours is, nearly everyone has a Chocolate Weak Point.

And there are certainly plenty of times when the perfect match for the CWP would be a Malteser or three at the end of a meal, or a square of the dark stuff with your coffee. No chocophile would complain. But there are also times when something a little more formal is called for, so here are some favourites.

If you're going to cook with chocolate there are two things to bear in mind.

Look for the percentage

Somewhere on the wrapper there will be a declaration of the percentage of cocoa solids in the chocolate. The higher the number, the 'darker' it is and the more intense its flavour. Since you'll be mixing chocolate with lots of other things when cooking, you need to use one with a high cocoa solids level if your final dessert is to have a pronounced chocolate flavour.

When cooking, look for chocolate with at least 50% cocoa solids. I prefer somewhere between 60% and 70%, but that's a personal matter. (A Cadbury's Bournville

bar, that stalwart of so many childhood chocolate mousses, has only 34%; if you look for something with a higher percentage, you'll get more flavour and a better result.) Avoid so-called cooking 'chocolate'; it's artificially chocolate-flavoured vegetable fat. It has neither the true melting qualities nor the flavour of real chocolate.

Melt with care!

Chocolate is strange stuff. If it overheats, it will be ruined, so melt it carefully. These are the rules:

- Break or chop chocolate into small even-sized pieces for melting. Put it in a thick heatproof bowl — a Pyrex bowl or a pudding bowl is ideal.
- Find a saucepan into which the bowl will sit, with its base a fair bit clear of the bottom of the pan. Put a little hot water into the pan and put it on the hob.
- Keep the water just below simmering point and put the bowl of chocolate above it — it shouldn't touch the water.
- After a few minutes the chocolate will begin to soften at the edges. Stir it now, and keep stirring until it has melted, and don't overheat it or it will 'seize', going lumpy and greasy-looking.
- If it seizes, try stirring in 1 tsp of sunflower oil; it may save it.
- The microwave is great for melting chocolate: melt on high for 2 minutes, then leave in the hot bowl to finish melting.
- The oddest thing about chocolate is the way it

behaves with liquids. It can be melted in a lot of liquid (cream, butter, milk, etc. — see the sauce below). But if it encounters just a drop or two while it's melting, it will seize. Try the tip above to rescue it. And be sure always to put it in a dry bowl (or a dry microwave), and not to allow the water 'bath' under it to bubble up.

- If you're having trouble with a chocolate recipe where you're melting it with just a little liquid, check the quantities. Never use less than 1 tbsp liquid for every 60 g chocolate.

GLOSSY CHOCOLATE SAUCE

For when you have no time at all:
- Buy a premium vanilla ice cream. Make this chocolate sauce. Serve.
- 50% cocoa solids is really the minimum, although a bar of Bournville will certainly do in an emergency. 70% solids will give you the most chocolatey flavour.

SERVES 6 (OR FEWER, DEPENDING ON THE NUMBER OF CHOCOLATE LOVERS PRESENT)

150 g dark chocolate, preferably at least 50% cocoa solids

200 ml cream

Break up the chocolate and put it in a heavy-based saucepan with the cream. Over a very low heat, stirring all the time, melt the chocolate. Keep stirring until the sauce is glossy and hot. Serve immediately or set aside. Err on the side of caution with the heat, especially if reheating; the sauce will curdle if it gets too hot. If you have a microwave, you can make the sauce in it.

chocolate

To serve with ice cream and chocolate sauce
Roasted hazelnuts — roast in a moderate oven until toasty-smelling and golden, then get the skins off by putting the nuts in a tea towel and rubbing. **Chocolate chip cookies** are a winner if you have access to good ones. Good delis should have them. And of course, **banana** makes for a banana split.

WIZARD DARK CHOCOLATE MOUSSE

This is my favourite.

SERVES ABOUT 6

175 g dark chocolate (70% cocoa solids)
2 tbsp light muscovado sugar
3 tbsp cream
2 tbsp brandy or rum
4 yolks and 5 whites from large, fresh, free-range eggs

To serve: cream and crème fraîche

Note: If you prefer a less intense chocolate flavour, use 50% solids chocolate instead.

Melt the chocolate with the cream and brandy in a fairly large heatproof bowl set over a pan of not-quite-simmering water. Stir to a smooth glossy paste. Allow to cool a little, then beat in the egg yolks.

Whisk the egg whites to a firm but not stiff foam. Stir 4 heaped tbsp of this into the chocolate to loosen it, then fold the rest into the chocolate. Don't leave big white blobs, but don't beat all the air out of the mix either.

Pour into individual bowls and leave in the fridge for several hours to set.

This is tastiest served with lightly whipped cream into which you have stirred a few tbsp of crème fraîche. This gives it a fresh flavour, which balances the dark chocolate well.

Variation: Chocolate Mocha Mousse: add 1 tsp best-quality instant coffee to the melting chocolate.

THE NO-BAKE CHOCOLATE MOCHA MOUSSE CAKE

This is a cake which you assemble, rather than bake. You will need a large loaf tin (about 21 x 11 x 6 cm) and some cling film. Make sure the cake is a nice, butter-made version or the whole thing will taste rather cheap. This is a variation of an Italian dessert called 'Il Diplomatico' which I first encountered in Marcella Hazan's *Classic Italian Cookbook*.

SERVES 8

The ingredients for the Wizard Dark Chocolate Mousse above plus:
300 g Madeira or rich, plain sponge cake
about 300 ml espresso-strength coffee (not instant)
about 100 ml brandy
3 tbsp caster sugar
200 ml cream
2 squares dark chocolate

Line the loaf tin with cling film (it doesn't matter if it isn't neat). Make the chocolate mousse as in the recipe above and put it in the fridge. When you're making the coffee, remember it must be very strong indeed, nearly bitter.

Slice the cake (about $\frac{1}{4}$–$\frac{1}{2}$ cm thick). In a large, shallow dish mix the coffee and brandy, and stir in the sugar to dissolve. One by one, dip cake slices in the coffee mix, then when they are soaked through, quickly use them to line the base and sides of the loaf tin.

You should have about a third of the cake left over. If at any stage of the making you need a few tbsp extra of the coffee mix, just make up some more, using 3:1 coffee to brandy, and a little sugar.

When the tin is lined with coffee-soaked cake, scrape in the chocolate mousse to fill it. Now make a layer of coffee-soaked cake to cover the mousse. Cover it all tightly with cling film and leave it to chill and set in the fridge overnight.

To serve, turn the cake carefully out onto a plate. Whip the cream and cover the cake entirely with a layer, dabbing it on to make peaks all over. Grate the chocolate over the top. Cut into slices and serve.

VELVET CHOCOLATE CREAMS

Smooth, melt-on-the-tongue wickedness in tiny little pots, and they take exactly 1 minute to make. This is one of those recipes which everyone begs for. You will need small little bowls, ramekins or espresso cups.

SERVES 6–8

200 g best dark chocolate, 70% cocoa solids
2 tbsp light muscovado sugar
1 large, fresh free-range egg
125 ml whole milk
175 ml cream
1 tbsp brandy or rum

Put the chocolate and sugar in the food processor and whizz to tiny grains. Add the egg and whizz to a slush. Put the milk and cream in a heavy-based pan, heat until boiling, and slowly, carefully, pour it onto the chocolate in the food processor with the blade turning. Then add the brandy or rum to make a kind of hot chocolate soup.

Lift off the lid, and then take the bowl off the processor. Swirl it gently to disperse as many of the surface air bubbles as you can, before pouring it into tiny bowls or espresso cups. Cover with cling film and set in the fridge for several hours or overnight.

Note: This really is best with 70% solids chocolate. If all you can get is about 50%, then leave out the sugar.

THE AMAZING 25-MINUTE CHOCOLATE CAKE

It's amazingly quick, amazingly simple and amazingly good.

200 g chocolate, preferably 70% cocoa solids

200 g butter, plus a little extra

4 large free-range eggs

175 g caster sugar

150 g plain flour

1 rounded tsp baking powder

icing sugar (preferably golden), for dusting, optional

Turn on the oven to 220C/425F /Gas 7 and butter the base and sides of a 26 cm springform cake tin.

Break the chocolate into small pieces, and put it and the butter into a heatproof bowl set over a pan of simmering water. Stir from time to time until you have a smooth, glossy sauce, then leave it to cool a little.

Meanwhile, in a large bowl whisk the eggs and sugar until light (about 5 minutes with electric beaters). Stir the cooled chocolate sauce into the eggs, then sift the flour with the baking powder onto this mix and fold it in. Scrape the cake mix into the tin and put it into the centre of the fully preheated oven.

Bake for about 25 minutes. This is the only slightly tricky part; all ovens are different, so yours may do the cake in 20 minutes, or 30. (I've even known some hot ones to do it in 15.) The usual tests for doneness don't apply, since you take this cake out of the oven while it's still gooey in the centre. It should be set at the edges, however, and to about half way in. The gooey centre will sink a little as it cools, and will make this the moistest cake you've ever made. It needs no adornment, though some golden icing sugar sprinkled through a sieve on to the cracked top is lovely.

There are few things as gratifying in winter as a wedge of steamed pudding, topped with a syrupy pouring sauce or a cold trickle of cream. Its crumb is more soft and moist than any cake you've ever eaten, and there's something about its sweet tenderness that deals most effectively with January miseries.

The idea of putting a cake mix in a bowl and then putting the bowl in a pot of water to boil does seem rather surprising, and I suspect that this is the bit that puts many people off.

While most pudding recipes involve creaming butter and sugar and all the usual kerfuffle of cake-making, there are some which only require to be stirred together before being poured into their bowl. And since they're the ones I like to cook, here's a favourite for you.

STICKY ORANGE STEAMED PUDDING

Here's a good reason to fill your pudding bowl again and get steaming. It's one of those wonderful just-stir-it-all-together recipes — and the result? The result is moist, sticky, toffeeish and intriguingly spicy, considering there are no spices in it. All it needs is a trickle of very cold pouring cream, pure and simple.

SERVES 4–6

85 g butter, plus extra for the bowl

150 g fresh white breadcrumbs

150 g light muscovado sugar

3 large eggs

150 g best bitter marmalade (Seville, preferably)

cream, to serve

You also need: a 1-litre pudding bowl, a little bit of greaseproof paper, aluminium foil, a big thick elastic band (or string) and a large saucepan.

Put the 85 g butter in the freezer. In the meantime, assemble the gear (see the tips below if you're a novice at steamed puddings). Butter the pudding bowl, use a small piece of greaseproof paper to cover the base of the buttered bowl, then butter the paper too.

In a large mixing bowl, rub the breadcrumbs and sugar with your fingertips until no lumps remain. Crack in the eggs, spoon in the marmalade and mix it all together with a fork. On the wide holes of a grater, grate the semi-frozen butter and very quickly stir it through with the fork as well. Pour the mix into the buttered pudding bowl. Cover securely with foil and steam it for 1½ hours. Then lift the bowl out of the pot but let it sit for a couple of minutes. Remove the foil, run a table knife round the sides of the pudding and turn it out onto a plate. Serve with cold pouring cream.

Note: You really do need the very best marmalade for this recipe; if it isn't intensely flavoured and somewhat bitter, the pudding may taste rather muted. In which case I'd recommend stirring the **grated zest of an orange** into the pudding mix as well.

Tips on steaming a pudding

- First, find your **pudding bowl**. There are plastic ones with handy clip-on lids, but I believe that the old-fashioned ivory-coloured delph ones do the job better — there's much more insulation so the pudding cooks more evenly.
- Then find a **large lidded saucepan** — it must be just a tiny bit taller than the pudding bowl. You also need something for the pudding to stand on, to protect it from the intense heat of the base of the pan. Trivets are often recommended but my saucepans aren't tall enough, so I just scrunch up a piece of foil and sit the pud on that.
- Of course, if you have a tall enough steamer, then you'll just put the pudding in that, set it over a pan of boiling water, and you're away.
- To **cover the pudding bowl**, use foil. (If the pudding mix reaches near the top of the bowl, fold a pleat in the centre of the foil to allow it to expand as the pudding rises, like putting a bit of 'give' in a waistband.) Next, you have to keep the foil in place. I find a large, stout rubber band does the job best.
  If you haven't got a rubber band, you'll need to use string. As you tighten it under the pudding bowl's collar, lift the foil's edges. This helps to persuade the string to stay up there where it should as you wrestle with the knot.
- **When the pudding's in the pan**, standing on its bit of scrunched-up foil or on the trivet, carefully pour boiling water from the kettle into the pan, to reach halfway up the pudding bowl. Simmer gently, with the lid on the pan, for the required time. Check every now and again that the pan isn't about to boil dry.
- And finally . . . you can **microwave** a pud in just a few minutes. Check your manual for tips. Remember, though, that you won't get quite the same depth of flavour in minutes as can develop in hours.

cakes

They don't come simpler than this cake. Its crumb is tender, fragrant and buttery. Its beauty lies in its lack of adornment — just a squidge of lemony curd in the centre, a powdery drift of icing sugar settling on top. Yet for all its plainness, it has a flavour which money can't buy: that fresh, moist, real-butter, just-baked flavour. All you have to do is invest in the best ingredients — including half an hour of your own time.

Which is all very well. After all, half an hour isn't that onerous. But unless you got the cake-making low-down at your mother's elbow, or had it beaten into you with wooden spoon and delph bowl in Domestic Science class at school, you're likely to end up floundering with many standard shorthand cake recipes. Not everything means quite what it says, and many terms just don't explain themselves properly. So after the recipe, check out the detail on this page and the next . . .

ZESTY LEMON SPONGE WITH LEMON CURD FILLING

MAKES 1 SMALL CAKE WHICH SERVES ABOUT 6

The cake

3 large free-range eggs

about 200 g each of:

    soft butter

    caster sugar

    self-raising flour

grated rind of 1 lemon & 3 tbsp lemon juice

icing sugar, to serve

You will also need two 20 cm shallow round cake tins and non-stick baking parchment

The lemon curd

1 large egg

30 g caster sugar

30 g butter

grated rind of 1 large lemon & juice of ½ lemon

To make the cake:

Preheat the oven to 180C/350F/Gas 4. Butter the tins and line the bases with baking parchment.

Weigh the eggs in the shell; they will come to about 200 g. Measure out the same weight as the eggs each of the soft butter, the caster sugar and the self-raising flour. Sieve the flour.

Cream the butter until pale. Add the sugar and grated lemon rind; cream again until very light. Crack the eggs into a bowl, whisk lightly with a fork, then beat them into the butter and sugar 1–2 tbsp at a time. Gently fold in the sieved flour and stir in the lemon juice to achieve a soft dropping consistency. Scrape the mix into the tins and bake for 25–30 minutes, until springy in the centre. Remove from the oven, turn out after 1 minute onto a wire rack, carefully peel off the paper, and leave to cool.

Meanwhile, make the lemon curd:

In a heatproof bowl, whisk the egg and sugar to mix. Set the bowl over a saucepan which has some simmering water in it (the base of the bowl should not touch the water). Add the butter to the eggs and sugar and stir. When it has dissolved, add the lemon rind and juice. Continue to stir until the mix has thickened to a near-jellied, custardy curd (about 5–10 minutes). Set it aside to cool.

To serve the cake:

Sandwich the two cakes with the lemon curd. Dust the top with icing sugar shaken through a sieve.

Get to know your oven

An oven thermometer costs a few pounds in cookware shops. You may be amazed. Some ovens are miles out; others have hot and cold spots. And cake recipes will work well for you only if the temperature is reasonably accurate.

The eggs

Egg sizes have changed, putting many recipes slightly out of kilter. So here I've returned to the old-fashioned pound cake method: an equal weight of all 4 main ingredients.

If using pre-1997 recipes which call for size 2 or 3 eggs, use smallish 'Medium' eggs to substitute.

The secret ingredient

The secret ingredient in a cake is air. And it comes free, so you may as well try to get as much in as possible. The next 3 steps are all about getting the air in, then keeping it there.

'Cream the butter and sugar' . . .

No — don't. This standard cake recipe phrase is misleading. Always 'cream' the butter on its own first, beating it for several minutes until it's much paler; then add the sugar and beat again until pale. You're adding air all the while.

— To do this, the butter must be soft. Take it out of the fridge several hours beforehand (and

cakes

the eggs too, while you're at it). Of course, most of us don't think of this in time. What then?
— If you have a microwave, soften the butter for 5–10 seconds on high, being sure to stop before it turns oily.
— Otherwise, chop the butter very small, spread the bits out and leave at warm room temperature. Avoid the temptation to put it near a heat source — it'll just melt.

'Beat in the eggs' . . .
Add them a little at a time. Beat until the mix changes — first it will be slithery, then it will turn back to a stiffer, resistant cream. You are stabilising the structure. If you shoot the egg in too quickly, the mix may curdle. So don't get impatient towards the end, just when it's most fragile.
— If you fear the mix may curdle, beat in 1 tbsp flour with every addition of egg.
— If the mix has curdled, try putting it in the food processor and beating with the blade for 1 or 2 minutes at high speed to restore it to a smooth cream.
— If nothing works, never mind. A curdled mix won't rise quite as well, but it will still taste good.

'Fold in the flour'
— Don't forget to sieve it first. Not just once, but twice! (More air.)
— To 'fold', sieve the flour onto the wet mix. Use a flexible plastic spatula or a large metal spoon. Slide it to the bottom of the bowl, then turn your wrist to scoop the mixture from underneath up to the top. Keep at it until the flour is incorporated.
— Handle with care! The mix is fragile, with hundreds of pockets of air trapped in it. Don't batter them out again . . .

'Soft dropping consistency' . . .
Always check for this. Holding a spoonful of the cake mix, flick your wrist over the bowl. The mix should drop slightly reluctantly from the spoon. If the mix is too sticky, add another tbsp of the liquid specified in the recipe. Gently.

Bake until it's done!
These are the signs: it is retracting very slightly from the edges of the tin; when pressed in the centre, it's springy; when a toothpick or skewer is inserted into the centre, it comes out without raw dough streaked on it.

And finally . . . can you open the oven door?
There's a lot of hype about this one. Opening the oven door is not guaranteed to make the cake fall. But if there's a big draught while the expanding air bubbles are not yet held in place by solidified cake mix, the delicate structure may collapse. Better not to risk it until $\frac{2}{3}$ of the baking time is over.

The tin(s)
— Use the size given in the recipe, or everything will be wrong.
— **Grease with butter**, not a cheaper fat which will taint the flavour.
— **Do tins really need to be lined?** Lining the sides is often optional — you can slide a knife in, to loosen the cake after baking — but lining the base is a very good idea indeed. Sit the tin on the greaseproof paper or baking parchment, draw round its outline, cut that out. After you've buttered the base, slip the paper in, then butter the paper.

Cake-making equipment
Best are hand-held electric beaters or a mixer. Unless you're in great training, it's incredibly hard work to do the job by hand, though of course it's perfectly possible. A food processor works fine, but the results are never as light.

The ingredients
Use the best. Free-range eggs, real butter. Forget the begrudgers. You're not going to be eating cakes every day.

CHOCOLATE CAKE WITH FRAGRANT SPICES

This is the darkest, most chocolatey cake I've ever tasted which uses no chocolate at all. The spicy flavour is sweet. You can bake it in a single loaf tin, or in 2 sandwich tins. Either way, be sure to serve it with plenty of crème fraîche or softly whipped cream.

SERVES 6–8

3 eggs
about 200 g soft butter, plus a little extra
about 200 g caster sugar
50 g cocoa powder
about 150 g self-raising flour
4 cardamom pods
$\frac{1}{2}$ tsp grated nutmeg
$\frac{1}{2}$ tsp finely ground black pepper from the pepper mill
3 tbsp milk
1 tsp vanilla extract
You will also need two 20 cm shallow round tins or a 1 kg loaf tin (about 21 x 11 x 6 cm) and non-stick baking parchment

Preheat the oven to 180C/350F/Gas 4. Butter the tins and line the base(s) with non-stick baking parchment.

Weigh the eggs in the shell. Measure out the same weight as the eggs of the butter and of the caster sugar. Weigh out 50 g cocoa powder, then add self-raising flour to the cocoa on the scales, until the flour and cocoa together weigh the same as the eggs did.

Release the black seeds from the cardamom pods: lie a large knife blade flat on the cardamom, lean heavily on the knife, and the pod will spring open. Pound the seeds to a powder in a pestle and mortar. Sieve the flour and cocoa with the ground cardamom, nutmeg and pepper into a bowl.

Cream the butter until pale. Add the sugar; cream again until very light. In a bowl, lightly whisk the eggs with the milk and vanilla, then beat them into the creamed butter and sugar, 1–2 tbsp at a time. Gently fold in the sieved flour and cocoa. The batter should have a soft dropping consistency; add a little more milk if it's too stiff.

Scrape the mix into the tin(s). If it's in 2 sandwich tins, bake for 25–30 minutes; if it's a loaf, it'll take about 40–50 minutes. It's done when it's springy in the centre and when a toothpick slid into the centre comes out without any streaks of uncooked dough on it.

Turn out after 1 minute onto a wire rack, carefully peel off the paper, and leave to cool.

SCRUFFY CAKE WITH PECAN AND BROWN SUGAR TOPPING

One of my mother's specials, this is a soft moist cake with a scruffy, nutty, crusty, crunchy topping, which half sinks into the cake as it bakes. It's perfect to finish brunch, or for afternoon tea, with a big, big bowl of *café au lait*.

A nice variation: add some rhubarb. Use 240 g rhubarb stalks (trimmed weight). Cut into small chunks and scatter over the cake along with the topping.

A deep gratin, lasagne or rectangular casserole dish is just right for this; it should measure about 33 x 23 x 5 cm. Butter it well and turn the oven on to 180C/350F/Gas 4.

Topping

130 g light muscovado sugar
2 tbsp plain flour
½ tsp ground cinnamon
2 tbsp butter at room temperature
140 g roughly chopped pecans

Cake

120 g butter at room temperature
200 g caster sugar
3 large eggs
250 g self-raising flour
1 rounded tsp baking powder
1 rounded tsp bread soda
½ tsp salt
220 g crème fraîche or sour cream

First make the topping. Mix the sugar, flour and cinnamon in a bowl with your fingers. Rub in the butter and stir in the nuts.

You can make the cake in a food processor, with electric beaters, or (if you're feeling energetic) by hand. Cream the butter until very light, then beat in the sugar and continue beating until very light. Whisk the eggs, then beat them in a little at a time. Sieve the flour, baking powder, bread soda and salt into a bowl. Beat them into the mix, a few tbsp at a time. After each flour addition, beat in a few tbsp of the crème fraîche.

Scrape the mix into the prepared dish. Scatter with the topping and bake in the preheated oven for about half an hour, or until a skewer inserted into the centre comes out clean. Allow to cool a little before cutting into squares to serve. It's at its absolute best when still slightly warm, but keeps very well too.

QUEEN CAKES

I've adapted this recipe from Darina Allen's *Irish Traditional Cooking*. These darling little soft cakes are fragrant from the butter and just a little crunchy on the outside.

MAKES ABOUT 20

110 g butter, plus extra
110 g caster sugar
140 g plain flour
½ tsp baking powder
2 free-range eggs
1 tsp vanilla essence, or a little orange or lemon rind
approx. 1 tbsp milk

Turn the oven on to 200C/400F/Gas 6 and smear shallow bun or patty tins with the extra butter.

Cream the 110 g butter until really soft. Add the sugar and beat again until white and creamy.

Sieve the flour and baking powder into a bowl, and in a separate bowl, whisk the eggs and your chosen flavouring. Gradually beat the eggs into the creamed butter and sugar. Add a little of the sieved flour between additions of the eggs to help prevent it curdling, then gently stir in the rest of the flour sieved with the baking powder. Add a little milk as necessary for a dropping consistency.

Put the mixture in spoonfuls into the patty tins until two-thirds full and bake for about 20 minutes in the preheated oven. Cool on a wire rack.

select bibliography

I have confined myself to a quite personal selection of those favourite books which inspired or taught me most along the way, or which I think would be most useful if you'd like to explore cooking a bit further.

Allen, Darina, *Irish Traditional Cooking* (Gill & Macmillan, 1995)
— *A Year at Ballymaloe Cookery School* (Gill & Macmillan, 1997)
Allen, Myrtle, *The Ballymaloe Cookbook* (Gill & Macmillan, 1977)
Beck, Simone, Louisette Bertholle and Julia Child, *Mastering the Art of French Cooking* (Penguin, 1966)
Bhumichitr, Vatcharin, *Vatch's Thai Cookbook* (Pavilion, 1994)
Collister, Linda and Anthony Blake, *The Bread Book* (Conran Octopus, 1993)
Cost, Bruce, *Bruce Cost's Asian Ingredients* (William Morrow, 1998)
Costa, Margaret, *Four Seasons Cookery Book* (Grub St, 1996)
David, Elizabeth, *French Provincial Cooking* (Penguin, 1986)
— *English Bread and Yeast Cookery* (Penguin, 1987)
— *Italian Food* (Penguin, 1987)
— *Summer Cooking* (Penguin, 1987)
— *Mediterranean Food* (Penguin, 1987)
Davidson, Alan, *The Oxford Companion to Food* (OUP, 1999)
del Conte, Anna, *Secrets from an Italian Kitchen* (Bantam, 1989)
— *The Classic Food of Northern Italy* (Pavilion, 1995)
Gray, Rose and Ruth Rogers, *River Cafe Cook Book* (Ebury Press, 1995)
Grigson, Jane, *Jane Grigson's Fruit Book* (Penguin, 1988)
— *Jane Grigson's Vegetable Book* (Penguin, 1988)
— *Fish Cookery* (Penguin, 1994)
Hazan, Marcella, *The Classic Italian Cookbook* (Macmillan, 1980)
— *The Second Classic Italian Cookbook* (Macmillan, 1982)
Henderson, Fergus, *Nose to Tail Eating* (Macmillan, 1999)
Hom, Ken, *Fragrant Harbour Taste* (Bantam, 1991)
— *Ken Hom's Hot Wok* (BBC, 1996)
Hopkinson, Simon, *Roast Chicken and Other Stories* (Ebury Press, 1994)
Jaffrey, Madhur, *Indian Cookery* (BBC, 1982)
— *Eastern Vegetarian Cooking* (Jonathan Cape, 1983)
— *A Taste of India* (Pavilion, 1985)
— *Far Eastern Cookery* (BBC, 1989)
La Place, Viana, *Verdura* (Macmillan, 1994)
Lepard, Dan and Richard Whittington, *Baker & Spice Baking with Passion* (Quadrille, 1999)
Little, Alastair, *Keep It Simple* (Conran Octopus, 1993)
McGee, Harold, *On Food and Cooking* (Collier, Macmillan, 1984)
Madison, Deborah, *The Greens Cookbook* (Bantam, 1987)
— *The Savoury Way* (Bantam, 1990)
Norwak, Mary, *English Puddings Sweet and Savoury* (Grub St, 1996)
O'Shea, Bernadette, *Pizza Defined* (Estragon Press, 1997)
Owen, Sri, *Indonesian Food and Cookery* (Prospect Books, 1976)
— *The Rice Book* (Frances Lincoln, 1998)
Rosengarten, David, Joel Dean and Giorgio Deluca, *The Dean & Deluca Cookbook* (Ebury Press, 1997)
Sahni, Julie, *Classic Indian Cooking* (Grub St, 1998)
So, Yan-kit, *Classic Chinese Cookbook* (Dorling Kindersley, 1987)
— *Classic Food of China* (Macmillan, 1992)
Stein, Rick, *English Seafood Cookery* (Penguin, 1988)
— *Taste of the Sea* (BBC, 1995)
— *Fruits of the Sea* (BBC, 1997)

— *Seafood Odyssey* (BBC, 1999)

Stobart, Tom, *Herbs, Spices and Flavourings* (Grub St, 1998)

Tatlow, Maureen, *Good Enough to Eat* (Gill & Macmillan, 1998)

Thompson, David, *Classic Thai Cuisine* (Simon & Schuster, 1993)

Treuille, Eric and Ursula Ferrigno, *Bread* (Dorling Kindersley, 1998)

Waters, Alice, *Chez Panisse Menu Cookbook* (Random House, 1982)

— *Chez Panisse Vegetables* (HarperCollins, 1996)

— *Pasta, Pizza & Calzone* (Pavilion, 1996)

Watson, Lyall, *Jacobson's Organ and the Remarkable Nature of Smell* (Allen Lane, 1999)

Wells, Patricia, *Bistro* (Kyle Cathie, 1999)

— *Trattoria* (Kyle Cathie, 1999)

Wolfert, Paula, *The Cooking of South West France* (Papermac, 1989)

— *Good Food from Morocco* (Murray, 1990)

index

aioli, 100, 101
  cheat's aioli, 100
almonds
  almond meringues, 107
  with couscous, 29
anchovies
  and fish sauce, 79
  fresh tomato Puttanesca, 14
  Janssons temptation, 25
  and lamb roasts, 48
  1-minute lemon and chilli
  sauce, 41
  quicker tomato sauce, 12
  rich savoury dressing, 71
  roasted red relish, 33
  salsa verde, 94
  and stir-fried cabbage, 80
apples
  apple tart with trembling
  custard, 120
  cider-apple sauce for pork (or
  chicken), 42
  'Dimpas' baked apple slices
  with butter cinnamon crunch,
  105
  tarte tatin, 121
asparagus, 76
aubergines, with roast courgettes
  and young onions, 75
avocado
  and rocket salad, 71
  and spiced beef salad, 71
  and prawn cocktail, 100

bacon
  classic Carbonara, 14
  classic quiche, 120
  peas, Prosciutto and cream, 15
  peasant omelette, 7
  stir-fried cabbage with
  rashers, 80
  streaky rashers with white
  fish, 33
  yellow pea and marjoram
  soup, 87
baking, 110–16
  basic soda bread or scones,
  111
  corn bread, 112
  orange and poppy seed
  muffins, 112
  sour-skons, 111
  see also cakes; pastry
basil
  mussels with Thai green curry
  sauce and fresh herbs, 37

quick-fried squid with olive
  oil, basil and cherry tomatoes,
  39
  wonderful pesto, 15
beans
  black bean soup, 86
  dried, 86
  steamed French, 76
  salade not-quite-Niçoise, 5
  stir-fried green beans, 78
beef
  Anne's salad: seared beef
  ribbons and parsley, 67
  avocado and spiced beef
  salad, 71
  beef daube Provençal, 59
  beef tagine, 61
  roast, 50–51
  steak, 40
    char-grilled, 65
  stewed, 59–61
  Thai beef salad, 66
  see also sauces, for meat
berries: summer berry salad, 124
breads, 110–16
  corn bread, 112
  flavourings for, 111, 112
  soda bread, 110–11
  yeast breads, 113–116
broccoli, 76
  jade broccoli, 80
  purple sprouting, 81
  stir-fried vegetables with
  spices, coconut milk and
  toasted peanuts, 79
bulgar, 29
  bulgar salads, 30
  15-minute bulgar, 29
  tabbouleh, 30
butter, 6
  country butter sauce, 33
  Derry Clarke's Café de Paris
  butter, 41
  'Dimpas' baked apple slices
  with butter cinnamon crunch,
  105
  flavoured, 41
  1-minute lemon and chilli
  sauce, 41
  Sri Lankan roast butter
  chicken, 46

cabbage, 76
  stir-fried, 80
    with spices, coconut milk
    and toasted peanuts, 79

cakes, 129–31
  amazing 25-minute chocolate
  cake, 127
  chocolate cake with fragrant
  spices, 130
  no-bake chocolate mocha
  mousse cake, 126
  queen cakes, 131
  scruffy cake with pecan and
  brown sugar topping, 131
  zesty lemon sponge with
  lemon curd filling, 129
caldo verde, 87
capers
  tender simmered lamb with
  green parsley and caper sauce,
  57
  yoghurt, garlic and caper
  dressing, 72
cardamom, 131
  creamy cardamom, yoghurt
  and black pepper sauce, 60
  melon and cardamom cream,
  124
carrots, 82–3
  roast, 74
    vegetables with olive oil
    and thyme, 75
  roll-cutting, 78
  stir-fried vegetables with
  spices, coconut milk and
  toasted peanuts, 79
  spiced carrots with sultanas
  and pine nuts, 83
  turnip and carrot purée, 83
  velvet root soup, 85
cauliflower, 76
  cauliflower cheese, 97
  Indian gingered cauliflower
  with spices, 81
  stir-fried vegetables with
  spices, coconut milk and
  toasted peanuts, 79
celery: lamb with celery and
  coriander, 64
char-grilling, 65–7
  Anne's salad: seared beef
  ribbons and parsley, 67
  courgettes, 67
  fish, 67
  marinades for, 66
  Thai beef salad, 66
cheese
  aromatic cheese omelette, 7
  cauliflower cheese, 97
  cheese soufflé, 109

feta, 13
fresh herb and goats' cheese
tart with a Pecorino crust, 120
goats' cheese, 75
gratin, 25
in omlettes, 6
macaroni cheese, 97
Milleens and marjoram pizza,
117
Parmesan, 12
pizza, 117
potato, courgette and piquant
cheese soup, 85
toasted goats' cheese salad, 73
chicken, 44–7
barbequed, 46
bon bon chicken, 56
char-grilling, 66
chicken in a creamy
cardamom, yoghurt and black
pepper sauce, 60
chicken mayonnaise, 56
Chinese five-spice chicken, 47
marinades for, 46–7, 66
marinated chicken salad, 56
poached, 54–6
poached chicken with ginger
and scallion dipping sauce, 56
roast, 44–6, 51
roast chicken with lemon grass
and lime, 47
and salsa verde, 55
sesame garlic roast chicken
with sweet chilli dipping
sauce, 47
Sri Lankan roast butter
chicken, 46
stewed, 59
stock, 89
Vietnamese chicken salad, 55
see also sauces, for meat
chillies, 39
1-minute lemon and chilli
sauce, 41
and pizza, 117
squid à la plancha, 39
stir-fried cabbage with red
chilli and balsamic vinegar, 80
stir-fried cabbage with red
chilli and ginger, 80
sweet chilli dipping sauce, 47
Thai dipping relish with lime,
garlic and chilli, 93
Chinese five-spice chicken, 47
chives
chive champ, 18, 42

simple green salad with
chives, 70
chocolate, 125–7
amazing 25-minute chocolate
cake, 127
chocolate cake with fragrant
spices, 130
chocolate soufflé, 109
chocolate tart, 121
glossy chocolate sauce, 125
no-bake chocolate mocha
mousse cake, 126
velvet chocolate creams, 126
wizard dark chocolate mousse,
126
chorizo, 28, 87
fried potatoes with chorizo,
21
cider: cider-apple sauce for pork
(or chicken), 42
cinnamon: 'Dimpas' baked apple
slices with butter cinnamon
crunch, 105
coconut
mussels with Thai green curry
sauce and fresh herbs, 37
stir-fried vegetables with
spices, coconut milk and
toasted peanuts, 79
coriander, fresh, 15
lamb with celery and
coriander, 64
mussels with Thai green curry
sauce and fresh herbs, 37
quickest coriander and lemon
fish, 33
salsa verde, 94
spicy yoghurt relish with mint
and coriander, 94
zesty green coriander and
lime salsa, 92
coriander seeds: roast lamb with
crushed coriander crust, 48
courgettes
potato, courgette and piquant
cheese soup, 85
roast courgettes, aubergines
and young onions, 75
roll-cutting, 78
seared, 67
steamed, 76
stir-fried courgette slivers and
parsley, 14
stir-fried vegetables with
spices, coconut milk and
toasted peanuts, 79

with yoghurt, garlic and caper
dressing, 72
couscous, 29
couscous salads, 30
10-minute couscous, 29
cream
horseradish herb cream, 51
peas, Prosciutto and cream, 15
curry: mussels with Thai green
curry sauce and fresh herbs, 37
custard: apple tart with trembling
custard, 120

desserts
almond meringues, 107
amazing 25-minute chocolate
cake, 127
apple tart with trembling
custard, 120
chocolate dishes, 109, 121,
125–7
'Dimpas' baked apple slices
with butter cinnamon crunch,
105
fruit salads, 122–4
glossy chocolate sauce, 125–6
no-bake chocolate mocha
mousse cake, 126
pancake fans with indulgent
orange sauce, 104
plum clafoutis, 104
steamed puddings, 128
tarte tatin, 121
tender meringues, 107
velvet chocolate creams, 126
wizard dark chocolate mousse,
126
dill
couscous and herb salad, 30
waxy potatoes with dill, 17
dips
simple dip, 23
Thai dip, 28
duck
with 2-minute green
peppercorn sauce, 41
warm salad of duck, grapes
and walnuts, 72

eggs, 4–9
boiled, 4–5
classic quiche, 120
freshness of, 5, 8, 106
fried, 9
with peanut sambal, 77
poached, 8–9

index

salade not-quite-Niçoise, 5
scrambled, 9
see also mayonnaise;
meringues; omelettes;
pancakes; soufflés
equipment, 9, 51, 99, 106
char-grills, 65–6
food processors, 18, 85, 130
knives, 81
steamers, 34, 76, 99, 128
woks, 62–3

fish
char-grilled, 67
clear-steamed fish with ginger
threads, 34
Thai-style, 35
and country butter sauce, 33
fried, 31–3
quickest coriander and lemon
fish, 33
salsas and relishes for, 33
steamed, 34–5
stock, 90
streaky rashers with white
fish, 33
Thai green curry sauce and
fresh herbs, 37
see also mussels; squid
focaccia, 115–16
fruit salads, 122–4
boozy orange, 124
flavoured syrups for, 123
melon and berries, 124
melon and cardamom cream,
124
melon and grapes, 124
melon, lychee and lime, 124
melon, two-tone, 124
mixed citrus, 124
Moroccan orange salad, 123
orange salad with
strawberries, 123
peaches in wine, 124
pineapple and mango with
lemon grass syrup, 124
strawberries, 124

garlic
in lamb roasts, 48
mayonnaise, 100–101
parchment-baked new
potatoes, 23
peeling of, 77
sesame garlic roast chicken
with sweet chilli dipping

sauce, 47
Thai dipping relish with lime,
garlic and chilli, 93
yoghurt, garlic and caper
dressing, 72
ginger, 34
clear-steamed fish with ginger
threads, 34
Thai-styled, 35
golden mash with ginger, 83
poached chicken with ginger
and scallion dipping sauce, 56
simplest fried rice with onions,
ginger and peas, 28
stir-fried cabbage with red
chilli and ginger, 80
stir-fried gingery pork with
squeaky greens, 64
grains *see* bulgar; couscous
grapes
melon and grapes fruit salad,
124
surprising green salad, 71–2
warm salad of duck, grapes
and walnuts, 72
gratins, 24
cheese gratin, 25
gratin dauphinois, 25
Janssons temptation, 25
pommes boulangère, 25
gravy, 52–3, *see also* sauces, for
meat

ham, 15
in omlettes, 6
peas, Prosciutto and cream, 15
in pizza, 117
yellow pea and marjoram
soup, 87
herbs
couscous and herb salad, 30
fresh herb and goats' cheese
tart with a Pecorino crust, 120
horseradish herb cream, 51
Italian herb roast pork, 49
mayonnaise, 100
no-cook fresh tomato and
fresh herb sauce, 13, 75
olive oil and herbs marinade,
66
potato, herb and parsnip
mash, 19, 42
Thai green curry sauce and
fresh herbs, 37
horseradish herb cream, 51

Janssons temptation, 25
kale: caldo verde, 87
kombu vegetable stock, 91

lamb
chops, 40
flavourings for roasts, 48
lamb daube Provençal, 59
lamb in a creamy cardamom,
yoghurt and black pepper
sauce, 61
lamb with celery and
coriander, 64
poached, 57
roast, 51
roast lamb with crushed
coriander crust, 48
roast shoulder of lamb
boulangère, 49
stewed, 59–61
tender simmered lamb with
green parsley and caper sauce,
57
see also sauces, for meat
lemon grass
in fruit salad, 123, 124
roast chicken with lemon grass
and lime, 47
lemons, 112
lemon curd, 129
1-minute lemon and chilli
sauce, 41
quickest coriander and lemon
fish, 33
zesty lemon sponge with
lemon curd filling, 129
limes, 112
pineapple and lime salsa, 93
roast chicken with lemon grass
and lime, 47
Thai dipping relish with lime,
garlic and chilli, 93
zesty green coriander and
lime salsa, 92

macaroni cheese, 97
marjoram
Milleens and marjoram pizza,
117
yellow pea and marjoram
soup, 87
mayonnaise, 98–101
aioli, 100, 101
cheat's aioli, 100
and chicken, 56
herb mayonnaise, 100

very slightly lighter
mayonnaise, 100
meat
buying, 40, 45, 48–9, 51, 54,
59–60
char-grilled, 65
curried, 60
roasting, 44–6, 48–51
stewed, 58–61
stir-fried, 62–4
see also beef; chicken; duck;
lamb; pork; sauces, for meat
melon
in fruit salads, 124
surprising green salad, 71
meringues, 106–7
almond meringues, 107
tender meringues, 107
mint
couscous and herb salad, 30
spicy yoghurt relish with mint
and coriander, 94
tabbouleh, 30
wonderful pesto, 15
mussels, 36–7
moules marinière, 37
with Thai green curry sauce
and fresh herbs, 37
mustard, Dijon, 69

olive oil, 69
in mayonnaise, 99
olive oil and herbs marinade,
66
quick-fried squid with olive
oil, basil and cherry tomatoes,
39
roast vegetables with olive oil
and thyme, 75
rosemary and olive oil roast
potato wedges, 23
steamed greens with olive oil
and balsamic vinegar, 76
stir-fried cabbage shreds in
olive oil, 80
stir-fried red peppers with
olive oil, 78
olives, 13
beef or lamb daube Provençal,
59
cos salad with black olives, 71
fresh tomato Puttanesca, 14
salade not-quite-Niçoise, 5
omelettes, 6–7
aromatic cheese omelette, 7
classic omelette, 6

Indian omelette, 7
peasant omelette, 7
onions
how to chop, 42
orange and onion sauce, 41
roast, 74
roast courgettes, aubergines
and young onions, 75
with roast meat, 52
simplest fried rice with onions,
ginger and peas, 28
oranges, 112, 122–3
in fruit salad, 123–4
orange and onion sauce, 41
orange and poppy seed
muffins, 112
pancake fans with indulgent
orange sauce, 104
to segment, 123
sticky orange steamed
pudding, 128

pancakes, 102–5
buttermilk pancakes, 104
'Dimpas' baked apple slices
with butter cinnamon crunch,
105
pancake fans with indulgent
orange sauce, 104
plum clafoutis, 104
parsley
Anne's salad: seared beef
ribbons and parsley, 67
country butter sauce for fish,
33
fried plaice, 32
green parsley sauce, 96
parsley sauce, 95
potato, herb and parsnip
mash, 19
with roast vegetables, 75
salsa verde, 94
stir-fried courgette slivers and
parsley, 14
tabbouleh, 30
tender simmered lamb with
green parsley and caper sauce,
57
winter pesto, 15
parsnips, 83
golden mash with ginger, 83
potato, herb and parsnip
mash, 19, 42
roast, 74
roasted vegetables with olive
oil and thyme, 75

velvet root soup, 85
pasta, 10–15
classic Carbonara, 14
fresh tomato Puttanesca, 14
macaroni cheese, 97
no-cook fresh tomato and
fresh herb sauce, 13
peas, Prosciutto and cream, 15
quicker tomato sauce, 12
simplest simmered tomato
sauce, 12
stir-fried courgette slivers and
parsley, 14
winter pesto, 15
wonderful pesto, 15
pastry, 118–21
peaches in wine, 124
peanuts
dry-roasted, 79
peanut sambal, 77
stir-fried vegetables with
spices, coconut milk and
toasted peanuts, 79
peas
peas, Prosciutto and cream, 15
simplest fried rice with onions,
ginger and peas, 28
yellow pea and marjoram
soup, 87
pecan: scruffy cake with pecan
and brown sugar topping, 131
peppercorns, 30, 69
creamy cardamom, yoghurt
and black pepper sauce, 60
2-minute green peppercorn
sauce for beef, duck or pork,
41
peppers
red and yellow salsa, 93
roasted red relish, 33
roast peppers, 75
stir-fried red peppers with
olive oil, 78
pesto, 15
coriander pesto, 15
winter pesto, 15
wonderful pesto, 15
pine nuts
in couscous, 29
marinated chicken salad, 56
spiced carrots with sultanas
and pine nuts, 83
wonderful pesto, 15
pineapples
in fruit salads, 124
pineapple and lime salsa, 93

index

pizza, 115–17
  ham and rocket, 117
  Milleens and marjoram, 117
  mozzarella and chilli, 117
plum clafoutis, 104
poppy seeds, and orange muffins, 112
pork, 40, 49–50
  Italian herb roast pork, 49
  roast, 51
  stewed, 59–60
  stir-fried gingery pork with squeaky greens, 64
  see also sauces, for meat
potatoes, 16–25
  boiled, 17
  caldo verde, 87
  cheese gratin, 25
  chive champ, 18, 42
  fried, 20–21
    with chorizo, 21
  gratin dauphinois, 25
  gratins, 24–5
  irresistibly spiced fried potatoes, 21
  Janssons temptation, 25
  mashed, 17–19
  parchment-baked new potatoes, 23
  peasant omelette, 7
  pommes boulangère, 25
  potato cakes, 19
  potato, courgette and piquant cheese soup, 85
  potato, herb and parsnip mash, 19, 42
  potato salad, 71
    with yoghurt, garlic and caper dressing, 72
  roast, 22–3, 74
  roast vegetables with olive oil and thyme, 75
  rosemary and olive oil roast potato wedges, 23
  spicy potato wedges, 23
  varieties of, 17, 43
  velvet root soup, 85
  waxy potatoes with dill, 17
prawn cocktail, 100
prunes: beef tagine, 61
puddings, steamed, 128
  sticky orange steamed pudding, 128
pumpkins, roast, 74

quail: roast quail with balsamic

vinegar and rosemary potatoes, 47
quiches and tarts, 120
  classic quiche, 120
  fresh herb and goats' cheese tart with a Pecorino crust, 120

relishes, see salsas and relishes
rhubarb: in scruffy cake with pecan and brown sugar topping, 131
rice, 26–8
  fried rice, 28
  simple spiced basmati rice, 28
  simplest fried rice with onions, ginger and peas, 28
  utterly simple spiced rice, 27
rosemary
  Italian herb roast pork, 49
  with lamb roasts, 48
  and roast chicken, 45
  rosemary and olive oil roast potato wedges, 23

salad dressings, 69–72
  Asian dressing, 71
  balsamic dressing, 70
  blue cheese dressing, 72
  buttermilk dressing, 71
  golden lemon dressing, 76
  purest dressing, 70
  rich savoury dressing, 71
  vinaigrette, classic French, 70
  walnut and balsamic dressing, 72
  yoghurt, garlic and caper dressing, 72
salads, 68–73
  Anne's salad: seared beef ribbons and parsley, 67
  avocado and rocket salad, 71
  avocado and spiced beef salad, 71
  bulgar salads, 30
  chicken salad, 55
  cos salad with black olives, 71
  couscous salads, 30
  little gems in a puddle, 72
  potato salad, 71, 72
  prawn cocktail, 100
  salade not-quite-Niçoise, 5
  simple green salad with chives, 70
  surprising green salad, 71
  Thai beef salad, 66
  toasted goats' cheese salad, 73

Vietnamese chicken salad, 55
warm salad of duck, grapes and walnuts, 72
see also salad dressings
salsas and relishes, 92–4
  for fish, 33
  for meat, 42
  peanut sambal, 77
  pineapple and lime salsa, 93
  quickest corn salsa, 93
  red and yellow salsa, 93
  ripe tomato salsa, 92
  roasted red relish, 33
  salsa verde, 55, 94
    milder, 94
  spicy yoghurt relish with mint and coriander, 94
  Thai dipping relish with lime, garlic and chilli, 93
  Thai tomato dressing, 93
  zesty green coriander and lime salsa, 92
salt, 30, 69
sauces, for meat
  cider-apple sauce, 42
  creamy cardamom, yoghurt and black pepper sauce, 60
  ginger and scallion dipping sauce, 56
  gravy, 45, 52–3
  green parsley and caper sauce, 57
  horseradish herb cream, 51
  1-minute lemon and chilli sauce, 41
  orange and onion sauce, 41
  quick wine sauce, 40
  satay, 56
  sweet-and-hot Chinese sauce, 56
  sweet chilli dipping sauce, 47
  2-minute green peppercorn sauce, 41
sauces, white, 95–7
  cauliflower cheese, 97
  green parsley sauce, 96
  macaroni cheese, 97
  parsley, 95
scallions
  clear-steamed fish, Thai style, 35
  clear-steamed fish with ginger threads, 34
  peas, Prosciutto and cream, 15
  poached chicken with ginger and scallion dipping sauce, 56

potato, herb and parsnip mash, 19
scallion champ, 18
tabbouleh, 30
scallops: clear-steamed with ginger threads, 34–5
scones and muffins
    basic soda scones, 111
    orange and poppy seed muffins, 112
    sour-skons, 111
seaweed: kombu vegetable stock, 91
sesame oil: sesame garlic roast chicken with sweet chilli dipping sauce, 47
sesame seeds, with stir-fried green beans, 78
soufflés, 108–9
    cheese, 109
    chocolate, 109
soups, 84–7
    black bean soup, 86
    caldo verde, 87
    potato, courgette and piquant cheese soup, 85
    Thai-style hot and sour soup, 86
    velvet root soup, 85
    yellow pea and marjoram soup, 87
soy sauce, 34
    ginger and soy marinade, 66
sprouts, stir-fried, 80
squid, 38–9
    a la plancha, 39
    char-grilled, 67
    quick-fried squid with olive oil, basil and cherry tomatoes, 39
stew, 58–61
    beef or lamb daube Provençal, 59
    chicken or lamb in a creamy cardamom, yoghurt and black pepper sauce, 60
    beef tagine, 61
stir-frying, 62–4, 78–81
stock, 88–91
    chicken, 89
    fish, 90
    kombu vegetable, 91
    vegetable, 91
strawberries, in fruit salad, 124
sultanas
    in couscous, 29

marinated chicken salad, 56
spiced carrots with sultanas and pine nuts, 83
swedes
    golden mash with ginger, 83
    turnip and carrot purée, 83
sweetcorn: quickest corn salsa, 93

tabbouleh, 30
tapenade, 13
tarts, sweet
    apple tart with trembling custard, 120
    chocolate tart, 121
    tarte tatin, 121
Thai dishes
    Thai beef salad, 66
    Thai dip, 28
    Thai dipping relish with lime, garlic and chilli, 93
    Thai fish sauce (nam pla), 79
    Thai green curry sauce and fresh herbs, 37
    Thai-style clear-steamed fish with ginger threads, 35
    Thai-style hot and sour soup, 86
    Thai tomato dressing, 93
thyme: roast chicken, 45
tomatoes
    fresh tomato Puttanesca, 14
    no-cook fresh tomato and fresh herb sauce, 13, 75
    in omlettes, 6, 7
    and pizza, 116
    quicker tomato sauce, 12
    quick-fried squid with olive oil, basil and cherry tomatoes, 39
    ripe tomato salsa, 92
    simplest simmered tomato sauce, 12
    tabbouleh, 30
    Thai tomato dressing, 93
tuna, 5
    salade not-quite-Niçoise, 5
turnips see swedes

vegetables, 74–83
    cauliflower cheese, 97
    golden mash with ginger, 83
    Indian gingered cauliflower with spices, 81
    jade broccoli, 80
    organic, 75
    and peanut sambal, 77

roast, 74–5
roast courgettes, aubergines and young onions, 75
roast vegetables with olive oil and thyme, 75
roll-cutting, 78
sauces for, 76–7, 79
seasonal, 101
spiced carrots with sultanas and pine nuts, 83
steamed, 76–7
steamed greens with olive oil and balsamic vinegar, 76
stir-fried cabbage, 80
stir-fried gingery pork with squeaky greens, 64
stir-fried green beans, 78
stir-fried red peppers with olive oil, 78
stir-fried sprouts, 80
stir-fried vegetables with spices, coconut milk and toasted peanuts, 79
stir-frying, 78–81
stock, 91
turnip and carrot purée, 83
vinegar, balsamic
    balsamic dressing, 70
    roast quail with balsamic vinegar and rosemary potatoes, 47
    steamed greens with olive oil and balsamic vinegar, 76
    stir-fried cabbage with red chilli and balsamic vinegar, 80
    walnut and balsamic dressing, 72

walnuts
    walnut and balsamic dressing, 72
    warm salad of duck, grapes and walnuts, 72
    winter pesto, 15

yeast, for bread-making, 113–14
yoghurt, 75
    creamy cardamom, yoghurt and black pepper sauce, 60
    simple dip, 23
    spicy yoghurt relish with mint and coriander, 94
    yoghurt, garlic and caper dressing, 72